The Complete Marketer

The Complete Marketer

60 essential concepts for marketing excellence

Malcolm McDonald
and Mike Meldrum

KoganPage

LONDON PHILADELPHIA NEW DELHI

First published in Great Britain and the United States in 2013 by Kogan Page Limited

120 Pentonville Road	1518 Walnut Street, Suite 1100	4737/23 Ansari Road
London N1 9JN	Philadelphia PA 19102	Daryaganj
United Kingdom	USA	New Delhi 110002
www.koganpage.com		India

© Malcolm McDonald and Mike Meldrum 2013

The right of Malcolm McDonald and Mike Meldrum to be identified as the authors of this work has been asserted by them in accordance with the Copyright, Designs and Patents Act 1988.

ISBN   978 0 7494 6676 3
E-ISBN   978 0 7494 6677 0

British Library Cataloguing-in-Publication Data

A CIP record for this book is available from the British Library.

Library of Congress Cataloging-in-Publication Data

McDonald, Malcolm.
   The complete marketer : 60 essential concepts for marketing excellence / Malcolm McDonald, Mike Meldrum. – 1st Edition.
      pages cm
   ISBN 978-0-7494-6676-3 – ISBN (invalid) 978-0-7494-6677-0 (ebk.)   1. Marketing.   I. Meldrum, Mike.   II. Title.
   HF5415.M37953 2013
   658.8–dc23
                                                                                    2012046365

Typeset by Graphicraft Limited, Hong Kong
Printed and bound in India by Replika Press Pvt Ltd

CONTENTS

List of Figures   x
List of Tables   xii

PART ONE   Understanding the basics of marketing   1

TOPIC 1   The discipline of marketing   3

TOPIC 2   A market orientation   8

TOPIC 3   The marketing mix   11

TOPIC 4   Customer retention strategies   18

TOPIC 5   Marketing and ethics   24

TOPIC 6   Marketing: concept, function or process?   29

TOPIC 7   World-class marketing   33

PART TWO   Different types of marketing   41

TOPIC 8   Marketing consumer products   43

TOPIC 9   Marketing industrial products   48

TOPIC 10   Marketing service products   52

TOPIC 11   Marketing high-tech products   57

TOPIC 12   Marketing capital goods   62

TOPIC 13   Trade marketing   66

TOPIC 14   Category management   70

TOPIC 15   Relationship marketing   74

TOPIC 16   International and global marketing   79

PART THREE   Marketing in the digital age   85

TOPIC 17   Internet marketing   87

TOPIC 18   Social media marketing   94

TOPIC 19   Mobile marketing   99

TOPIC 20   Databases for marketing   104

PART FOUR   Understanding customers   111

TOPIC 21   Consumer buying behaviour   113

TOPIC 22   Organizational buying behaviour   118

TOPIC 23   Market segmentation   123

TOPIC 24   International market segmentation   130

PART FIVE   Understanding markets   135

TOPIC 25   Marketing information and research   137

TOPIC 26   Preparing a marketing research brief   143

TOPIC 27   Auditing a market   146

TOPIC 28   Constructing a SWOT   150

TOPIC 29   Competitor analysis   155

TOPIC 30   The Boston Matrix   160

TOPIC 31   The Directional Policy Matrix   164

TOPIC 32   The Ansoff Matrix   171

PART SIX   Managing the marketing mix   177

TOPIC 33   Branding   179

TOPIC 34   The product life cycle   183

TOPIC 35   Diffusion of innovation   189

TOPIC 36   Developing new products   193

TOPIC 37   Pricing strategies   198

TOPIC 38   Setting a price   204

TOPIC 39   Sales promotion   208

TOPIC 40   Advertising   213

TOPIC 41   Public relations   218

TOPIC 42   Sponsorship   222

TOPIC 43   Personal selling   228

TOPIC 44   Managing the sales team   232

TOPIC 45   Key account management   238

TOPIC 46   Implementing key account management   244

TOPIC 47   Channel strategy   248

TOPIC 48   Channel management   252

TOPIC 49   Customer service strategies   257

TOPIC 50   Multi-channel integration   261

TOPIC 51   Integrated marketing communication and distribution channels   266

PART SEVEN   Planning and control   271

TOPIC 52   Forecasting sales   273

TOPIC 53   Marketing planning   277

TOPIC 54   Barriers to implementing marketing planning systems   282

TOPIC 55   International product planning   287

TOPIC 56   Organizational structure and marketing   291

TOPIC 57   Budgeting for marketing   297

TOPIC 58   Legal issues in marketing   301

TOPIC 59   Marketing due diligence   305

TOPIC 60   Marketing metrics   310

Index   316

LIST OF FIGURES

FIGURE 1.1   Marketing as a business process   7
FIGURE 3.1   Channel options for the produce of a market gardener   17
FIGURE 4.1   Net Promoter Score   20
FIGURE 5.1   Consumerism's way to better marketing   28
FIGURE 6.1   Marketing as a process   32
FIGURE 7.1   Ensuring a market orientation   34
FIGURE 7.2   Striving for competitive advantage   34
FIGURE 7.3   Monitoring the environment: key areas   35
FIGURE 7.4   Developing competitor profiles   36
FIGURE 7.5   The process of market segmentation   36
FIGURE 7.6   Identifying strengths and weaknesses   37
FIGURE 7.7   The dynamics of product/market life cycles   38
FIGURE 7.8   Portfolio of products and markets   38
FIGURE 7.9   Contents of a strategic marketing plan   39
FIGURE 7.10   Core professional curriculum   40
FIGURE 9.1   Continuum of industrial marketing   49
FIGURE 10.1   Continuum of tangible–intangible products   54
FIGURE 11.1   The technology life cycle   60
FIGURE 14.1   Category management evolution   73
FIGURE 15.1   Expanded marketing mix   76
FIGURE 15.2   The relationship marketing six markets model   77
FIGURE 19.1   M-Marketing enhancements   101
FIGURE 20.1   Information flows in a marketing system   109
FIGURE 21.1   Components of a consumer's purchase decision   114
FIGURE 22.1   Organizational buying behaviour model   119
FIGURE 23.1   Cooking appliances market   125
FIGURE 23.2   Micro-segments   125
FIGURE 23.3   Example of segmentation of consumer market for toothpaste   127
FIGURE 23.4   Example of segmentation of the industrial market for a technical service product   128
FIGURE 23.5   Understand the different category buyers   129
FIGURE 28.1   Establishing competitive positions using critical success factors   152
FIGURE 28.2   Strengths and weaknesses analysis   152
FIGURE 28.3   Opportunities matrix   153

FIGURE 28.4 Threats matrix 153

FIGURE 29.1 Competitor analysis framework 158

FIGURE 30.1 The Boston Matrix 160

FIGURE 30.2 The experience curve 161

FIGURE 30.3 The Boston Matrix – cash flow implications 163

FIGURE 31.1 The Directional Policy Matrix (DPM) 164

FIGURE 31.2 Four strategic categories 168

FIGURE 31.3 Programme guidelines suggested for different positioning on the DPM 169

FIGURE 32.1 The Ansoff Matrix 172

FIGURE 32.2 An extended product/market matrix 176

FIGURE 34.1 Standard product life cycle curve 183

FIGURE 34.2 Phases in the product life cycle 185

FIGURE 34.3 Alternative product life cycles 186

FIGURE 35.1 The diffusion of innovation curve 190

FIGURE 36.1 New product classification 194

FIGURE 36.2 Cultural blockages to new product initiatives 196

FIGURE 36.3 Risk and new product development 197

FIGURE 38.1 The price continuum 204

FIGURE 42.1 Sponsorship types 223

FIGURE 42.2 Sponsorship management cycle 224

FIGURE 45.1 Evolutionary nature of KAM relationships 239

FIGURE 45.2 The basic KAM stage 240

FIGURE 45.3 Co-operative KAM 241

FIGURE 45.4 The interdependent KAM stage 241

FIGURE 45.5 The integrated KAM stage 242

FIGURE 46.1 Customer satisfaction: virtuous circle 245

FIGURE 50.1 Choosing channels: the value curve 263

FIGURE 50.2 Channel-chain analysis: the corporate PC market 264

FIGURE 51.1 Communications plan 266

FIGURE 51.2 Value chain and associated communications activities 268

FIGURE 53.1 Strategic and tactical marketing plans 280

FIGURE 53.2 Strategic and operational planning cycle 281

FIGURE 56.1 Organizational structure and marketing 292

FIGURE 56.2 Matrix marketing department 294

FIGURE 58.1 Three faces of the law 302

FIGURE 59.1 Marketing due diligence process 309

FIGURE 60.1 Map of the marketing domain 311

FIGURE 60.2 CSFs in the marketing process 312

FIGURE 60.3 Critical success factor analysis template 313

LIST OF TABLES

TABLE 3.1   Product variables   12
TABLE 3.2   Pricing variables   13
TABLE 4.1   Industries with traditionally high defection rates, where customer retention improvements can have a significant impact   21
TABLE 10.1   Major examples of service industries   52
TABLE 10.2   Variations in product tangibility   53
TABLE 15.1   Tendencies inherent in a transaction approach to marketing   75
TABLE 16.1   Environmental factors affecting global marketing   80
TABLE 16.2   Business factors making marketing globally more complex   81
TABLE 16.3   Key questions in international marketing   84
TABLE 20.1   Myths and realities about databases   105
TABLE 20.2   Problems of reconciling internal and external market audits   106
TABLE 20.3   Examples of business objectives and segmentation methods   108
TABLE 20.4   The main components of a marketing database system   110
TABLE 25.1   Main areas of market research   138
TABLE 25.2   Top ten marketing research topics   138
TABLE 27.1   The marketing audit checklist   148
TABLE 29.1   Guide to market competitive position classifications   157
TABLE 29.2   Alternative business directions   158
TABLE 29.3   Individual competitor analysis   159
TABLE 31.1   Criteria which might make a market attractive   166
TABLE 31.2   Factors that might be considered, or which may yield, business strengths   167
TABLE 31.3   The ten steps involved in producing a DPM   170
TABLE 32.1   Kinds of new products and markets   175
TABLE 33.1   Bipolar scales for brand positioning   181
TABLE 34.1   Typical marketing-mix strategies for different life-cycle stages   188
TABLE 37.1   Appeal of a cost approach to pricing   202
TABLE 37.2   Problems of a cost approach to pricing   202

TABLE 39.1   Types of sales promotions   210

TABLE 40.1   Suggested pro-forma for an advertising plan   216

TABLE 43.1   The advantages of personal selling   231

TABLE 44.1   Further quantitative objectives for a sales force   233

TABLE 44.2   Setting objectives for an individual sales representative   234

TABLE 45.1   Key questions for the future of KAM   243

TABLE 47.1   Major forms of intermediaries   250

TABLE 49.1   Example of customer service trade-off matrix   259

TABLE 54.1   Barriers to the integration of strategic marketing planning   282

TABLE 55.1   Areas requiring attention in international product planning   290

TABLE 59.1   Factors contributing to risk   308

TABLE 60.1   Typical responsibilities of a marketing department   314

PART ONE
Understanding the basics of marketing

The discipline of marketing

Marketing has long been recognized as important for the long-term survival and success of organizations, be they commercial, government or third sector activities. Indeed, any analysis of the more successful companies in the world usually confirms their use of sound marketing principles or disciplines within their management processes. In less successful organizations, it is often observed that marketing is something not done particularly well.

To understand marketing, it is helpful to understand where it came from. In essence, it started when entrepreneurs began experiencing difficulties selling their wares. When putting ever increasing efforts into sales proved ineffective, smart traders instead put effort into identifying what they would have to do differently to keep trading. People like Josiah Wedgwood (1730–95) became known for their ability to 'sense' what the market wanted in terms of design, quality and price; and then to organize production and distribution accordingly.

Although this was not called marketing, it is the formalization of these processes that evolved into the discipline of marketing. And even then, it did not become a widely recognized discipline until well into the second half of last century.

Thus, the focus of marketing is on creating an environment in which sales can be made. Selling is therefore part of marketing. Where there is an excess of demand over supply or a monopoly of some kind, it is often all that is needed. Even where this is not the case, for some businesses smart or hard selling are their main competitive weapons.

This is not to say that organizations *cannot* survive without marketing. They can and sometimes do – usually because they have some natural advantage over competitors such as a patent or a monopoly, or there is excess demand for their products. In the long run, however, these advantages are rarely sustainable.

There are many definitions that try to provide a clear insight into what marketing is all about. One of the best describes marketing as 'the way in which an organization matches its human, financial and physical resources with the wants and needs of its customers'. This is a bit of a mouthful and, on the surface, does not mention any of the things we usually associate with marketing such as advertising, mail shots, loss-leaders and so on. The definition does, however, focus attention on the crucial elements that the whole organization has to manage correctly – the mechanisms by which a relationship is developed between the organization and its customers so that mutually beneficial exchanges will take place.

Success, of course, requires attention to more than just marketing. Other activities such as operating efficiency, financial matters and supply chain management are also important, not least because they have an impact on an organization's relationship with its customers. This makes implementing the discipline of marketing difficult as it implies influencing the co-ordination of a wide range of organizational activities.

Underlying this, however, is a set of ideas, principles and concepts that are relatively simple to understand, but which (like most simple things) are quite deep in their meaning. Getting to grips with marketing is thus a two-stage process: first, the development of an understanding of the discipline and its principles; and second, the application of these principles to individual circumstances.

At the heart of the relationship between an organization and its customers is the product or service the organization offers or sells, which must match the wants and needs of its target customers. If one company offers a closer match, this will be to the disadvantage of its competitors. The process of creating this match, however, is complex. The substance of a matching relationship and the factors that affect it are at the heart of any understanding of marketing.

The key question this approach generates is thus: 'What will make a potential customer want to enter into an exchange with our organization as opposed to another?' In other words: 'Why will they buy our product, give to our charity or co-operate with our service, given that they have plenty of choice?'

The answer to this question is a long list of different factors. Some of these will be under the control of the supplying organization, while others will be beyond their control but can still fundamentally affect their chances of completing the exchange. No matter how good a product is, other factors such as interest rates, new laws, fashion, etc, can affect its attractiveness to customers. In order to make sense of these factors and to put them into an understandable form, they are usually classified as the marketing mix and the marketing environment. The marketing mix is the offering we control; the environment is the set of uncontrollable variables within which the marketing process takes place.

The marketing mix is usually classified as product, price, promotion, or place – the four Ps:

Products can be varied in terms of quality, tangibility, size, functionality, range, etc.

Price can be high or low, can involve a discount or can be affected by credit terms.

Promotion can utilize television advertising, the domain of sales people, or can involve branding, public relations or social media.

Place includes the channels through which we choose to make a product available plus the service elements involved in delivering the offering, such as after-sales service or quality of accompanying documentation.

The importance of the marketing mix is that successful matching depends on customers being aware of the products or services on offer, finding them available and favourably judging their attractiveness in terms of both price and performance. If any important element is missing or wrong from the customer's point of view, a long-term relationship will be difficult to sustain. Effective marketing management welds these variables into a co-ordinated whole in the market place in exactly the right combination and positioning for the targeted customer.

The marketing environment features a similarly complex set of factors, which can be considered under five distinct headings:

Social or cultural factors, which can include fashion, religious preferences, population trends and other developments such as more working women and an increasing awareness of green issues – all of which will affect people's perception of the appropriateness and value of a product or service.

Competition, which exists whenever an organization places an offering in the market place – there will always be some form of substitute somewhere. This may be direct, such as a Ford Focus versus an equivalent Citroen, or it may be indirect such as a holiday versus a home extension. Organizations should never underestimate the power of different sources of competition.

Technological change, the pace of which appears to be increasing at an ever-faster rate. It is therefore dangerous to assume that existing products will continue to be demanded by customers. There are many examples of products being superseded by advances in technology elsewhere, for example, slide rules, mechanical watches, copper pipes, fax machines, and more recently CRT televisions and video recorders. At the time of writing, cameras are under threat from mobile phones and printed books are under threat from portable tablets. Technological developments will determine what is both possible and attractive in all markets.

Government activities, which include political, fiscal, environmental, economic and legal activities. All of these will affect what can be done in a particular market. Interest rates will affect the willingness to purchase on credit; deregulation will alter entry barriers to a market and the nature of competition; exhaust emissions requirements will affect the saleability of motor vehicles, and so on. Governments, even if they do nothing, will still be a significant influence on an organization's marketing environment.

Institutional changes will impact marketing activities and it is therefore important to understand the effect of institutions and to predict the consequences of any change. Important examples include the changes that have occurred in food distribution, from small local outlets to large out-of-town supermarkets to internet shopping; the role of the standards institutes; the influence of the press; the rise of consumer associations and popular pressure groups; and the expansion of the activities of telecommunications companies.

Both consciously and subconsciously, customers are constantly performing a matching exercise between their needs and wants, and the products and services they see in the market place. When the match is sufficiently good they will purchase. The methodology for creating a match is the manipulation and management of the marketing mix and the monitoring and evaluation of the environment.

To clarify what marketing is, it is necessary to understand that it operates at three levels.

The first is what might be termed the 'philosophical' level. If the people who control an organization do not believe that striving for superior customer value is critical to long-term customer retention, marketing will never be anything other than a trivial functional department. There needs to be a culture that supports a positive customer orientation.

The second level is what is often called the 'strategic' level. Here, many of the disciplines of marketing such as market analysis and understanding, market segmentation, positioning, product development and relationship strategies become major determinants of success, and are clearly essential ingredients of business unit strategy.

Finally, there is the 'tactical' or implementation level of marketing, at which more detailed issues relating to the offer and customer satisfaction are considered.

The discipline of marketing thus covers a wide range of topics and ideas. If depicted as a process, it would have a clear starting point: understanding customers, markets and competitors. Based on this understanding, target markets and customers would be identified and an appropriate strategy and competitive position established. These would be delivered through the marketing mix and then monitored for effectiveness. This is depicted in Figure 1.1.

Thought of in this way, the discipline of marketing becomes a core organizational process, and in the words of Peter Drucker, something too important to be left to the Marketing Department. As a consequence, marketing professionals become experts in reading and understanding markets, or specialists in marketing communications. Both are complex specialisms within marketing. The other areas are more general in nature and vital aspects of management elsewhere in the organization: an integral part of what is sometimes referred to as 'general management'.

Thus, marketing is a discipline in that it is a body of thought, a managerial process, an approach to managing a business, and it involves some specific professional skills.

FIGURE 1.1   Marketing as a business process

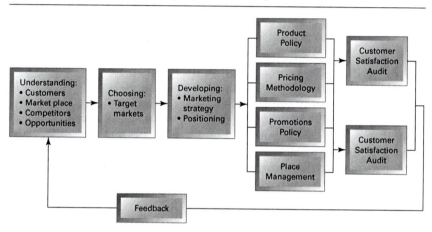

A market orientation

Many organizations have experienced the introduction of a rallying cry from their senior management to the effect of 'we will now become a marketing-led organization'. What they really mean is that they wish to become a *market-driven* organization, not that the marketing department should now lead the business. Turning this statement into reality requires more than just the pronouncement of the principle and the employment of a few people with marketing titles. It requires something much more difficult: the creation of a desire within the entire organization for principles, policies and practices that anticipate and meet the needs of markets and the customers who collectively form that market. These principles, policies and practices are all core to the discipline of marketing (See Topic 1).

To gain a better understanding of the difference between marketing and a market orientation, it is sometimes helpful to think of marketing as occurring in three distinct forms. These can be characterized as: *marketing tasks*; *marketing management*; and, in addition, *a market orientation*.

The first form, *marketing tasks*, will involve a number of specialized activities requiring a degree of experience and expertise to be performed well. Some of these will be tasks that are normally associated with successful marketing, such as designing brochures, advertising, commissioning market research and brand management. A 'professional' marketing person should have expertise in these areas. However, there are a large number of other areas of activity that will have an impact on marketing success, but will often be the responsibility of managers in other functional areas. These can include calculating volume discounts, stock control, after-sales service activities and product development. Each area will usually be the responsibility of different parts of an organization, but each will affect the nature of relationships with customers and, therefore, the possibility of new and continued sales.

The second form, *marketing management*, is thus not only the management of specialist marketing tasks but also working across the business to influence the management of these other activities. If there are many activities that can affect an organization's success in the market place, then it follows that a degree of co-ordination has to be applied to them. In the absence of any co-ordination, these tasks will be performed according to the beliefs and preferences of the individuals involved. It does not stretch the imagination to foresee the problems that this might cause. In Topic 1, we referred to this as the 'strategic' level of marketing.

The function of marketing management is to provide co-ordination by whatever mechanism is appropriate to the organization. Their job is to ensure a common direction; an agreement between the various activity centres on what the organization is trying to achieve; a clear leadership task. The outcome sought from such leadership would be an agreed set of policies or guidelines for the individuals engaged in performing the various tasks that affect the marketing mix. The overall outcome would be a better degree of organizational integration in relation to its markets. This implies that providing cross-functional leadership becomes a significant requirement for a good marketing manager.

Such leadership will occur at different levels within an organization. It will range from the strategic positions adopted or defined by the senior leaders of the organization, through the specific responsibilities of a marketing director, to the various operational marketing managers and section heads. At whatever level this occurs, however, it will still have the same purpose: co-ordinating and integrating activities across the business to achieve a good match with customer requirements.

A *market orientation* is, then, the third form of marketing found within organizations. It is something that goes beyond marketing tasks and management leadership, and is the most intangible aspect of marketing. Orientations are to do with the values, attitudes and beliefs of the people working within an organization. In this, they are an aspect of an organization's culture. Orientations are very powerful influences since they will determine what are considered to be legitimate concerns in management action.

The phrase 'we are a market-driven organization' should therefore be a reflection of the organization's culture. It encompasses the way in which priorities are determined and what sort of questions managers and operatives feel they should be asking each other. It also includes the type of management information readily available, the ease with which budgets are obtained for various types of expenditure and the processes by which decisions are made.

The focus of a market orientation is, of course, the customer. More important, however, is a focus on an organization's *relationships* with its customers. Since marketing is about matching resources with the wants and needs of customers, a market orientation exists when all personnel view activities in terms of their likely impact on relationships with customers. Important questions include:

- why will these customers want to obtain this product from us?
- what impact will this action have on our customers?
- what is happening out there in our markets that will affect our activities?

A market orientation exists when people make sense of their business, justify actions and authorize spending by reference to customers.

Instilling a market orientation within an organization is a difficult job. It is easy to accept intellectually that long-term survival depends on creating and keeping customers, whether they are paying customers or otherwise, but it is quite another matter to introduce this philosophy into managerial processes. This is because people are subject to a large number of influences and pressures in their work that will tend to counter the pursuit of marketing principles.

As an example, pressures will derive from people's professional backgrounds where problems are often tackled using different methodologies from those involved in marketing. As an art, rather than a science, marketing is sometimes difficult for people from technical, operational or scientific backgrounds since there are few constant input/output relationships. It is hard to evaluate the returns on investing in developing a market- and customer-oriented culture. In addition, most people's work is performed away from the customer interface. When people go to work their direct concerns are with their jobs and their e-mail inbox, not with matching customer needs.

Other orientations that can exist side by side with market orientation include: production, design, technology, financial, sales and social orientations. These are not 'wrong' and indeed are all required at certain times to a greater or lesser extent. If, for example, a company has profitability problems, it will be important that a financial orientation should emerge as a priority to enable the short-term survival of the business. Alternatively, an organization that relies on product innovation and development for its success in the market place should encourage a technology and/or innovation orientation within its ranks in the way that 3M, Google and Amazon have famously done.

The problem with these various types of orientation is obtaining the right balance between them to match the market conditions within which the organization operates. Successful organizations are good at matching, not only in terms of the four Ps, but also in terms of the ways in which they manage and set priorities for themselves. In good times, marketing tends to be forgotten and other priorities dominate. Marketing then becomes the way forward in bad times, but by that point is often perceived as a threat to the other traditional values already well-embedded in the organization.

As with other disciplines, a market orientation needs to exist in an organization. It does not have to stem from a marketing department. Indeed, many successful marketing organizations do not have a formal marketing department beyond some specialists in market communications. It is therefore important that *all* general managers are aware of the need for, and are active in the promotion of, a marketing philosophy alongside the other orientations necessary for continued success.

The marketing mix

The marketing mix is the name given to the main *demand-influencing variables* that are available to an organization. This is because, when a customer makes a purchase or engages in an exchange with a supplier, what they are responding to is not just the product but a whole range of variables that constitute the offer. The classic description of the marketing mix, although something of a simplification, is 'the four Ps'. The four Ps and the fundamental questions associated with them are:

- **Product:** What type and range of product or service should we provide?
- **Price:** What price should be set for each product or service and how should it be constructed?
- **Promotion:** How do we best communicate with our target customers and persuade them to buy our offer?
- **Place:** What channels of distribution and what levels of service are appropriate?

Each of these elements is capable of influencing demand either separately or in combination. When considering the marketing mix, it is important to look at some of the general principles underlying decisions about the actual mix that an organization might choose to implement.

Product (including service products)

Although customers and their needs form the focal point of the marketing process, few organizations started with this in mind. Invariably somebody had a good idea for a product and this became the germ of the business idea.

Not surprisingly, then, many enterprises see the product as being at the heart of their firm's marketing efforts. There may be nothing intrinsically wrong with this attitude as long as managers can see that their product does not have to remain as a fixed, unchanging entity: a sort of organizational straitjacket. Instead, the company must learn to see its output as flexible, being subject to development and adaptation, just like any other component of the marketing mix. Because the world is never static, an organization should keep asking itself the question: 'Does each product we offer provide relevant and desired benefits for today's customers' needs?'

Some of these benefits can be provided by other elements of the marketing mix, such as availability, after-sales service and value for money. Aspects of the product that can provide appropriate benefits are shown in Table 3.1.

TABLE 3.1   Product variables

Technical features	Complexity of the product and range of features included
Design	Extent to which the product is made to be attractive and easy to use
Durability	Extent of built-in obsolescence or expected life of the product
Robustness	Ability of product to function in a harsh environment
Innovativeness	Extent to which the product includes new features or things done in a different way
Functional performance	Number of tasks the product can do and the quality to which it can do them
Interference	Extent to which the product affects people and processes such as electrical interference, noise or time
Range	Availability of different colours, sizes, functionalities, prices and so on
Ease of maintenance	Complexity and/or frequency of maintenance, or extent to which the user can maintain the product
Environmental friendliness	Extent to which the product will cause pollution or use non-sustainable resources
Packaging	Can be simply functional to protect the product or used to advertise or enhance the appeal
Compatibility	Can it be used with previous investments or products from other suppliers
Degree of customization	Level of detail to which a purchaser can vary the product to suit their own needs and preferences

TABLE 3.1 *continued*

Flexibility	Ease with which the product can be applied to a range of tasks or circumstances
Upgradability	Potential for the product to be enhanced by the addition of newly developed features
Quality	Can be derived from the materials used, incidence of faults, efficiency and so on
Volumes available	Amount that can be purchased at a time and/or continuity of supply
Safety	Safety standards conformed to, both statutory and voluntary
Ease of use	Degree of training or familiarity required to be able to take advantage of the product plus quality of instructions

Price

Pricing is an area of marketing with tremendous potential for increasing short-term profits, but unfortunately, if managed badly, it can equally quickly bring a business to its knees. Pricing is both an art and a science. The options open to an organization for using pricing as a flexible 'connector' that helps to position a product and match efforts to the needs of the customer are many, as shown in Table 3.2.

TABLE 3.2 Pricing variables

Discount structure	Volume discounts, retrospective discounts, early-order discounts, discounts for cash
Discount amounts	Percentages, flat rates, cash-backs
Special offers	Coupons, 'buy one and get one free'
Sales	Seasonal sales, end of line sales, closing down sales
Cost of ownership	Fuel costs, other consumables, longevity, maintenance costs

TABLE 3.2   *continued*

Credit terms	From payment in advance to x months credit with or without interest penalties
Stage payments	Number of payments and period over which payments may be made
Residual value	What the item is worth after its useful life to the original owner, second-hand value
Leasing arrangements	Operating leases, finance leases, hire purchase
Financial deals	Trade-in of old equipment, sale and lease back, rent-free periods
Psychological elements	Keeping within price bands, price comparisons, low up-front costs, presenting elements separately to avoid big numbers

There is a fear among many managers that unless they offer the lowest possible price they will not win the order. While this can be true for some businesses, it is rarely the case with market leaders. Take the case of the really successful construction companies that tend to rely on quality, innovation and carefully managed business relationships to win contracts. Other companies without these advantages have to use price to obtain work. As a consequence, their main hopes for profit rest on keeping costs to a minimum and loopholes in the contract. Such adversarial approaches never seem to last.

As an alternative, take the example of a shopper who prefers to buy goods from a local shop rather than a supermarket or via the internet where cheaper prices can be obtained. Why? Quite apart from the convenience factor, the shopper knows and values the personal service from a local shop, and is prepared to pay for this. Thus, in the 2012 economic downturn in the UK, John Lewis – a high service and quality retailer – fared better than many of its cheaper competitors.

When a customer buys, he/she or the organization purchases a 'package' of benefits and the price should reflect the value of the *total package*. Clearly, price is an important element of the business transaction and, appropriately chosen, it can not only have a big impact on a company's market positioning, but can also help to differentiate the product or service from those of competitors.

Promotion

The promotional element of the marketing mix is concerned with ways of communicating with customers and potential customers. In practice the promotional element of the marketing mix falls into two broad categories: personal promotion and impersonal promotion.

Personal promotion

This is the role of selling, which is usually accomplished through a sales force, sales assistants, or via a call centre. Person-to-person selling has a number of advantages over impersonal methods:

- as it is a two-way process it gives the prospective purchaser the opportunity to ask questions about the product;
- the sales message can be tailored to the needs of individual customers;
- the sales person can use in-depth knowledge about the product to identify new customer needs and overcome objections;
- the customer can be prompted to buy by being asked for an order;
- the sales person can negotiate on price, delivery or special requirements;
- personal relationships with customers can be developed and thereby lay the foundations for longer-term business.

However, selling also involves a lot of 'dead' time such as preparing sales aids, telephoning for appointments or simply making a telephone sale, travelling or waiting for a customer to drop in, failing to win an order, administration and research. These are costly activities and need to be regularly monitored to ensure they provide a good return for the cost and effort that goes into it.

Impersonal promotion

Typically, this area of promotion takes the form of advertising and sales promotion. Advertising is often felt to be the province of only the very large organizations and something that is best left to the 'experts'. In fact, advertising can be addressed by any competent manager, and can encompass: the traditional slots on television; newspaper and magazine adverts; billboards; radio; leaflets; brochures; stories in the papers and trade journals; Yellow Pages; local buses and taxis; and gifts such as calendars and pens. It can also include the more modern: e-mail campaigns; product placement in films and TV programmes; banners on websites; pages on social media; text messaging; and the ubiquitous spam.

Advertising can be appropriate for any organization. To be managed well, however, it needs to be looked upon as an investment rather than a cost and like any other investment, it is only going to be any good if it achieves a return. To obtain this, it is important to address the following questions:

- At whom is it aimed? (target customers)
- What is it trying to achieve? (objectives)
- What should it say? (message)
- How should the message be communicated? (medium)
- How will the result be measured? (monitoring)

These questions can only be answered if an organization has a good understanding of its customers and potential customers: what interests them; what motivates them to buy; and how messages can reach them.

Although the various advertising media mentioned above vary in terms of their costs and potential for reaching customers, different combinations of message and media will provide a very flexible advertising repertoire that can be tailored to fit most budgets.

Sales promotions

Sales promotions are essentially short-term campaigns to influence customers (perhaps a competitor's customers, or even intermediaries) to buy more of a product or to use it faster. Some companies use promotions to encourage their own sales force to sell more. Generally, promotions take the form of offering a monetary incentive, such as a price reduction or a coupon against the next purchase, goods such as two for the price of one, or services such as free estimates and holidays.

Place

If a market gardener started a business farming organically-grown vegetables, he or she would be faced with several different routes for getting these vegetables to the consumer; some direct, and some through intermediaries, as illustrated in Figure 3.1.

This example provides a good illustration of the 'place' element of the marketing mix and how this needs to be integrated with delivery, consignment 'packaging' and the service elements associated with delivery. Clearly, the cheapest channel is the 'pick your own' option, where getting the consumer to bear the harvesting costs while receiving no customer service will save the farmer money. But suppose that does not appeal to people in the catchment area, or suppose the farm is in a sparsely populated area? A farm shop would have the advantage of appealing to passing trade as well as to regular customers, but involve infrastructure and staff costs. Mail order websites have become more popular as a consequence, but add distribution costs that make total purchase costs high when compared to supermarkets. Such costs make wholesalers look attractive, but will inevitably squeeze margins. And so on. To make the best of things, most suppliers safeguard their interests by using more than one channel to reach different customer segments.

FIGURE 3.1   Channel options for the produce of a market gardener

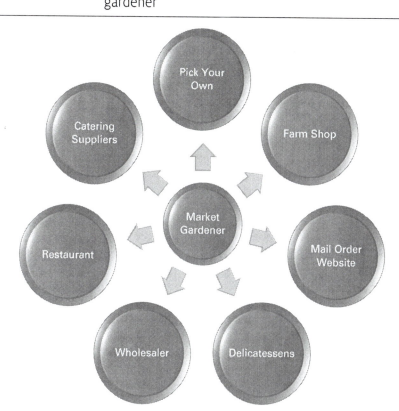

The choice of channel can also help enterprises to differentiate their product. Classic UK examples include Avon Cosmetics taking their products into the home of the consumer while the competition continued to trade in department stores and chemists' shops, and HSBC creating First Direct to offer telephone banking at a time when other banks relied on High Street branches. Latterly, the internet has enabled many businesses to offer very different services to traditional retailing.

When developing policies for the various elements of the marketing mix, it is important to be comprehensive, but also to identify those areas that are significant in the markets in which an organization operates. Thus, some organizations use an expanded marketing mix for managerial and planning purposes. This can involve isolating sales plans, processes, people or customer service for special attention. Whatever the case, the key task of any manager is to ensure that the mix presented to the market place is internally consistent and provides a set of benefits that target customers will find preferable to the offerings of other organizations.

Customer retention strategies

Many organizations concentrate on developing strategies to expand sales through market share dominance, market penetration, finding new markets and product range expansion. The main reason for focusing on these is that research has shown that size, revenue growth and dominance are usually positively correlated with long-term survival and profitability. Recent work, however, has questioned the universality of these approaches, arguing that the cost of winning new customers is high and that, for many organizations, it will be more cost-effective to concentrate on retaining existing customers than attracting new ones.

For some industries, the increased profitability that can be gained from higher rates of customer retention are quite startling. Improvements of a few percentage points in customer retention yield large percentage increases in profits. The basis of this is the mathematical relationship between retention rates and the average life of a customer. Thus, a 90 per cent retention rate implies that 10 per cent of a business's customers are lost each year. In 10 years, the equivalent of its entire customer base will have to have been recruited just to maintain its current size. The average life of a customer can thus be seen to be 10 years. If retention rates are increased to 95 per cent, the average life of a customer doubles to 20 years, since only 5 per cent will be lost each year. Where recruiting new customers costs significantly more than selling to existing customers (five times more in many cases), customer retention may prove a more profitable strategic objective.

Apart from the costs of recruitment, retained customers can also benefit supplier organizations in a number of other ways, although this assumes that such customers become loyal out of choice rather than through some device that 'locks them in'. Such benefits will be obtained because:

- regular customers will tend to spend less time comparing prices with those of competitors and can become less price-sensitive, providing the opportunity for premium pricing;

- voluntarily retained customers are more likely to be a source of positive referrals, which can provide a cost-effective source of new customers;
- administrative procedures and other activities that affect the cost of a sale will be more routinized and, for the supplier as well as the customer, less expensive;
- there is a tendency for loyal customers to make a larger proportion of their purchases with a single supplier and thus boost turnover.

Before focusing on customer retention as a strategic objective, however, it is important to understand the relevance of customer retention activities for an organization's customer base. In some markets, customers value the ability to move between suppliers for similar purchases and would resent efforts on the part of suppliers to develop longer-term relationships. Internet 'surfers' who pride themselves on finding the 'best deal' would be an example of this. In other markets, many customers are unprofitable, or merely contribute to overheads rather than adding to the 'bottom line', as is the case for many bank current accounts that are effectively dormant from one year to the next. In addition, the nature of some products means that the majority of sales are only ever going to be 'one-offs', or at least very infrequent purchases, as is the case for double glazing, some large projects and time-share holiday accommodation. Under these circumstances, strategies designed to improve customer retention are likely to reduce customer satisfaction levels and have little impact on profitability.

Where it appears that customer retention is an appropriate strategy, the next step is to identify the type of customers the business wishes to retain. This will provide the focus for both customer recruitment and retention endeavours. In general, the 'right type' of customers will have a particular need in common, so that the costs of servicing these customers can benefit from economies of scale and the organization's positioning will not become too diffused. This essentially requires a benefit segmentation exercise, with the identification of associated needs and benefits enabling sub-segments to be developed. Many such sub-segments can be adequately managed via the advances being made in database marketing.

Other types of customer that will be a suitable focus for retention strategies include ones who like a stable relationship; are reasonable in their demands of suppliers; and who have the potential for long-term purchase or usage.

Customers not attracted to stable relationships, often referred to as 'promiscuous customers', will tend to be those who are very price-sensitive, who value change and variety, or who respond well to sales-promotion initiatives. Predictions of 'promiscuity', however, do not tend to be very robust and characteristics such as income, sex and socio-economic class cannot be easily used for this purpose and, indeed, will vary from one industry sector to another.

What *is* true, however, is that loyalty is sometimes a 'default situation' caused by the inability of a customer to purchase elsewhere through legal restrictions, company policy, poverty, or awareness limitations and who may well turn out to be 'promiscuous' under other circumstances.

The term 'reasonable customers' refers to those who do not cause a supplier to incur costs significantly beyond those associated with the provision of the product. Unreasonable customers would include those for whom the cost of sale was high, who made excessive use of warranty or after-sales services, or who were late payers. Those with the potential to be 'long-term customers' would include customers who recognize that they have a long-term need, who can be easy to locate or keep in touch with and who are likely to experience or maintain an appropriate level of disposable income.

These characteristics highlight the importance of personal recommendations, which have been found to generate more of the better-quality customers than other sources of new customers. They also emphasize the need to target consumers with stable lifestyles or organizations that do not suffer wild fluctuations in their activities, who seem to be well-positioned for growth, or who are diversified enough to survive changing market circumstances. In this context, the value of identifying and developing campaigns for referral markets becomes apparent.

A popular measure to establish the 'loyalty' of customers is the Net Promoter Score. This is established through regular collection of customer feedback that asks them how likely they are to recommend the organization to others, as illustrated in Figure 4.1.

FIGURE 4.1   Net Promoter Score

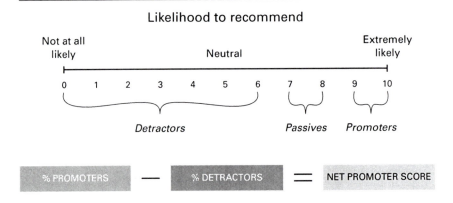

In addition to identifying potentially loyal and profitable customers, it is also important to understand the causes of customer defection since these will underpin the development of any strategies for retention. Essentially, there are only two causes of customers ceasing to purchase: their need ends, or the product offering fails in some way or another.

Needs can end for a number of reasons, such as children growing up; retirement; death; bankruptcy; legislative changes; in-house provisions; and so on. Together, these will be either a move from one stage in a life cycle to another, or changed circumstances.

A failure in a product offering will be due to the product failing to deliver the performances required, a failure in customer service or a competitor offering superior benefits in terms of product performance, service or value. Table 4.1 provides examples of industries with traditionally high defection rates. It is, therefore, very important for an organization to monitor defection patterns as clues to the causes both of customer satisfaction and dissatisfaction levels. These can be supplemented by the use of 'root cause analysis' to get to the heart of defections, rather than just accepting stated reasons, which are not always the real ones.

TABLE 4.1 Industries with traditionally high defection rates, where customer retention improvements can have a significant impact

Personal, home and motor insurance
Credit and charge cards
Hotels
Airlines
Grocery retailing
Travel and real estate agencies
Courier services
Management training and consultancy

Once the rationale and focus for customer retention has been identified, attention must then turn to the choice of strategic options. The main aim will be to convert a potential or actual purchaser into a loyal, long-term customer. This is the process of converting the relationship from that of a simple transaction to something approaching a partnership, which is then maintained over time. The options available fall into three different categories: validating the customer's choice of supplier; enhancing the value of the exchange; or creating interdependency.

Validating choice means finding ways of reassuring a customer that they have chosen wisely and providing them with clear views as to why their decision was, and is, correct. This will reduce the likelihood of them considering alternative offerings and will enhance their ability to explain their choice to others. Verbalizing the reasons for using a supplier is, in itself, a powerful means of reinforcing personal opinions and beliefs, but does require a high degree of clarity. Validation can be achieved via:

- influencer markets such as the media, trade associations and intermediaries;
- customer communications such as advertising, PR and direct mail/e-mail;
- post-purchase service activities, including instruction manuals, product maintenance or emergency assistance.

Perceptions of enhanced value will result from building something extra into the overall product offer that will increase the utility the customer derives from its consumption. Value is provided in either tangible or intangible form. Tangible value can be:

- monetary, such as loyalty discounts, or terminal bonuses;
- gifts donated on a periodic or cumulative basis, such as Air Miles schemes;
- Christmas shopping deals;
- some form of points collection activity.

Intangible value is more likely to be provided through customer service or database marketing, which makes purchase, use or ownership of the product satisfying and/or ego boosting. This may be a simple acknowledgement or 'thank you', or can be something grander such as some sort of status award.

Interdependency requires both the supplier and the purchaser to recognize that they rely on each other for either product or revenue. This can be achieved on the part of the supplier by:

- acknowledging, both publicly and privately, the contribution a customer makes to their business;
- seeking help from customers so that they become more involved in the organization's activities;
- finding ways of demonstrating commitment to customers by 'bending rules', public pronouncements or extraordinary efforts to meet individual requests.

Focusing on interdependency is probably the issue closest to ideas of partnership, since any partnership should involve the sharing of risk, information and commitment.

As a final point, and as previously noted, it must be remembered that customer retention should not be taken to involve schemes which 'lock customers' into a supplier. While the idea has appeal in terms of reducing competition and enhancing supplier power, the long-term impact on customer perceptions can be dysfunctional. Locking mechanisms include: financial exit penalties; propriety technology that is incompatible with other products;

or just the sheer administrative problems involved in abandoning a supplier. One only has to think of the problems involved in transferring a house-purchase mortgage from one lender to another to understand the frustrations such barriers can cause.

Recent research has also indicated that an alternative way of approaching customer retention is to ensure product offerings match purchasers' values: values are deep-seated responses that categorize things as 'good' or 'bad', 'right' or 'wrong', and so on. When an offer or brand mirrors the values of a target market above and beyond a competitor product, loyalty is much easier to sustain.

Marketing and ethics

As marketing has assumed a greater role in business, concerns about the ethicality of marketing have also increased. In response, several measures to protect the consuming public have been introduced to counter the danger of exploitative marketing practices. Thus, children are seen as a vulnerable target throughout the world, and so there is often legislation to protect them from unfair practices. As an example, there are advertising standards authorities in many countries to help regulate the advertising industry; and consumer protection legislation often exists to prevent organizations making false claims about their products or colluding to fix prices. In addition, the long-running debates such as the ones about the promotion and selling of tobacco and alcohol products promoted opposition among a number of people and interest groups.

In spite of these, concern about unethical trading practices and irresponsible marketing remains. To a large extent, these have been amplified by a number of significant events over the first part of the 21st century. Thus, it is increasingly accepted that 'global warming' is a problem that is exacerbated by carbon emissions. In response, and with great difficulty, nations have agreed that if they are to be viewed as responsible, they have a role in helping to reduce these emissions. At the same time, the notion of responsible governance has assumed a higher profile as corporate scandals such as Enron in 2001, followed by the collapse of Lehmann Brothers and RBS in 2008, have focused attention on ethical trading practices. In particular, the 'banking crisis' of 2008, caused by decisions to reduce lending standards for mortgages leading to excessive levels of sub-prime mortgages and unwarranted risk levels for banks, has reinforced the need to monitor the way businesses create and market products and services.

Other stories that have kept the debate going include:

- the accusation by some advocacy groups that Nestlé inappropriately promotes its infant formula over breast milk in a number of developing countries;
- Greenwashing – the marketing tactic of misleading consumers about a product or service's environmental friendliness;

- Dannon having to pay up to $35 million in damages to consumers who said they'd been bamboozled into buying Activia for its purported nutritional benefits; when it was actually pretty much the same as every other kind of yoghurt;
- the mis-selling of PPI (Payment Protection Insurance) to UK mortgage applicants and HSBC's $1.92 billion fine for money laundering in the US.

To behave ethically, an organization and its members need to adhere to a collection of principles of right or moral conduct that shape the decisions they make. Ethical marketing is about whether a firm's marketing decisions are morally right or wrong. Practicing ethics in marketing means deliberately applying standards of fairness or moral rights and wrongs to marketing decision making and the resultant behaviours and practices in the organization. The morality of a marketing decision can encompass any aspect of marketing from advertising to the pricing of products or services or to the sourcing of raw materials.

The American Marketing Association promotes ethical conduct by advocating that professional marketing managers be careful to:

1 **do no harm:** by consciously avoiding harmful actions or omissions by embodying high ethical standards and adhering to all applicable laws and regulations in the choices we make;

2 **foster trust in the marketing system:** by striving for good faith and fair dealing so as to contribute toward the efficacy of the exchange process as well as avoiding deception in product design, pricing, communication and delivery of distribution;

3 **embrace ethical values:** by building relationships and enhancing consumer confidence in the integrity of marketing by affirming these core values: honesty, responsibility, fairness, respect, transparency and citizenship.

The range of criticism that is brought against marketing is that it can (and sometimes does):

- Play on people's weaknesses such as envy, fear, uncertainty and doubt to persuade consumers that they must use a particular brand of washing powder or own that brand of mobile phone.
- Deliberately hide practices that would devalue a product or service's image such as the use of child labour, poorly sourced ingredients or excessive and unnecessary packaging.
- Inappropriately use stereotypes that reinforce prejudices or societal divisions; or that play on sexual imagery to sell a product.
- Employ 'high pressure' sales techniques to sell to consumers or to pressure vendors to buy more than they need and push items that will result in higher commissions for the sales person even though they are not right for the customer.

- Infringe people's privacy through using overly invasive market research or holding data about individuals that they do not want held. While data protection legislation provides safeguards, people do not always know about the databases they are on.

- Promote excessive materialism through making products and services appear attractive by associating them with traits that people desire or that they think they have. In addition, the over promotion of credit, it is argued, encourages people to consume more than they need.

- Use 'Dark Patterns' that exploit psychological attributes such as a tendency to scan read terms and conditions or information pages, or to pursue the path of least resistance. This is particularly relevant to internet site user-interface design where: the default for an extra (insurance or special delivery) is 'opt-in' rather than 'opt-out'; extras are automatically added to one's 'basket'; it is easy to sign up but very difficult to get out of or return a purchase.

- Move from information and persuasion into manipulation; so that people purchase something they don't really want.

All these can be supported with recent examples and some with long-standing examples. However, they do imply that consumers' powers of perception are limited and that their intelligence is sufficiently low that they will be 'fooled' forever. In the longer run, no matter what 'marketing' is performed, the consumer will always be sovereign as long as he or she is free to make choices – either choices between competing products, or the choice not to buy at all. Indeed, it could be argued that by extending product choices and the range of techniques used to sell products, marketing is enhancing consumer sovereignty rather than eroding it.

It should be noted, too, that although 'clever' marketing activity may persuade an individual to buy a product or service for the first time, it is unlikely to be the persuasive factor in subsequent purchases unless there is real value in the product. Thus, many customers complain about the methods used by some budget airlines to boost their revenue on the back of very low cost ticket prices, but stick with them because they see them as value for money in spite of their poor customer service and suspect marketing practices.

It is also suggested that skilful marketing can create needs. The argument to support this would be that nobody wanted an Apple iPhone before it was invented and that marketing has created it as a 'must-have' product that has provoked a number of competitive 'look-alikes'. This, however, confuses needs and wants. Clearly, nobody specified an iPhone before it was invented; but there has always been a need for portable communications, entertainment and useful applications. Previously, these needs had been met by a number of separate devices such as mobile phones, digital audio players, sat-navs, newspapers, games consoles, and so on. Now technology has made available a means of satisfying these needs using one device. Creating further applications and greater functionality has produced something that consumers find very useful. It is common to find people extolling the virtues of this product at the same time as they admit to not having wanted one before they experienced it. At the time of writing, similar views can be found about tablet computers and e-book readers.

In these examples, the contribution of marketing was to identify in as much detail as possible what a customer needed and then to persuade him or her that a specific product or brand would provide the most effective means of satisfying the latent and expressed needs. The key is in providing a unique set of benefits that match real needs.

Underlying this view of marketing is the belief that consumers seek satisfactory solutions to their buying problems: first, by acquiring information about available goods and services and their attributes and, eventually, by choosing that product which comes closest to solving their problem.

Much of the criticism levelled at marketing is in fact directed at one aspect of it: advertising. Advertising practitioners themselves are fully conscious of these criticisms, which include the ideas that advertising:

- makes misleading claims about product or services;
- uses hidden, dangerously powerful techniques of persuasion;
- by encouraging undesirable attitudes, has adverse social effects;
- works through the exploitation of human inadequacy.

Advertisers themselves would point to the fact that advertising in all its forms is heavily controlled in most Western societies and cannot by itself achieve sustained patterns of repeat purchase.

The debate about the ethics of marketing also often confuses marketing institutions with the people who work in them. Clearly, there are dishonest business people who engage in activities that are detrimental to their fellow citizens. However, it seems a grave error to criticize marketing institutions because of the practices of a small number of unethical marketers. It is clear, for example, that there are advertisers who engage in deceptive practices designed to mislead and possibly defraud consumers. Nevertheless, the institution of advertising can be used not only to inform consumers about potentially beneficial new products, such as new energy-saving technologies, but also to promote non-profit community services, such as theatres and state education. This argument can, of course, be applied to all marketing activities.

Consumerism and marketing

Closely connected with the issue of the ethics in marketing is the issue of consumerism. This can be defined as the process of fostering an emphasis on, or preoccupation with, the acquisition of consumer goods. The consumerist movement seeks to moderate this process by promoting such practices as honest packaging and advertising, product guarantees and improved safety standards. In this sense it is a movement or a set of policies aimed at regulating products and services, and standards in manufacturing, selling and advertising in the interests of the buyer.

Ironically, the aims of consumerist movements are pro-marketing in that what they want is for marketing in business to be implemented in a sincere rather than cynical spirit. Cynical implementation of marketing practices, which consumerists claim has been all too common, is no better than high-pressure salesmanship or misleading puffery. The sincere implementation of a marketing approach entails respect for each individual customer served. An interpretation of the consumerist desire is that the sort of relationship found between a manufacturer and a customer in, say, a capital goods market should be created in consumer markets. In so far as that it is both economically feasible and what the consumer really wants, marketers should also want a more satisfactory relationship between organization and customer (see Figure 5.1).

FIGURE 5.1   Consumerism's way to better marketing

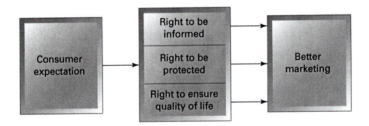

The marketing of children's toys provides an example of how customers, consumers and company objectives can all be satisfied by careful business practice. The successful toy companies of today are those that inform parents that their products are not potentially dangerous, not coated with lead paint, and not destroyed the hour after they are first pressed into active service. At the time of writing, Fisher-Price is still one of the most successful toy manufacturers. Since 1968 it has eschewed child-manipulative promotion, carefully tested its products with children for durability, safety and purposeful play, and charged the prices necessary to make and market 'good' toys. The consequent sales and profit margins have been impressive.

On the other side of the coin, McDonald's, one of the strongest brands in the world, has been forced to make its food offering healthier to comply with changing customer tastes and the demands of consumer lobbyists.

In the end, the difference between ethical and unethical marketing is in the intent. The judgement about the ethicality of the intent is, however, down to the individual. In this, the extremes of intent never create problems; it is the grey or middle ground that is hard. To be an ethical marketing manager, it is therefore important to be 'honest with yourself' as well as others as to motivations and the moral codes you have decided to adhere to.

Marketing: concept, function or process?

It doesn't take long for any business practitioner or student of marketing to recognize that many people are confused about the status, value and role of marketing within organizations. This is mainly due to the focus of the discipline: the satisfaction of customer needs by the organization, which means that the value marketing has to offer has implications across the whole of an enterprise. Thus, it can be hard to recognize marketing's role simply by looking at the activities normally conducted by a marketing department.

The problem is compounded by the bad press that marketing had towards the end of the last century. Headlines such as 'Has Marketing had its Day?' and 'P&G Disband their Marketing Departments' appeared with uncomfortable regularity. As the 21st century unfolds, developments in the internet, communications technology and social media are also fundamentally changing the business models organizations have available to them. Added to this is the fact that one only has to poll a small number of managers within most organizations to find widespread agreement about the low status of their marketing colleagues. Phrases such as 'not sure what they do' and 'waste of time and space' are all too frequently to be heard.

In reality, the problem is not that marketing has outlived its usefulness as business models change, or is fundamentally flawed in some way, but that there is often a failure to distinguish between marketing as a concept, a business function or department, and the business processes the marketing concept implies. To exploit marketing's potential, managers needs to be clear about the distinctions between these three different facets of the discipline.

The basic error has been to assume that all the ideas, analytical tools and approaches contained within the discipline of marketing (and this book) define the job of a marketing department or marketing professional. If they did, then marketing managers would effectively be running all businesses. In the vast majority of organizations, this would not usually be acceptable. It is hard to imagine a business unit's executive board delegating competitive strategy and cross-function co-ordination to the marketing function. Most managers and strategists see these as key tasks for a business's executive – if they don't do this, what else do they do? It is they who should be running the business, not the marketing function.

The marketing concept

The marketing concept, or the concept of marketing, is derived from the realization that organizations only survive if they satisfy customers. Theodore Levitt was one of the first to formalize this idea. In his seminal work, he draws attention to the importance of viewing a business in a way that is appropriate to the markets in which it operates. His classic example was the railroads, which defined themselves as being in the railway business, rather than in the transportation business:

> The railroads did not stop growing because the need for passenger and freight transportation declined. That grew. The railroads are in trouble today not because the need was filled by others (cars, trucks, aeroplanes, even telephones), but because it was not filled by the railroads themselves.
> (Levitt, T, 'Marketing Myopia', *Harvard Business Review*, July/August 1960)

Levitt contrasted the railroads with companies such as DuPont, which saw their activities in a very different light. Instead of defining themselves in terms of their products, they concentrated on finding 'customer-satisfying' applications for them. They did not abandon the search for technical excellence, but combined it with an awareness of its relevance to market needs.

These examples focus attention on contrary aspects of the business. Seeing oneself as being in the railroad business implies that knowing, understanding and being proficient in running railways is the key to success. If, however, the business is seen as finding the best means of transporting people and freight from one location to another, business management takes on another dimension. The priority then becomes, not running a railway, but providing transport and communication services.

The significance of the marketing concept, then, is that it places duties on managers across the business to think in a certain way, to adopt a certain approach to doing business, and to foster a culture that puts customers at the heart of the organization.

Marketing as an organizational function

The activities in which a marketing department or function engage are distinct and require a well-developed set of professional skills to be performed properly. Its two areas of unique expertise are delivering high quality and impactful market and customer intelligence, and well executed marketing communications.

Market and customer intelligence covers a range of topic areas. These include strategic contributions such as defining and segmenting markets, understanding perceptions of value, recommending value propositions to business unit management, identifying gaps in the market, proposing new products, positioning competitors and understanding customer behaviour. The more operational or tactical activities here are concerned with conducting market research, an area where considerable expertise is required, and monitoring the impact of an enterprise's efforts such as customer service assessment.

Marketing communications similarly cover a range of activities, some of which are strategic while others are tactical. The main strategic activity is brand or impression management, which covers a range of areas but tends to be communications led. Tactical activities include advertising, public relations, conferencing, mail and exploiting the opportunities offered by e-media. Sales promotions are also often part of a marketing department's tactical responsibilities, which can involve special offers, coupons and other forms of merchandising. Also included here might be responsibility for the launch of new products.

Marketing as a process

A business process is a series of actions that will deliver a predetermined outcome. Marketing can therefore be mapped as a process that will deliver value to an organization's customers. The process can be captured in Figure 6.1 and is similar to the diagram used to explain the discipline of marketing in Topic 1 of this book.

The starting point for mapping the discipline as a process is a definition of the markets in which an organization wishes to compete and an understanding of how value is perceived by members of that market. Once established, appropriate value propositions can be formulated. Delivering value, however, requires customers to know about the proposition, see it in a favourable light, be able to afford it and be able to source it. Delivering value also necessitates providing appropriate sales and after-sales service and the product or service performing to the expectations set by the market and the provider.

Customer experience and market changes must subsequently be monitored to gain assurance that value continues to be delivered. It is vital for any organization that a supplier's understanding of the market is constantly updated. This 'virtuous circle' is constrained and/or enhanced by an organization's assets, both tangible and intangible.

FIGURE 6.1 Marketing as a process

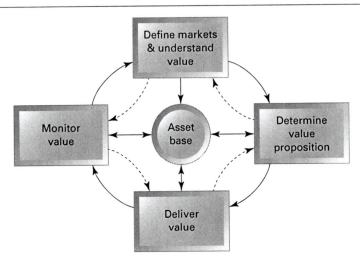

Concept, function or process?

The discipline of marketing, then, is at once a concept, a function and a process. The concept is clear and represents a way of thinking about the purpose and management of an organization. Parts of the discipline, however, form the basis of a professional activity that can be logically contained within a specialist department or departments. Nevertheless, those departments cannot be expected to run the business any more than a sales function, engineering division or finance department can (even though it sometimes feels that they try to). Similarly, they are in a weak position to provide the cross-functional co-ordination that the breadth of the discipline implies.

On the other hand, the discipline of marketing and its associated processes do have a significant contribution to make to the strategic management of an organization. As has been demonstrated many times, business decisions need to be made in the light of market developments and customer needs. Insight into these are delivered by good quality, well founded, market research. All people who reach a general management level in any organization require these insights plus the ability to understand and influence the value creation and delivery activities encompassed within marketing as a process. Unfortunately, and all too regularly, managers seem to forget the marketing aspects of their strategic roles, and marketing defaults to the 'stuff' of a marketing department. Hopefully, continued education will make this an increasingly rare condition.

World-class marketing

R esearch conducted by the Cranfield School of Management in the late 1990s with the assistance of some of Europe's best companies, large and small, produced key indications of how successful companies use marketing to create sustainable competitive advantage. Over the years, the results of this work have remained true as illustrated by the offers from large 'leading edge' marketing consultancies.

The challenges such companies address to create this competitive advantage include the pace of change; process thinking; market maturity; the expertise and power of customers; and the internationalization of business. Studying the way these organizations have met these challenges has enabled the identification of 10 guidelines for world-class marketing.

1 A market orientation

In the economic downturns of the 1990s, and again in the world financial and economic crises at the end of the first decade of the 21st century, created restricted markets for most organizations. Typical responses have been financial husbandry, ratio management, disinvestment and downsizing. In companies that are not market driven this has led to *anorexia industrialosa* (an excessive desire to be leaner and fitter, leading to emaciation and eventually death).

An alternative response has been attempts to create the 'agile organization' or to manage the business on the basis of the 'balanced scorecard'. In many cases, an over-focus on the systems aspect of these initiatives has led to increased bureaucracy and difficulty in garnering the potential benefits of such moves.

Successful companies might have tried these initiatives but have always come back to the necessity to lift their heads above the parapet and look at their markets and their customers rather than wasting their energy tinkering with their own internal workings. World-class companies believe passionately, from the Board downwards, that creating superior value for clearly defined groups of customers is the best way of creating wealth for all stakeholders. Only then do the initiatives referred to above work; otherwise they become fads. This leads to the first guideline as shown in Figure 7.1:

as far as possible, ensure that a strong market orientation exists within your organization.

FIGURE 7.1   Ensuring a market orientation

- Develop customer orientation in all functions. Ensure that every function understands that they are there to serve the customer, not for their own narrow functional interests.
- This must be driven from the Board downwards.
- Where possible, organize in cross-functional teams around customer groups and core processes.
- Make customers the arbiter of quality.

2 Competitive advantage

Successful organizations avoid offering an undifferentiated product or service in too broad a market, and they use one or any combination of different aspects of the marketing mix to earn superior positions. Without something different to offer (provided the market requires it), companies will continue to struggle, relying on being in a growth market and/or the inadequacies of their competitors rather than their own competitive strengths for survival. Advantage within these approaches can come from any of a number of different sources including technological leadership, superior service, wide distribution coverage, strong positioning or any other value-creating proposition.

World leaders continuously strive to serve customer needs better and more cost-effectively, and work relentlessly towards the differential advantage that this brings. The foundations of this process are summarized in Figure 7.2.

FIGURE 7.2   Striving for competitive advantage

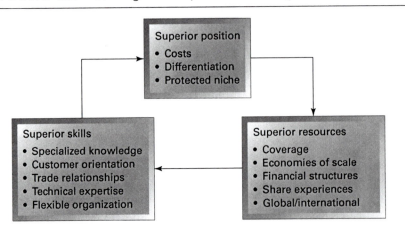

3 Environmental scanning

It goes without saying that failure to monitor hostile environmental changes is the most common reason for companies going to the wall. Had anyone at the end of the 1980s predicted that IBM would be losing billions of dollars by the mid-1990s, they would have been derided. But it was IBM's failure to respond to the changes taking place in their markets that caused just such problems. Now, in the 21st century, global giants such as General Motors are facing similar problems and, at the time of writing, it remains to be seen whether the mighty Intel can survive the transition to mobile devices from PCs.

Clearly, marketing plays a key role in this process. For successful organizations, this means devoting at least some of the time and resources of key executives to monitoring formally the changes taking place around them. The key areas requiring environmental scanning are summarized in Figure 7.3.

FIGURE 7.3   Monitoring the environment: key areas

Macro environment	Market/industry environment
• Political/regulatory	• Market size and potential
• Economic	• Customer behaviour
• Technological	• Segmentation
• Societal	• Suppliers
	• Channels
	• Industry practices
	• Industry profitability

Together these imply a formal marketing audit

4 Competitor surveillance

Excellent companies know as much about their close competitors as they know about themselves. This implies a structured competitor monitoring process covering the areas noted in Figure 7.4 in order to develop usable profiles. The results of this profiling exercise should be included in the marketing audit.

FIGURE 7.4   Developing competitor profiles

- Direct competitors
- Potential competitors
- Substitute products
- Forward integration by suppliers
- Backward integration by customers
- Competitors' profitability
- Competitors' strengths and weaknesses

5 Market segmentation

The ability to recognize groups of customers who share the same or similar needs and offer them appropriate value propositions has always been a major contributor to organizational success. However, the real secret is to change the offer in accordance with changing needs, and not to offer exactly the same product or service to everyone; an indication of a product-orientated organization.

This process of market segmentation is the basis for strategy formation and positioning. Without a good understanding of how needs within a market can vary, and how these variations can be used to identify different market segments, decisions about strategies and positioning become divorced from the markets in which they are supposed to secure competitive advantage. The process of segmentation is summarized in Figure 7.5.

FIGURE 7.5   The process of market segmentation

Steps in segmenting a market:

(a) Understand how your market works (market structure)
(b) List what is bought (including where, when, how, applications)
(c) List who buys (demographics, psychographics)
(d) List why they buy (needs, benefits sought)
(e) Search for groups with similar needs

The golden rule:
Select a segment and serve it.
Do not straddle segments and sit between them.

6 Strengths and weaknesses analysis

Successful companies usually have a well-established and excellent grasp of the opportunities and threats facing them (derived from the previous three guidelines) plus a good understanding of their relative strengths and weaknesses in each of the segments they are targeting as a result of the analysis outlined in the previous guideline. The process of identifying strengths and weaknesses is summarized in Figure 7.6.

FIGURE 7.6   Identifying strengths and weaknesses

For each segment in which an organization competes, understand:

- What the 'qualifying' features and benefits are
- What the 'differential' features and benefits are
- How relatively important each of these are
- How well your product or service performs against your competitors' on each of these requirements

7 Mirroring market dynamics

Good organizations use their understanding of their markets and their own positions within these markets to adapt their operations in line with environmental changes as they occur. Some changes will result from the marketing activities of the firms themselves; others will be beyond their control being a consequence of predictable but inexorable trends or unforeseeable events. The combination of these factors creates the dynamics of a product-based market as it evolves from birth through growth and maturity to its eventual decline.

World-class businesses manage their way through this life cycle so that they are in the best competitive position at each point in the evolutionary process. They build market share before maturity sets in; they try to ensure that they have a cost advantage when it does, and they recognize that different segments will have different life cycles. Typical responses to the different dynamics of each life cycle stage are illustrated in Figure 7.7.

FIGURE 7.7   The dynamics of product/market life cycles

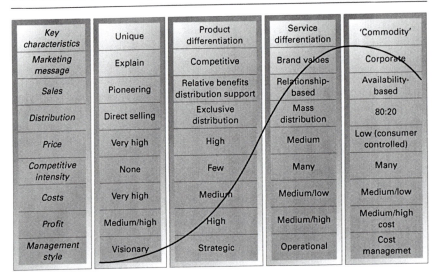

Key characteristics	Unique	Product differentiation	Service differentiation	'Commodity'
Marketing message	Explain	Competitive	Brand values	Corporate
Sales	Pioneering	Relative benefits distribution support	Relationship-based	Availability-based
Distribution	Direct selling	Exclusive distribution	Mass distribution	80:20
Price	Very high	High	Medium	Low (consumer controlled)
Competitive intensity	None	Few	Many	Many
Costs	Very high	Medium	Medium/low	Medium/low
Profit	Medium/high	High	Medium/high	Medium/high cost
Management style	Visionary	Strategic	Operational	Cost managemet

8 Adopt a portfolio management approach

Successful companies recognize that they cannot be all things to all people and that they have greater or lesser strengths in serving each of their various markets. This recognition enables the development of a portfolio approach to determining appropriate objectives and the effective allocation of resources. The portfolio approach is most easily conceived as a matrix, as illustrated in Figure 7.8.

FIGURE 7.8   Portfolio of products and markets

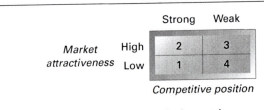

		Strong	Weak
Market attractiveness	High	2	3
	Low	1	4

Competitive position

Strategies for different boxes in the matrix:

- Box 1   Maintain and manage for sustained earings
- Box 2   Invest and build for growth
- Box 3   Selectively invest
- Box 4   Manage for cash

9 Set strategic priorities

The previous six guidelines effectively comprise a marketing audit; the basis of a strategic marketing plan. World-class companies usually engage in some form of planning of this nature. However, the best also take great pains to avoid stifling creativity through excessively bureaucratic planning procedures. The strength of a good planning process is that it provides a sound and logical foundation for defining key target markets, sources of differential advantage and intended sources of revenue and profits.

This implies something more sophisticated than forecasts and budgets. Commercial history has demonstrated that any fool can spell out the financial results they wish to achieve. It takes intellect to spell out *how* they are to be achieved. This identification of what needs to be done to achieve logically derived objectives will then highlight the strategic imperatives for the business. Only when such priorities are clear can they be used to create key performance indicators and drive other business processes. The key contents of a good strategic marketing plan are listed in Figure 7.9.

FIGURE 7.9   Contents of a strategic marketing plan

A written strategic marketing plan for three years usually contains:

- A mission statement
- A financial summary
- A market overview
- SWOT analyses on key segments
- A portfolio summary
- Assumptions
- Marketing objectives and strategies
- A budget

This strategic plan can then be converted into a detailed one-year plan.

10 Be professional

Professional management skills, particularly in marketing, are the hallmark of commercial success. Leadership and entrepreneurial skills, combined with hard-edged marketing skills, will see any company thrive in the new millennium. Leading companies maintain a corporate optimism because they believe that what they are doing and what they have to offer is worthwhile.

They recognize, however, that the increasingly hostile and dynamic environments within which they work demand professionalism at a number of different levels. It requires the courage to question strategic priorities that do not appear to have been adequately defined or refined. It requires conventional wisdom to be challenged if it appears to be no longer relevant. It requires the discipline to follow the logical processes of strategic analysis and planning rather than jumping at the first good idea that comes along. But at its base, it also requires professional marketing skills and formal training in the underlying concepts, tools and techniques of marketing as management discipline. The core of this curriculum is outlined in Figure 7.10.

FIGURE 7.10   Core professional curriculum

- Market research
- Gap analysis
- Market segmentation/positioning
- Product lifecycle analysis
- Portfolio management
- The four Ps
  - Product management
  - Pricing
  - Place (customer service, channel management)
  - Promotion (selling, sales force management, advertising, sales promotion)

PART TWO
Different types of marketing

Marketing consumer products

Consumer products are those that are sold to individuals and then consumed by them or someone they pass them on to. This distinguishes them from industrial products, which are purchased for their ability to help make or deliver another product.

Consumer products are therefore at the head of their value chains leading right back to the production of the basic raw materials. They rely on the whole chain performing well for their success. At the same time, those in charge of marketing consumer products also determine the survival of that value chain. As such they are interdependent.

Consumer services are similar. Thus a financial adviser or hairdresser will sell to individual consumers and will use tangible products and/or information supplies to deliver their service. Together, they will have a collective impact on their value, as will large retailers who will have a significant interdependency with their value chains.

Consumer markets

The key marketing issue for manufacturers or retailers of consumer goods, or providers of consumer services, is that they are faced with large numbers of potential customers. This applies equally to organizations that supply consumer durables such as refrigerators, and consumables such as grocery products. The main differences between these two categories tend to be:

- frequency of purchase;
- absolute cost;
- degree of involvement in the purchase.

For these reasons, consumable products are often referred to as 'fast moving consumer goods' (FMCGs) where acceptance or rejection occurs in a relatively short space of time, which has implications for the way these products are marketed. Consumer durables, such as 'white goods' (freezers, cookers, etc) or 'brown goods' (small appliances, furniture, etc), on the other hand, tend to be infrequent purchases but of some significance to a household. Their purchase therefore tends to be a much longer and more considered process, requiring a supplier to adapt their marketing accordingly.

Whatever their category, the fact of very large numbers of potential purchasers remains and presents the suppliers of these products with a significant problem: how to make contact with customers when there are so many people who might be persuaded to buy your products in preference to a competitor's? This problem is compounded when those potential consumers are geographically dispersed or where they represent a small proportion of each community within the market.

Main methods for marketing consumer products

Over the years, this difficulty has been addressed in a number of different ways and it's an area in which significant innovations have taken place at various times.

Personal selling

The most effective way to develop a sales relationship with a potential customer has always been for a person to meet with that customer to explore his or her needs and to explain the virtues of the offer to him or her. In most consumer markets, this would involve a sales person calling on individuals and engaging them in the sales process either over the phone or in person. Traditionally, this is known as cold calling or door-to-door selling. However, employing sales people in this way is a very expensive means of making a sale and, where the value of each sale is relatively small, not very profitable. For this reason, consumer goods sold in this manner tend to be:

- difficult to sell (ie the benefits are hard to explain as is the case for insurance, solar heating or time-shares);
- highly profitable (ie the margin per sale is large as is the case for double glazing, conservatories or changing utilities supplier);
- commodity items (ie where the only differentiating aspect is the sales process as can be the case for gardening services, new driveways or loft conversions).

The rapid expansion of call centres at the end of the last century and the beginning of the 21st has helped address the need for personal contact, although has been abused by some organizations on a 'cold calling' basis. Well-run call centres, such as those for Orange or First Direct, however, can be a powerful adjunct to face-to-face personal selling.

Direct mail

In parallel with the increasing sophistication of information technology and databases has come a significant increase in the use of direct mail. This is a cheaper means of placing a product in front of a consumer but enables a direct contact to be made. The increasing ability to target particular types of customer has encouraged many consumer products organizations to explore this route, and the 21st century has seen a proliferation of letters and catalogues arriving through consumers' doors. With advances in internet and mobile phone access, electronic direct mail has also increased.

The downsides of this method include: a relatively low response rate; progressive disillusionment on the part of consumers who begin to feel deluged with offers; and a loss of any personal contact with suppliers. Spam filters have also reduced the potential for e-mail.

Retail outlets

Given the number and dispersal of potential customers, suppliers of consumer products often rely on retailers to distribute and sell their goods and services. This emphasizes the need to select appropriate retail organizations and the requirement for maintaining good relations with them. Indeed, for some grocery products such as a new cook-in sauce, simply being on the right shelf in the right part of the right chain of supermarkets is almost enough to guarantee success for a product line. The power of such retailers has also given rise to a particular type of marketing referred to as trade marketing, and a supplier industry providing retail 'own label' products.

The internet has also provided opportunities for established retailers to have another shop window, and new retailers to access a much more dispersed group of customers. An innovative example of a retailer using advanced technology to meet customer needs is provided by Tesco in South Korea. Operating in one of the hardest working countries in the world, Tesco's South Korean branch – called Home Plus – encourages time-poor commuters to buy products through their mobile phones while waiting for their trains by building virtual aisles on the platforms. These virtual aisles display rich images of grocery items laid out in the same way as they would be in the shop. Every item has a corresponding QR barcode (Quick Response two-dimensional barcode). People waiting on the platform scan the codes of the items they want using their mobile, which are then immediately added to their Home Plus shopping basket.

Brands

Creating and maintaining a brand for a product or set of products is essentially a way of developing and keeping a relationship with a consumer without the need for personal contact.

Strong brands are those that have a personality with which consumers can identify or that evoke a feeling within a consumer that matches their personal values, aspirations and lifestyle. Consumers are therefore attracted to brands of this nature and will buy them in preference to lesser (commodity) brands or brands that are targeted at a different segment of the market.

Possessing a strong product or company brand provides their owners with power in the market place. Manufacturers and service suppliers who own such brands are able to exert considerable influence on retailers in terms of price, shelf location, competitor positioning, merchandising, promotions policy, acceptance of new products and many other areas. Distinct retail brands are similarly able to influence lesser branded suppliers and to gain favourable locations and terms for their outlets.

For these reasons, brands and brand strategy are often at the heart of a supplier of consumer products' marketing strategy.

Value chain management

The competitive world of consumer marketing has led many suppliers and retailers to pay closer attention to the value chain at whose head they sit. These organizations have recognized that advantage can be gained by exerting influence across all those who affect their products and their ability to supply. These advantages include: lower cost; higher quality; better availability; product innovation; speed to market; and a host of other important competitive factors.

In industries such as automotive manufacture, management of aspects of the value chain are sometimes delegated to a small group of key suppliers who are expected to influence and co-ordinate other suppliers in the chain. In others, such as the computer supply industry, businesses such as Dell are working directly with suppliers right down to component level and beyond in seeking efficiency and innovation for competitive advantage.

Micro marketing

Large numbers of potential consumers with similar needs leads many consumer marketing organizations to a mass marketing approach that tries to satisfy the majority of the market with an undiscriminating product, brand or approach as classically practised by Ford, Coca-Cola or McDonald's. Modern consumer marketers are, however, increasingly finding that markets are fragmenting as consumers become more sophisticated, individualistic and demanding. With the potential for varying the offer increasing as information technology becomes more sophisticated, micro marketing is increasing in significance.

One result has been a proliferation of new brands, or in some cases, existing brands being 'stretched' across a number of product variations. A recent example is provided by Neutrogena, which is now one of the biggest brands in the personal care portfolio of Johnson & Johnson. Originally, however, the brand was a skin-friendly range of mild glycerine soaps that only diversified into shampoos in 1980. Today the 'mild' associations of the brand have been used to stretch the name, which now covers a wide variety of products ranging from cleansers and moisturizers to hair care products, cosmetics and anti-aging creams.

Another initiative has been efforts to provide 'mass customization'. This involves consumers being able to configure their own product from a series of modular offerings added on to the core product or service. The relaunched 'Mini' designed and produced by BMW is a good example of this. The base product is devoid of most extras, which will add 50 per cent to the retail price once added, but which allows purchasers to create the car of their choice.

Personalized portfolios, where suppliers such as Amazon or Tesco target offers and information based on past purchases or expressions of interest, are also increasing in use.

Finding ways of keeping the cost of such practices down, and utilizing the growth of new direct consumer channels such as the internet to provide customization in innovative and consumer-friendly ways, remain important challenges for future consumer marketers.

Marketing industrial products

Whatever an organization is offering, be it public services, involvement in a charity or commercial products, the fundamental principles of marketing always apply. A market-orientated organization will seek an understanding of its customers, the markets of which they are a part, the opportunities which exist within that market, the best ways to compete with its rivals and so on.

In spite of these similarities, most organizations in industrial markets instinctively know that their markets are different and that marketing their products requires a different set of approaches. To operate effectively in industrial markets, it is important to understand what these differences are since they will highlight the areas on which the organization must focus.

Having accepted this, it is also important to note that there is no simple or clear divide between industrial and consumer products and markets. On the product side, some products are sold in the same form to both industrial and consumer markets. Examples of this include bank accounts, motor cars, personal computers and parts for washing machines. In terms of markets, some consumer-goods manufacturers will only sell directly to other businesses, ie trade sales. As a consequence, industrial marketing cannot be defined simply by the products involved or by the fact that it involves business-to-business selling.

Understanding industrial marketing

The best way to conceptualize industrial marketing is to look at it as a continuum with obvious slow-moving industrial products at one end and fast-moving consumer products at the other (see Figure 9.1). In the middle of the continuum are faster moving industrial products and slower moving consumer products.

FIGURE 9.1   Continuum of industrial marketing

Industrial markets			Consumer markets
Machine tools	Ball bearings	Furniture	Soap powder
Complex software	Printed circuit boards	Domestic appliances	Canned food

The existence of this continuum also illustrates the possibility of transferring marketing approaches between these different markets. While the context of their usage and the way in which they are applied may vary, no idea should be ignored because it is thought to be more appropriate to the realm of one market or product than another.

Brands, for instance, are usually thought of as most appropriate for consumer product marketing. However, efforts by Intel and the success of Caterpillar provide contrary examples. Earth moving equipment is an unlikely candidate for branding, yet Caterpillar have established the stylish yellow-tabbed CAT logo as the symbol of the leading global manufacturer of off-road trucks, tractors and other multi-terrain vehicles. The power of the brand is demonstrated by its easy transfer to a range of high-priced heavy-duty designer boots and associated apparel sold to the general public. The latter, though the smaller of the two businesses by far, trades off its sibling's well-established brand values of rugged, durable and dependable performance. Other examples of industrial corporations that have invested efforts in brand building include Johnston Controls and United Technologies Corp.

Issues in industrial marketing

The first issue concerns the way in which an industrial purchaser views a product it wishes to buy. Industrial products are often thought of as being more **complex** than the equivalent consumer products, which is obviously not always the case. What is different is the attention paid to the **details** of a product. Even a commodity product, such as sheet steel, cement or a simple component, will be considered in much greater detail by an industrial purchaser. This is because it will be used in more complex ways or that small variations will have potentially harmful consequences. As an example, the wrong grade of steel will not machine properly and may put cost up and quality down. Similarly, a personal computer with a slightly wrong specification may make previous software purchases obsolete or networking with existing machines impossible.

The implications of such detailed product evaluations are that industrial purchasers have greater **information needs** than consumer purchasers, both before and after a purchase is made. In turn, this implies larger numbers of people being involved in the purchase decision. Consequently, organizations marketing industrial products have to cope with a larger and more diverse **decision-making unit** and a greater degree of **formalization** in the procedures applied to a purchase.

It also implies that a greater degree of **personal contact** between the supplier and buyer will be necessary, since this is the best way of providing complete information. Personal contact is necessary to isolate *who needs to know what* and *at what point in the decision-making process*, in order to improve the chances of a sale, or continued sales.

Apart from costly and infrequently purchased capital goods, the **volumes** bought by an industrial purchaser are also likely to be higher than by individuals or families in a consumer market. This makes the loss of a supply agreement to both supplier and purchaser more significant. If a supplier fails to deliver the right quantity, the purchaser will find it difficult to continue their business.

On the other hand, if a purchaser stops buying, this will have a significant impact on the supplier's income. In industrial markets, therefore, there is often a high degree of **interdependence**. Both supplier and purchaser will rely on each other for their continued existence. The loss of one purchaser in a consumer market is not nearly so significant.

This situation is further complicated by the fact that it is difficult in the industrial context to find mass markets. Apart from there being **smaller numbers of customers**, one buying organization is likely to differ significantly from the next in their buying requirements. This means that **segmentation** in industrial markets has to be conducted on a different basis.

A further implication is that the degree of **product variability** required can also be greater. In some cases, a single customer can form an entire segment and can consequently demand a high degree of customization. In others, the consumer variables for segmentation such as demography, life-stage and lifestyle need to be replaced by alternatives such as size, applications and competitive positioning. Such **heterogeneity** is an important factor for the organization marketing industrial products.

In trying to understand, and give some structure to, the markets that industrial suppliers face, it must be recognized that their customers also have customers of their own, who may in turn have customers! Unless the customer is a country's Defence Ministry or some similar body, all industrial products will eventually translate into a consumer purchase. This means that the structure of the market in which an industrial organization operates can be complex, with a whole series of intermediaries or 'value adders' between them and the final consumer. Industrial suppliers are thus faced with a situation of **derived demand** for their goods and services. The way they perceive their market and the way in which opportunities are identified and defined can therefore become a very complicated process.

Paradoxically, these factors combine to make **market research** in industrial markets sometimes more problematic, and sometimes easier, than consumer market research. Because of their low numbers, potential customers are likely to be difficult to find, extract information from, and generalize about. One cannot simply stand in shopping centres and stop passers-by or ring at random from the telephone directory. In addition, the influences on demand are likely to be more complex and remote from each organization, making them difficult to interpret. Where an organization has existing customers, however, market research is often easier since the people who hold valuable information and opinions should already be known and are usually quite willing to be approached.

Industrial marketing and general management

One of the consequences of the complexities that exist in the buyer/seller relationship in industrial markets is that many different functions within the selling organization are required to interact with various aspects of the customer organization. This can include service or maintenance sections, the design team, installation group, training, delivery and finance departments, as well as senior directors and the sales people. While many of these are also points of contact in consumer marketing, these contacts tend to be extensive and of greater significance in industrial markets.

Such complexity has also given rise to a need for key account management. Supply relationships that are significant for both parties can easily falter if left on a simple transactional basis. Key account managers who take a relationship perspective on an organization-wide basis are more likely to ensure that potential problems are avoided.

The management of marketing in industrial organizations, therefore, tends towards a **general management** function with small decisions in one area having a greater impact on the customer and business success. This is not to say that such co-ordination is inappropriate for consumer markets, but that closer attention to building a marketing approach across the management functions has a higher profile.

In general, then, marketing industrial products is a diverse area that can utilize a number of the approaches developed by consumer marketing organizations. What is important is a recognition of the differences that exist in industrial markets and the implications these hold for the supplying organization. In particular, the way that the relationship between supplier and customer is managed takes on a different perspective, but one that must be well understood and nurtured over time for the achievement of continuing and successful business.

Marketing service products

Service businesses became an increasingly significant sector of most advanced economies towards the end of the last century and continue to be a dynamic sector as the 21st century unfolds. As a sector, it currently provides around 70 per cent of civilian employment in the United States and the United Kingdom. Table 10.1 illustrates the potential range of service activities involved. At the same time, there has been an accelerating trend to differentiate what were once considered to be simply 'goods' by highlighting the service elements of the offer. Together with the deregulation experienced by many professional and government services, these factors have forced organizations to consider whether any differences are required when marketing service-based products.

At one level, the answer is 'no' since the theory of marketing has universal application. At another, the nature of many service-based products dictates that more emphasis is placed on certain elements of the marketing process.

TABLE 10.1 Major examples of service industries

Retailing, wholesaling and distribution
Banking, insurance and other financial institutions
Real estate
Communications, information and multimedia services
Health services
Business, professional and personal services
Leisure and entertainment
Education
Public utilities
Government services and non-profit service organizations

It is very important that marketing organizations understand these elements and how they will affect the marketing tasks they face.

Defining a service

Defining a service for marketing purposes, however, is not easy. The diversity of organizations involved in services and the tendency to highlight the service elements of an 'offer' for competitive purposes means that they are sometimes hard to classify. One important element, however, is the degree of tangibility involved. Table 10.2 identifies four categories, varying from a 'pure' tangible product to a 'pure' service.

Looked at in this way, a continuum of tangible–intangible products emerges as illustrated in Figure 10.1. Point 'a' on the left-hand side of this figure illustrates an offer where there is no service element and the product is highly tangible. At the other end of the spectrum, point 'd' illustrates a product that is entirely a service and is therefore highly intangible. Points 'b' and 'c' show varying mixes. For example, point 'b' illustrates the mix of tangibility for a computer company.

TABLE 10.2   Variations in product tangibility

A pure tangible product	A tangible offer, such as sugar, coal or tea. No services are bought with the product
A tangible product with accompanying services such as commissioning, training, maintenance, etc	The offer has built-in services to enhance its customer appeal, eg computers, machine tools
An intangible product with accompanying minor goods	The offer is basically a service, but has a physical element, eg property surveyors, whose expert inspection is encapsulated in a report. Similarly, airlines offer in-flight meals or entertainment
A pure intangible product, where one buys expertise	The offer is a stand-alone service such as market research, psychoanalysis or ski-instruction

FIGURE 10.1   Continuum of tangible–intangible products

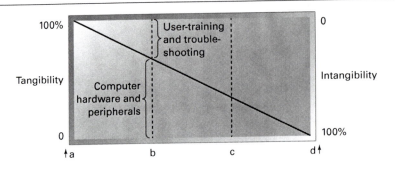

Computer hardware and peripherals are highly tangible and can be regarded as commodities, whereas the service elements of user-training and trouble-shooting are largely intangible.

The intangible nature of a service leads to a number of other differences of significance for marketing. These include the implications that:

- Services can easily be copied by competitors, since they cannot be patented and specified with drawings.

- Quality can be difficult to guarantee since services are not previously produced or 'manufactured' under controlled conditions. Instead, they are produced and delivered at the time of consumption.

- A service cannot be stored on a shelf or taken down and used at a later time. Services are therefore highly perishable.

- People are an intrinsic part of most services and are difficult to separate from the product.

- The true value of a service can only be assessed on consumption. Thus, the purchase of a service involves a high component of trust.

- Services are often very personal in their nature and can involve the customer in their delivery and consumption, as in the case of a golf lesson or making a purchase at IKEA.

An important area in marketing services is, therefore, the **relationship** between the customer and the supplier. The close link between production and consumption, and the personal nature of many service products, emphasize this aspect. Where no personal relationship exists, the contrast between membership-type organizations and 'hands-off' or automated services is stark and has led many businesses to seek a means of marketing more concrete affiliations as a substitute. In looking at ways and means of marketing the specific features of service products, the management of the relationship with the customer is, thus, always important.

The nature of a service also makes it hard for the customer to **evaluate** an offer prior to purchase. Unlike a car, it cannot be test-driven; it is difficult to encapsulate in a technical specification; and quality is uncertain. As examples, it is hard for a potential customer to assess a bank before opening an account with them, and a stay in a hotel can only be judged after one has checked out.

Thus, a crucial aspect of marketing services is to provide, as far as is possible, **tangible evidence** of the product quality. This highlights the need for careful attention to the 'product promise', such as the initial points of contact, descriptive literature and the peripherals that provide clues to the product's integrity. It is no coincidence that professional service businesses often have plush reception areas, holiday brochures are a masterpiece of presentation and spa-based health clubs make a big show of testing the water. The problems associated with service evaluation can also be addressed by focusing on reputation, or by enhancing the value of a service through the provision of extra benefits such as free offers. Here, word of mouth or third-party endorsements become particularly influential. These can come from existing customers, referral markets and media institutions, all of whom can provide powerful testimony to the quality or value of an organization's offering. The increasing use of the internet has enabled many more organizations to collect and display customer views.

Since many services rely heavily on a personal interaction between the service provider and the customer, or depend on individuals exercising judgement when creating the service, considerable **heterogeneity** between purchases becomes possible, so that customer experiences of the product may vary enormously. Thus, the performance of a waiter or a shop assistant will have a great impact on the way a customer experiences the core benefit they are seeking. Similarly, two customers in the same hotel can have completely different opinions of their visit if one found their towels unlaundered or had their breakfast delivered late. Since the quality of such elements is in the hands of the people performing the service, employees become a vital concern for marketing services effectively. This requires attention to service modelling to identify people-related 'fail points', as well as taking an interest in recruitment markets to ensure the right calibre of person. The process of **service delivery** thus needs careful specification, which should include an identification of the skills necessary to reduce the likelihood of product heterogeneity as a consequence of 'people problems'.

This is particularly important for providers of professional services where service delivery and marketing activities overlap and even spill over into informal client contact. Thus lawyers, accountants and other professionals need to use time with clients to improve their customer knowledge, identify appropriate levels of service and ensure post-purchase satisfaction. Indeed, the term 'marketing' could be seen as a term to describe professional service delivery.

At this point, it should also be noted that both the intangibility and heterogeneity of services mean that **attention to detail** becomes central to marketing effectiveness. This is, first, because it is often small factors that provide clues for the consumer about quality and, second, because such factors can have a major impact on customers' experience of service quality. Details, however, are also that part of the process of delivering the service most influenced by individual employees, thereby giving further weight to the focus on process design and human resource management.

The fact that a service will require the customer's involvement in its creation and delivery enhances the need for efficient management of this customer/provider **interaction**. Since manufacturers are able to check quality prior to delivery, service providers have to find substitutes for this. One solution has been to utilize technology to enhance consistency and improve accessibility, as was achieved by banks when they introduced automated tills or 'banking through the wall' and the introduction of e-tickets by airlines. Another approach has been to focus attention on front-line staff and to 'empower' them to negotiate service delivery to prevent excessive disappointment. Such a situation has worked well with in-store supervisory staff, receptionists and service engineers. A further method has involved better customer management to ensure satisfactory service delivery. Customer management can cover a number of different aspects, from setting appropriate expectations and encouraging customers to signify their satisfaction levels while utilizing a service, to getting them to behave in a way that enhances the service. A good example of the latter is the widespread improvement in the queuing technology that now ensures nobody waits longer than necessary in many banks, post offices and railway stations.

For marketing managers, the **perishability** of a service places extra emphasis on understanding demand patterns and why such fluctuations exist. However, **matching demand** at all times is rarely possible or, indeed, cost-effective. In the end, the only alternatives are to try to change patterns of demand or to generate increased capacity at peak times. The techniques for managing demand revolve around incentives, such as offering better value and other sales promotion activities to encourage off-peak use, or using pricing mechanisms, such as premiums or discounts. Capacity can be enhanced by using part-time staff, subcontractors and shared facilities, or by carrying overheads in the form of staff, or assets, which are redundant at certain times. Managers, therefore, have to ensure careful co-ordination to balance the overall offer with the market's preferred pattern of utilization.

Services are sold into a whole range of markets, including industrial, consumer, government and not-for-profit. While each market creates its own unique marketing requirements, for services it is the distinct characteristics of the product that provide the major marketing challenges. In particular, it would seem to demand an expanded marketing mix beyond the four Ps of product, price, place and promotion, to include **people, processes** and **customer service**. These three additional elements significantly affect the success or otherwise of a service-based offering and will benefit from discrete programmes and action plans being developed for them. The features of service products also underline the importance of third-party markets such as recruitment, referral, influencer and internal markets, plus the overall concept of relationship marketing. Indeed, it has been argued that the recent interest in relationship marketing first grew from developments initiated within service businesses.

Marketing high-tech products

Technology is now an important competitive tool for most organizations to help differentiate themselves from others in a market. Where technology is a significant part of the overall market offering, organizations must consider whether its inclusion requires a particular approach or whether the nature of the technology will have little impact on the way in which the product is marketed.

The key distinction here is between products that are high-tech for marketing purposes and products that simply involve advanced technology but do not require specific attention to that aspect of the offer. If the situation is the former, then there are a number of marketing issues that require special attention. If it is the latter, then other product and market issues are likely to be more important.

Distinguishing high-tech products

In deciding whether a product is high-tech for marketing purposes, it must be recognized that few products consist of a single technology. They are more usually a mixture of advanced, new and old technologies that, together, create the substantive product. Thus, for instance, automobiles, printers and cameras utilize a whole range of technologies, but will only be high-tech for marketing purposes if the new or advanced technology they incorporate acts as a focus for customers' evaluation of the product. The first criterion for classifying a product as high-tech is therefore how customers view the product.

Whatever the product, purchases involve a risk for the buyer. For high-tech products, the problem is that the **risk** for the purchaser is increased as a result of the uncertainties associated with a new or advanced technology. However, risk does not just exist for the buyer – the supplier will also experience a higher than usual element of risk. This is because both the supplier and the buyer, be they end-users or supply-chain intermediaries, will lack experience of applying, maintaining and using the technology. In turn, this will increase the chances of unforeseen problems arising, such as further cost, supply continuity, unanticipated side effects or quality problems.

The newness of a technology forming the key feature of a high-tech product will also contribute to marketing issues since the product is unlikely to be an accepted solution, yet, for the problem(s) it has been designed to solve. As such, there is unlikely to be widespread understanding of how a high-tech product can provide benefits for both customer and potential customer organizations. In addition, it is doubtful if there will be support structures in the market that supplying organizations can utilize in their marketing efforts.

A further implication of high-tech or 'state-of-the-art' technology is that supplying organizations will have to employ comparatively large proportions of highly skilled scientific and technical specialists. These will be necessary to obtain the developments needed for new products and to provide the know-how required for manufacture, sales and post-purchase support. This will be particularly important given the absence of external expertise to which such problems can be out-sourced. The downside is that large numbers of technical specialists may encourage a technically (rather than market) oriented organization.

The key features of high-tech products that have implications for marketing are therefore:

- advanced technology that acts as the focus for product evaluation;
- high degree of uncertainty on the part of both the supplier and the customer about the technology;
- products not yet accepted as a natural solution for the problems they have been designed to address;
- lack of any associated external infrastructure;
- likely to have been developed in a highly technical environment.

These do not negate the fundamentals of marketing management such as benefit analysis, segmentation and careful targeting via the marketing mix. They do, however, lead to the critical issues that marketing managers of high-tech products must address.

Critical marketing issues

Technology seduction

Since high-tech products tend to be derived in a technologically orientated organization peopled by large numbers of technical specialists, marketing managers must first be aware of the potential for **technology seduction**. Seduction will involve the internal promotion of a technology that is unwarranted by the market(s) that a business can realistically address. This can lead to either products whose performance exceeds market needs, or investment based on gaining technical improvements rather than market potential. The role of marketing managers is to recognize a case of technology seduction and to avoid becoming seduced, themselves, by the enthusiasm of others.

Credibility

As a second issue, if high-tech products are not yet accepted solutions and tend to generate a high level of uncertainty, customers will need to develop a greater degree of trust than might otherwise be the case. An important ingredient for the creation of trust is **credibility**. This can involve both the credibility of the supplying organization and the technology itself.

Establishing credibility may require:

- high-profile demonstrations;
- the offer of substantial guarantees;
- wooing 'lead users';
- fostering excellent media relations.

Creating or changing people's perceptions, however, can take a long time. This means that high-tech marketing managers need to foresee the potential for credibility problems well in advance to avoid them becoming barriers to entry into new markets or barriers to establishing them in existing ones.

Standards

In technology-based markets, **standards** have always had a significant impact on marketing strategy, but for high technology they can be very important. As an example, conforming to standards can enhance credibility while the absence of standards can increase the uncertainty felt by customers and can leave a supplier without frameworks within which to work. In addition, the creation of a standard that is based on an alternative interpretation of a technology can make an organization's products obsolete. When marketing high-tech products, attention must therefore be paid to:

- influencing the creation of standards;
- the possibility of becoming 'the standard';
- conforming to standards;
- gaining approval or being certified as meeting a standard, and so on.

Unfortunately, this usually requires a lot of time, money and effort, and will demand careful co-ordination to gain the maximum marketing benefits.

Technology life cycles

The 'newness' of a high-tech product and the uncertainty associated with it implies that managers should also place their marketing decisions in the

FIGURE 11.1   The technology life cycle

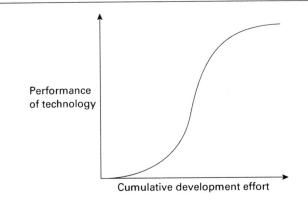

context of the technology's life cycle (see Figure 11.1). By definition, a high-tech product is at the early stages of its technological (as opposed to market) life. This means that marketing managers have to prepare for the transition from a situation where performance improvements have been hard to achieve to one where improvements become relatively easy to obtain. At the same time, the marketing task will change as risk and uncertainty reduce while technologies move through their life cycles. This also suggests that marketing should contribute to decisions about which element of performance should be prioritized for development, and how sufficient flexibility can be maintained for future product development.

Positioning

A further contributor to overcoming the problems associated with high-tech products is good **positioning**. Favourable product evaluation, reduced uncertainty and broadened supplier acceptance can be enhanced by positioning that implies leadership (to support credibility), customer service (to compensate for the lack of general knowledge about the technology) and a clear performance benefit (to make the risk of purchase worthwhile). This could involve positioning the supplier as the technology innovator and service leader, and the product's benefits as improved quality, cost savings or performance levels that were previously impossible.

Infrastructure

Finally, since a critical feature of high-tech products is the lack of associated market and technological **infrastructures**, marketing managers must also find a means of redressing this problem. Where they cannot be redressed externally, a business must seek an in-house solution and bear the associated costs. Alternatively, it will require an enterprise to select markets and, therefore, product development priorities, where limited infrastructure will have the least impact on commercialization and business development.

Overall, then, like other product-based marketing activities, marketing high-tech products requires a good understanding of their distinctive features and the marketing priorities they imply. If these are ignored, decisions and consequent actions will be taken according to other criteria such as: instinct; short-term considerations; ill-informed assumptions; or significant voices. The role of the marketing manager is to establish the marketing priorities associated with this type of product as an integral part of, and a timely contribution to, the managerial processes of the organization.

In addition, and unlike products in established and growing markets, high-tech products require a more proactive approach to the establishment of demand. The sheer newness of the product or its position will necessitate a 'supply-push' approach as opposed to the product being able to ride on the back of 'demand-pull' conditions. Latent demand will need to be sought and activated into purchasing activity.

Marketing capital goods

The marketing of capital goods presents suppliers with some special concerns. These are generated by the nature of the products and the circumstances under which they are bought and sold. Capital goods can be pieces of plant and equipment, such as large machines, boilers or storage facilities, or complete systems such as refineries, telecommunications networks or civil engineering projects.

Customers will similarly be large organizations and may be either private or public sector. Whichever the case, the purchase will be a significant event for both the customer and the supplier in terms of the amounts of money involved and the benefits that the products will be required to deliver. Such high stakes mean that a systematic approach to marketing is required so that the risks involved are carefully managed.

Consequences for marketing

By their nature, orders for capital goods tend to be few in number, even for the 'faster-moving' capital goods such as machine tools. In addition, their high cost also makes them very prone to economic fluctuations. Suppliers are thus often faced with a 'feast or famine' situation whereby they either have no orders and are standing around idle, or they are overwhelmed with enquiries and find it difficult to meet delivery or completion schedules.

This is further exacerbated by the fact that each purchase is usually supplied against a different specification. It is unlikely that such large and complex products will be used in the same way, or serve exactly the same purpose, from one customer to another. Such a situation prohibits the creation of finished stock except at a very early stage in the manufacture or construction process.

The risk associated with the supply and purchase of capital goods also creates pressures that militate against the use of innovative technologies or approaches. On the supplier side, the consequence of product failure in terms of financial penalties or loss of reputation can be very high. Similarly, from the customer's point of view, a capital purchase will frequently have strategic, or at least operational, significance and buyers are likely to be anxious to reduce the chances of something going wrong by sticking to proven technologies or methodologies. Where innovation does occur, its adoption is therefore likely to be a slow process and the recovery of development costs a long-term activity.

The consequences of these factors for marketing cover a number of areas. High levels of customization plus the complexity of (particularly) larger products will mean that a product specification will take time to evolve and will typically be the result of much negotiation between supplier and customer. This will require suppliers to resource such negotiations and to maintain the ability to understand a customer's perspectives so that they can translate the benefits that customers seek into a product specification. Protracted negotiations and the absence of finished goods stock will create long order lead times, which will also require suppliers to maintain sales relationships over time. Without this, suppliers may risk losing an order through issues such as:

- changes in personnel;
- loss of interest;
- situational changes that will alter the product specification;
- the activities of competitors.

The size of an order may also require suppliers to join together, sometimes as international consortia, to be able to fulfil the requirements of a customer. Managing such relationships in a way that presents customers with a unified face is a distinct skill, but one that is important for the maintenance of relationships with customers. Such relationships, however, will also need to be continued after a sale has been made since capital goods usually involve lengthy construction and/or installation. Although repeat business is not as significant a feature of capital goods marketing as it is for other types of industrial products, client or customer referrals and references *are* an important aspect of selling and good relationships will be needed to ensure that these are forthcoming.

Capital goods pricing

Since each product is unique, the price of a particular sale will also vary. In addition, since there is much negotiation about each specification, price is often one of the last factors to be considered. The complexity of supply also means that competing bids for a contract often vary significantly between competitors as a result of the way prices are calculated and the different methodologies that can be applied to the fulfilment of a specification. Indeed, finding alternative cheaper solutions to problems presented in an invitation to tender can be a significant competitive advantage.

At the same time, the variations in demand mean that organizations sometimes adopt a pricing strategy that is closer to marginal cost pricing. This may be done to maintain capacity during times of 'famine' in order to prevent the loss of resources that would make them uncompetitive when business becomes more buoyant. Alternatively, during periods of growth, organizations will often seek to recover cost and limit demand, which will tempt them to quote much higher prices.

Prices in capital goods markets, then, have a tendency to fluctuate quite widely, both between time periods and between different forms of the same product, which makes it difficult to decide how to use price as a competitive weapon. On the other hand, the amounts of money involved and the complexity of the product provide more scope than in other areas for variations on the pricing mix. This can involve:

- payment terms;
- payment penalties and bonuses;
- profit sharing;
- leasing arrangements;
- modular pricing;
- the way a price is presented;
- technology transfer agreements.

Decision making in the purchase of capital goods

The size and significance of a capital purchase will mean that large numbers of people are likely to combine to form the decision-making unit. Since relationships are an important factor in capital goods sales, personal contacts and the ability to keep and develop such relationships is a critical factor for success. Similarly, having the flexibility to maintain different types of relationships with different people is also important. The significance of capital purchases, however, can mean that governments will also have an interest in the product. Indeed, for some products, governments *are* the customer. Thus, there can be a political, as well as a commercial, influence in the decision to buy.

Thus, in some instances, such as a defence project, high levels of confidentiality may be required. In others, such as a large infrastructural civil engineering project, awareness of a country's development plans, the involvement of national suppliers or some 'tit-for-tat' investment by the supplier or the supplier's government may be a prerequisite for a successful sale. This political aspect, plus the complex nature of the 'buy-centre', may require a lot of 'politics' and building of credibility along a number of different dimensions for an organization to be a viable contender for a piece of business.

Marketing capital goods is, therefore, conducted in a complex market environment. Marketers are faced with long lead times and extended product life cycles, which make it difficult to innovate. In contrast, they are also faced with volatile demand and large variations between one purchase and the next. This is further complicated by the need to develop good relationships with customers, but with the likelihood that any relationship will only be temporary since any one customer is only likely to purchase once or, at best, infrequently. This demands that suppliers are able to be flexible in terms of relationships, capacity and the product they supply. It also demands that they take a long-term perspective on several counts including sales negotiations, product design and development, relationship management, profit planning and funding issues.

Trade marketing

In the marketing of consumer products and 'fast-moving' industrial goods, much effort is applied to 'pull' activities (ie creating demand among large numbers of users that will 'pull' products through the supply chain). This is the logic behind most branding strategies, sales calls and promotional activities such as couponing or distributing free samples through doors. An alternative, or even complementary approach, is to adopt a 'push' strategy focusing on intermediaries (the trade) and 'pushing' products through the supply chain to consumers.

The power and influence of these trade intermediaries in developed economies has grown significantly over the last 30 years. Indeed, the ability to have your product on the shelves or in the catalogues of the more prominent intermediaries is often a key factor to gaining position and advantage in many end-use markets. Focusing marketing effort on these intermediaries is termed trade marketing. As its significance has increased, many organizations have had to develop new approaches to marketing and relationship management to be effective.

The rise of intermediaries

Factors that have contributed to the increasing importance of trade intermediaries for suppliers of mass market goods and services are as follows.

Retail power

As has already happened in North America and much of Western Europe, retailing and some aspects of industrial distribution have become dominated by a small number of large organizations such as Wal-Mart in the United States, Tesco in the United Kingdom and Carrefour in France. Suppliers relying on these intermediaries for sales to end users can easily be denied access to such markets even if only one intermediary decides not to stock their products. Effective marketing to these intermediaries therefore takes on much greater significance. The strategy can no longer be a reliance on large sales forces placing their products in a wide range of different retailers or distributors in a 'hit or miss' fashion, but one that sustains effective presence in these outlets.

Brand differentiation

In some markets, consumers are finding it increasingly difficult to differentiate between leading brands or suppliers. This is particularly true in markets for banking, mobile telephony or personal computing, but it is also observable in traditional fast-moving consumer areas such as washing powders or tinned foods. The result of this growing brand parity is that consumers more frequently purchase on the basis of availability and price within their chosen 'retail set'.

Market fragmentation

As markets become more competitive and customers grow in sophistication, demands for individualized supply similarly increase. Demand consequently fragments making it less effective to adopt mass marketing techniques. While this has encouraged organizations such as Heinz, Amazon and wine importers to experiment with more direct and individualized marketing methods, it has also emphasized the value of reaching out to customers at the point of purchase. This requires trade promotions to encourage preferential stocking and point-of-sale support.

E-commerce

Advances in information technology have meant that suppliers can be in direct contact with an intermediary on a real-time basis. This has enabled retailers and other intermediaries to reduce cost and increase efficiency by effectively delegating inventory responsibilities to a small number of key suppliers. Establishing oneself as one of these key suppliers in the eyes of intermediaries therefore becomes a priority for many manufacturers.

Brand management deficiencies

Brand managers in many organizations are often young and ambitious people trying to leave their mark on a brand's performance. The most effective way of achieving short-term position is often through trade promotions since brand value enhancement in the eyes of the consumer is more difficult and inevitably a longer-term proposition. Trade marketing therefore becomes more valuable to a brand manager's career than brand development.

Trade marketing tactics

Traditionally, tactics for trade marketing have centred on the marketing mix elements of promotion and price. These have taken the form of:

Promotion	Price
Incentives to staff of intermediaries	Additional discounts
Point-of-sale material	Supplying to retailer price points
Merchandising support	Supporting buyer margin targets
Co-operative advertising	Price promotions such as 'buy two and get a third free'
Joint trade fair representation	

Trade marketing strategies

As intermediaries have become an increasing focus for suppliers, so tactical approaches have given way to more strategic marketing approaches. At the heart of this is an understanding of how both supplier and intermediary can mutually benefit from a well-managed long-term relationship.

One manifestation of this are product profitability studies that analyse in great detail the way that cost attaches itself to a product during manufacture, distribution and handling within the retail environment. Thus, packaging that allows items to be transported around a retail outlet and deposited straight onto the shelves without the need to unpack and stack will save time, effort and therefore cost for the retailer. Another is the development of category management whereby a single supplier takes responsibility for a product category such as hair care or chocolate bar confectionery within a retailer's store. They will check the display effectiveness, restock routines and generally ensure they and the retailer are making the most from stocking the product.

Where category management has become widespread, as is the case in the United States, Germany and the United Kingdom, suppliers vie with each other to become 'category leaders', which has caused a need to adjust significantly the structure of many suppliers' brand portfolios.

The strategic importance of trade marketing has also led to heavy investment in information technology by many suppliers to enable logistics and communications to proceed as smoothly as possible. Other aspects of the relationship will be enshrined in joint product development plans, the sharing of 'best-practice' information and a long-term view of category development such as the introduction of new products, range extensions, brand development, supply arrangements, managing seasonal variations, and so on. A typical example might be a decision to introduce more organic produce, different labelling information or recyclable packaging.

The future

The factors that have led to the expansion of trade marketing have also stimulated many suppliers to reassess their relationship with end users. While some suppliers have concentrated on better marketing relationships with intermediaries, others have sought to strengthen their brand franchise so that retail or product categories will be weakened without the inclusion of their brand. This is quite apparent in a number of areas such as fashionable sportswear, pet foods and some aspects of the soft drinks market. It is also a major part of Intel's long-term strategy with their global 'Intel Inside' campaign.

At the same time, there has been an upsurge of 'direct' provision in many areas, particularly in the financial services arena. The advent of the internet is dramatically fuelling this trend. While some retailers have added this to the range of services they offer, the possibility of direct provision for manufacturers is an attractive proposition. Not only does it imply higher margins but it also reduces their reliance on retailers who may not always approach supply relationships in a true 'spirit of partnership'.

The increase in global retailing and the emergence of 'category killers' are also good and bad news for suppliers. The global expansion of stores such as Toys-R-Us, Wal-Mart and Carrefour means access to expanded markets and growth in line with the retailers. However, such stores are usually situated out of town and offer focused category goods at heavily discounted prices. Their predatory nature often decimates local retail competition, reducing suppliers' routes to a market, and putting them in a stronger position to demand lower prices from suppliers. At the time of writing, there is a big debate about the viability of traditional High Street retailing.

Managing the conflicting demands of these powerful intermediaries, including the need for independence and long-term profitability on the part of a supplier and the continuing possibility for creating a consumer or brand franchise, will be an important determinant of the way trade marketing develops in the future.

Category management

Category management is a concept that has been developing as a radical alternative to brand management in retail marketing since the mid-1990s. The process of category management can be summarized as: The strategic management of a group of products clustered around a specific customer need with the group, or category, being managed as a strategic business unit with clearly defined profitability goals.

The importance of category management is that it shifts attention from individual brands to the management of overall categories as defined by local customer needs.

Category management emerged from the development of ideas within the concept of Efficient Customer Response (ECR) that was initiated industry-wide in the United States from the mid-1980s onwards. The emphasis of ECR is on sales profitability rather than sales volume and it spans the entire value chain from the purchase of raw materials to manufacturing, distribution and sale. It was enabled by improvements in technology and has allowed suppliers and buyers to reduce waste and stockholding as well as moving away from discounts as a means of generating sales. The focus of the concept is the business processes in retail organizations.

Growth of category management

Brand management focuses on individual brands from the manufacturer's perspective, grouping all functions that affect a brand's profitability under one manager. Retailers, however, will often group brands together by product (eg soap powder) because that is more convenient for their customers and reflects the way in which customers shop.

The resultant categories are therefore defined by customers, but can lead to problems of definition. For instance, when a customer wants a cleaner for the bathroom, does he or she categorize it as a bathroom product, a cleaner or a home safety product? In addition, categories tend to vary regionally and according to customer types, rather than on a broader cross-cultural basis. In response some manufacturers have had to recast their brands for categories, but this in turn has raised the question of whether some products should appear in more than one category (for instance, should herbs be categorized with fresh produce, baking goods or both?).

In the final analysis, what is important to retailers is that their shelf space sells more than it would if managed another way. Retailers' expertise lies in providing the retail brand plus the space to sell products and services that facilitate sales. Sometimes, an external supplier is appointed as category manager, who is then made responsible for optimizing sales from that space. By doing so, retailers are exploiting manufacturer skills in such areas as display, sales promotion and merchandising.

The retailer will normally set minimum standards for the category such as demanding that there must be at least one major brand name and one 'own label' product displayed. After that, the category managers make their own stocking and communications decisions on behalf of their assigned category. For example, if GSK or P&G were to identify opportunities for increased toothbrush sales within the oral hygiene category for which they acted as category manager, they could spend their own budget on promoting them.

Contrary to traditional practices, category management obliges manufacturers to consider the profitability of an entire product segment rather than that of just their own brands. The fact that retailers have forced this change is another example of the evolution of retailers from passive distributors to proactive marketers and the shift of power from manufacturer to retailer.

Where category managers are appointed internally, they usually have a similar role, ie the management of a partnership between a supplier or a number of suppliers with the objective of sales and profit enhancement. Their role becomes that of sourcing strategists and brings control of the category back within the retailer.

From brand management to category management

The trend towards category management has also required a shift from the traditionally narrow focus of brand management. Looked at from a category perspective, it is possible to see that consumer choice is not just about selecting from competing brands such as Coca-Cola or Pepsi, but involves an entire drinks portfolio of soft drinks, juices, beverages and alcohol. Heinz began realigning its business of over 150 leading brands along category management principles in 1997 into seven global categories: ketchups, condiments and sauces; infant feeding; seafood (tuna); organic and nutritional food; pet food; frozen food; and convenience food. By 2009, they had reduced this to three core categories: ketchup and sauces; meals and snacks; and infant/nutrition (HJ Heinz Company Corporate Profiles 2000 and 2009).

Rather than relying on the power of their brand names, organizations need to ensure that all of their support systems demonstrate to retailers that they are capable of managing categories to their advantage. This might mean a review of all of the organization's systems for retail supply such as the logistics of keeping the shelves fully supplied or maintaining efficient electronic data interchange systems for monitoring stock levels.

Limitations of category management

Viewed purely as a strategy to reduce waste and therefore costs, category management loses its focus on the end customer as the absolute priority. Concentrating on the maximization of shelf space profitability may not improve customer satisfaction levels, which, in the long run, may reduce profits.

One recent report concluded that the availability of a wide selection of goods is a major determinant in customers' decisions about where to shop. Category management limits the product choice to those that are most profitable for the retailer, and this can have a negative impact on the customers' shopping experience. If customers feel hindered in their purchase decisions by the inability to compare prices of different brands, the category management process will ultimately rebound.

Further difficulties arise from the issue of positioning different product categories. Should paper tissues, for instance, be categorized with bathroom products or health and beauty? And should the two categories be set next to each other or apart? In addition, different retailers and manufacturers could well work to different category definitions.

These limitations reflect the fact that much of the emphasis of category management has been on the manufacturer/retailer relationship. As far back as 1994, a *Financial Times* survey found that consumers have effectively been demoted as the focus of marketing strategy as retailers have grown in importance, with consumers attracting 30 per cent of marketing expenditure against retailers at 54 per cent.

Challenges for the future

One of the most difficult challenges facing category management is reducing the number of superfluous items on the shelves. This is in opposition to traditional brand marketing, which aims to prolong the life of the brand by extending the product range. Possible evolutionary pathways are demonstrated in Figure 14.1.

A further factor is mass customization. This has been made possible by the increased sophistication in consumer information and has allowed marketers to provide variations on the central product to suit each customer. The growth of retailers' own or private label products (eg Tesco's 'finest' and 'value' or Wal-Mart's 'Sam's Choice') reflects this, but further limits the

FIGURE 14.1   Category management evolution

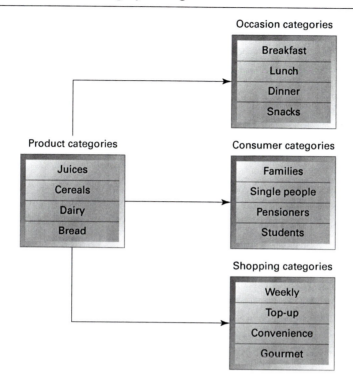

Occasion categories
- Breakfast
- Lunch
- Dinner
- Snacks

Product categories
- Juices
- Cereals
- Dairy
- Bread

Consumer categories
- Families
- Single people
- Pensioners
- Students

Shopping categories
- Weekly
- Top-up
- Convenience
- Gourmet

available shelf space for branded supplies. The difficulty for retailers is ensuring that limiting consumers' brand choice is not perceived as limiting their category choice just because they cannot find their favourite products.

The future of category management must necessarily take account of the distribution systems for an increasingly 'global village' market. Many mass retailers are unable to market so many products properly, even when redefined as categories. Providing marketing expertise is therefore one way in which manufacturers can hope to retain some kind of balance in the relationship with such international retailers.

In order to sustain a customer focus, manufacturers need free access to customer information. This can be obtained through large panel companies such as Nielsen or Taylor Nelson Sofres (TNS), or through the development of a manufacturer's own database, such as Heinz. Manufacturers can also try to establish a reputation for themselves as leaders in ECR.

Future emphasis will probably be on targeting customer satisfaction more effectively in order to maximize long-term profit. Category management can help by focusing on the retail audience and the way in which category sales are driven. This in turn helps retailers build an effective vehicle for appealing to the variety of customers' product decisions and needs. The challenge is to make this happen on a store-by-store basis, at an affordable cost.

Relationship marketing

The concept of relationship marketing has evolved as a consequence of some of the limitations of traditional approaches to marketing. The most important relationships for marketing purposes are those between the supplying organization and its customers. The focus of these relationships is the activities involved in delivering the marketing mix. Although the four Ps are probably the most universally accepted method for structuring the marketing mix, the idea of there only being four internal areas and one external requiring attention have been questioned. This has led to the propositions contained within the relationship marketing approach.

An expanded marketing mix

The four Ps of product, price, promotion and place constitute the 'offer' that an organization presents to the market place. If the offer is sufficiently well matched to customers' needs, it should lead to sales. In addition, if it is sufficiently well managed, these sales should be profitable to the organization. The potential downside of this is that an organization's attention becomes too focused on a 'profitable sale', leading to a transactional approach to marketing (see Table 15.1). The danger is that interactions based on transactions can ignore other aspects of supplier/buyer relationships that can provide something of greater substance for longer-term marketing success. The manifestation of this is the development of customer loyalty and commitment, which will survive the attempts of competitors to lure away customers.

The need for such relationships as a means of retaining customers has, in reality, long been recognized. Fast-moving consumer goods organizations have become very sophisticated in developing brands, which act as surrogates for personal relationships. Business-to-business selling has traditionally utilized both corporate image and sales teams to keep customers loyal. In general, however, growth and the winning of new customers have tended to attract the greater amount of managerial attention. The increasingly

TABLE 15.1 Tendencies inherent in a transaction approach to marketing

The priority is achieving a sale
The focus is on margins rather than profitability
Meeting short-term sales targets overrides other priorities
The product is 'pushed' at customer
There is limited commitment to the customer
Unrealistic terms of sale can be accepted
Responsibility is passed to customer at the earliest opportunity

volatile competitive environment, however, has required this approach to change. From a marketing perspective, attitudes towards managing existing relationships have, therefore, had to adopt a higher profile.

The key attitude shifts involved are:

- recognition of the value of retaining customers as well as attracting new ones;
- acceptance that there are elements within the components of the marketing mix that could have special significance in terms of managing relationships;
- acknowledgement of the influence that people and institutions outside customers can have in developing and maintaining relationships.

A closer look at those elements of the overall offer in terms of their impact on customer relationships indicates that certain elements should probably be separated out and treated as distinct elements of the marketing mix (see Figure 15.1). The first of these is customer service. This is normally included as part of the 'P' of place and consists of those activities that support the placement of orders, the delivery of goods or services, either directly or via third party channels, and any post-purchase assistance required. Such support is obviously an important aspect of an organization's relationships with customers and will help determine customers' experience of a purchase and product utilization. Indeed, in many service businesses, mature markets or markets where the products are technically complex, customer service is seen as a significant vehicle for competitive differentiation.

An organization's employees will inevitably interact with customers and other stakeholders at some point. When they do, their actions will affect customers'

FIGURE 15.1   Expanded marketing mix

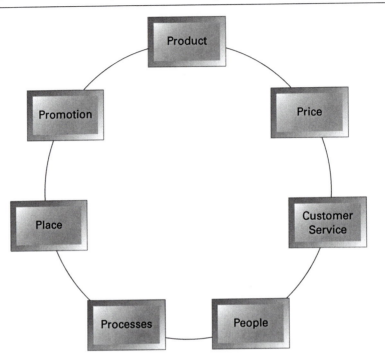

and other stakeholders' perceptions of the whole organization as they will often assume everyone in the organization is the same as the person they've just encountered. Staff, or people, should therefore be regarded as an additional element of the marketing mix.

Whenever a person is identified as a member of a particular establishment, he or she will perform an ambassadorial role, whether they like it or not. Similarly, people will be responsible for the majority of the variations in an organization's performance as experienced by the world outside. Since they will impact on all elements of the marketing mix, and since it is difficult to establish sustainable relationships with inanimate objects or intangible features, people become an important competitive aspect of the offer.

An additional element concerns the procedures, mechanisms and routines by which goods or services are created and delivered to the customer, ie the processes that structure an organization's activities. The importance of these is that, as a supplier unravels the various elements of its significant relationships, the quality of these elements will be determined by the integrity of the processes involved. Where such processes impact on external audiences, be they customers or other parties, they will influence the viability of a relationship and the way in which it develops.

The six markets model

Relationship marketing also recognizes that customer markets do not exist in isolation, but are members of a network of organizations and audiences for which marketing plans may need to be developed. These have been termed:

- influencer markets;
- referral markets;
- supplier markets;
- recruitment markets;
- internal markets.

This provides a six markets model, as shown in Figure 15.2. Customers, of course, remain the prime focus. The success of an organization in its customer markets, however, can be affected to a high degree by these 'other' markets and an organization's strength within them.

FIGURE 15.2   The relationship marketing six markets model

Influencer markets are important because customers are affected as much by independent third parties as they are by the direct activities of supplier organizations. These may be simple media channels, regulatory bodies that set standards, industry experts with influential opinions, or trade associations that shape practice. Influencer markets can therefore include banks, government bodies, and pressure groups, as well as media activities; all of which influence the perceptions of a supplier. Increasing access to information through the internet has also boosted the influence of product evaluation organizations such as Which?

People who will **refer** potential customers to a supplier, such as existing customers or professional advisers, are also an important market. They are particularly significant for the generation of new business, but also for the reinforcement of existing relationships. They can include consultants, other professionals, intermediaries, suppliers and so on.

Suppliers can also be a critical, separate, market for an organization, not just because they are a source of referrals, but because their performance can help or hinder a business to fulfil its promises. Thus, many businesses areinterested in better relations with their suppliers, particularly following the example set by the Japanese. In some quarters, this is described as 'reverse marketing'.

As well as capital and other physical resources, organizations need to **recruit** skilled people. The scarcity of skilled people is a consequence of the changing demographics in many developed nations, plus the increased specialization required for people to be able to work with many of the advanced technologies that are so important to organizational efficiency and effectiveness.

As skills become more specialized and less available, and as people themselves become a more significant element of the marketing mix, **internal** marketing must also be addressed both to retain scarce skills and optimize employees' interactions with external markets.

Traditional marketing is usually outwardly focused and has for too long ignored the people within the organization who have to turn a market promise into a reality. In this way, the concept of relationship marketing brings up to date the efforts of many organizations who have tried to take a broader view of the markets of which they are part and to develop a more sophisticated approach to profitable marketing.

International and global marketing

Global marketing, at its simplest, is the performance of the marketing task across national boundaries. Sometimes this takes the form of international marketing whereby organizations export their goods and services to another country or countries. At others, a more holistic approach is adopted whereby organizations look at the world as one market in the same way that a British business might look at the UK as a market or a German firm might look at the EU as a market. The basic approach, however, is no different from domestic marketing and the principles involved remain the same. Thus, a supplier has to perform market research, identify a target market, develop appropriate products, adopt a suitable pricing policy, promote sales, and so on. In spite of this, whenever organizations begin to operate outside their domestic markets, many otherwise successful enterprises seem to suffer.

This has led both academics and practitioners to wonder why. On examination, what becomes clear is that although the principles are the same, the context is different and adopting a similar mindset for the international market place as for a domestic market can create problems. What emerges, then, is the significance of the *differences* rather than the *similarities* involved when marketing abroad. Within this, it becomes important to recognize that:

- the market environment in other parts of the world can be significantly different in certain areas;
- there is a different dimension of complexity involved in planning the marketing process;
- the control it is possible to exercise over the marketing mix is reduced.

Environment

The environment in different parts of the world presents challenges that can make the transfer of a marketing strategy inappropriate. There are a number of factors potentially at play as outlined in Table 16.1. Thus, for instance, they

TABLE 16.1   Environmental factors affecting global marketing

Degree of political stability	The 'Arab Spring' starting December 2010 brought instability to many Middle Eastern countries
Legal systems	Contrast between common law, civil law and law based on religious systems
Political ideology of the government	Ranging from totalitarian dictatorships to liberal democracies
Historical links	Can be both positive and negative. Ex-colonies often have beneficial links while old enemies such as China and Japan can create difficulties
Attitude towards foreign investment	Some countries encourage it with financial inducements while others make it conditional requiring, say, technological exchange
North/South cultural divide	Most areas of the world see differences in attitude and behaviour and consumption
Technological infrastructure	Can include transport, telecommunications, research establishments, access to sources of power and so on
Economic development	The degree of industrialization will usually affect levels of prosperity, infrastructure development, public health and so on
Role and influence of government	Some governments legislate widely, such as Singapore, with others have low levels of state enterprise and intervention, such as the US

may find that culture inhibits their ability to borrow money; that they are required to use a local partner as a distributor; or that prices are controlled by the government. There may also be different technical standards operating in the country and ethical standards may vary considerably. In addition, fiscal practices such as tariffs, exchange controls and customs duties may require different economic models to be used or that profits be calculated in different ways. Together with such factors as political volatility, an additional element of risk and uncertainty is added to the marketing task.

As one example, the United States is a highly developed free market economy that has a strong car culture and distinctive shopping habits. Tesco moved into this market in spite of a similar move having proved a nightmare for both Marks & Spencer and Sainsbury's before it. They introduced a new brand; Fresh and Easy stores, modelled on the Tesco Express stores in Britain and majored on a limited range of 'wholesome food that doesn't cost your whole paycheck'. However, local stores for major grocery shopping were counter culture; highly competitive markets promoted choice as an expectation for the US consumer, and focusing on price and convenience is what the 'Yanks' do better than anyone else. At the time of writing, Tesco is still present in the United States but has not fulfilled its strategy and is still making heavy losses on the initiative, and is actively considering withdrawal.

Complexity

Many organizations acknowledge the differences in consumer behaviour in other parts of the world; and indeed Tesco sent 50 executives to live with families in the United States before launching their Fresh and Easy chain. However, like many others, Tesco did not manage to translate that experience into a winning strategy and a productive implementation processes. Tesco is not alone and there are many other examples of mistakes that have cost organizations millions of dollars as a result of inadequate rigour in investigating and understanding such differences. Some are the result of inflexible mindsets while others are careless, such as Toyota's launch of the MR2 in France while not realizing that, when spoken in French, the letters and numbers made a rude word. Still others are just silly, such as the poor translations often found in technical instructions. All are based on not dealing with the complexity that makes marketing globally a more challenging task. A number of these factors are shown in Table 16.2.

TABLE 16.2   Business factors making marketing globally more complex

Language
Tastes and fashions
Packaging requirements
Physical environment (temperature, humidity)
Power supplies
Security arrangements
Family structure and size

TABLE 16.2   *continued*

Business hours
What is polite and impolite
Social niceties
Literacy levels
Communications infrastructure
Distribution practices
Methods of transaction

International control

The degrees of freedom an organization has when operating abroad, and the consequent control they can exert over their marketing activities, will mostly be determined by the method chosen for entering a foreign market. The two main forms can be described as simply exporting or alternatively, actually operating abroad.

Straightforward *exporting* can be either indirect or direct. Indirect exporting is when a third party arranges the documentation, shipping and selling of an organization's goods or services abroad, which usually represents the lowest level of commitment to marketing internationally. As foreign sales grow, however, an organization often begins to make a greater commitment, frequently in the form of taking on the documentation task for itself. It is usually at this stage that overseas agents or distributors are appointed to perform the selling task abroad. The business is now a direct exporter, although it is likely that the commitment is still limited to marginal production or process capacity with no additional fixed investment.

Recognition of the importance of overseas trading really happens when a limited fixed investment occurs, not just in the form of production capacity, but also in the form of a marketing subsidiary abroad in recognition of the need for a local presence and often a more aggressive marketing approach.

Foreign production can take the form of opening a branch or licensing; or in the case of tangible products, contract manufacturing, local assembly or full manufacture, either by joint ventures or wholly-owned subsidiaries. With licensing, the company is hiring out its brand name, technical expertise, patents, trademark or process expertise. The licensee offers the service or manufactures and markets abroad on behalf of the licensor. While this avoids the need for a heavy investment, it can lead to over-dependence on the licensee, who quickly builds up process, manufacturing and/or marketing expertise. Disney, Warner Brothers, Phillips-Van Heusen (who own the Calvin Klein brand), Westinghouse and Pilkington Glass are just a few of the many organizations with a successful record of licensing abroad.

Contract manufacturing is the use of someone else's production capacity. This is often difficult for technically complex products where local assembly is a preferable solution. Such an approach is a useful way of getting round tariff barriers as well as gaining experience of a foreign market, without the need for investment in capital and labour. Local assembly can similarly be a learning opportunity and tariff avoidance device, but is more attractive to the host country as it also helps local employment. Car manufacturers such as Honda and Toyota have successfully employed this technique to enter attractive foreign markets.

As such approaches are usually backed by a strong and/or global brand, the marketing task is to protect the brand's values while leaving other aspects of the marketing mix to the licensee or assembler. However, where more control is required and local laws forbid 100 per cent foreign ownership of assets, companies have to consider joint ventures, either with a foreign government or with local partners. This is a good way of gaining greater (but probably not complete) influence over marketing activities and has the added advantages of sharing risk and gaining experience using local expertise.

One-hundred per cent ownership of foreign offices or production facilities is the best way to retain control over marketing activities but also represents a major commitment and should only be done after much research and consideration. Most foreign ownership occurs as a result of a factor associated with that market. As an example, Nissan and St Gobain have both built manufacturing plants in the United States and the United Kingdom because this was the best way to overcome barriers to entry. Likewise, GKN's big stake in the German components industry gave them a market share that could not have been achieved by direct export from the United Kingdom due to the German need for short delivery lead times.

Since the method of market entry used to gain presence in foreign markets is the major determinant of the degree of control a company has over its marketing, each of the different options should be carefully considered before a decision is made. In doing so, there are a number of key questions that need to be answered as shown in Table 16.3.

Overall, then, international or global marketing can be seen to involve a number of issues that make decision making a difficult task. Focusing on the differences involved when marketing in non-domestic markets is important, but merely recognizing the differences and the complexities involved is not enough. In the Tesco example provided earlier, the company was well aware of the dangers of trying to expand into the US market but failed to

TABLE 16.3 Key questions in international marketing

Whether to sell abroad. Geographical diversification may be more desirable than product diversification, depending of course on circumstances. However, the decision to sell abroad should not be taken lightly.

Where to sell abroad. This is one of the major decisions for international marketing. Choosing foreign markets on the basis of proximity and similarity is not necessarily the most potentially profitable option to go for.

What to sell abroad and the degree to which products should be altered to suit foreign needs is also one of the major problems of international marketing.

How to sell abroad is concerned, not just with the issue of how to enter a foreign market, but also with the management of 'the four Ps' once a business arrives. It also involves the difficult question of how to co-ordinate the marketing effort across a number of different countries.

overcome a mindset that led them to replicate approaches that had been successful elsewhere. As one learned commentator, Professor John A Quelch, put it: 'Although they spent a lot of money researching the market, they were probably seeking information that confirmed their strategy was right rather than truly looking for a marketing mix that was right for the market.'

PART THREE
Marketing in the digital age

Internet marketing

The internet or net is the abbreviated name for the 'interconnection of computer networks'. It consists of a massive hardware combination of millions of personal, business and governmental computers, all connected like a set of international roads and highways. The world wide web, or 'web', is a subset of the internet dedicated to broadcasting HTML pages. The web is viewed by using free software called web browsers. Born in 1989, the web is based on the hypertext transfer protocol, a language that allows users to 'jump' (hyperlink) to any other public web page. There are over 40 billion public web pages on the web today.

The term 'Internet marketing' can therefore be summarized as: The promotion of goods and services using the world wide web to communicate and receive information via the internet that will enable direct sales and support an integrated marketing strategy.

The three most important internet applications for marketing are world wide web sites (websites), electronic mail (e-mail) and instant messaging. Recent developments that have the potential for marketing are Rich Site Summary (RSS) feeds that syndicate information from many sites, and Voice over Internet Protocol (VoIP) services such as Skype. The most extreme example of internet marketing, 'electronic commerce', is the sale and purchase of goods and services over the internet. Its success to date indicates that the internet is likely to remain a significant media for the provision of interactive communication and commerce for some time to come.

As a basis for electronic commerce, the fundamental requirement is an internet website. The difficulty for suppliers is that websites attract a continuum of visitors. At one end are passive users simply 'passing through' or seeking information on a 'mildly curious' basis. At the other are browsers looking to evaluate alternative offers and make a purchase. The challenge is to satisfy these 'browsers' while finding innovative ways of attracting active users to your site and getting them to stay; and then getting them involved in *your* product rather than a competitor's. Important in this is the integrated use of different internet applications.

Thus, many consultancy organizations such as Booz Hamilton or McKinsey rely on regular subscriber e-mails to keep their organizations in the forefront of people's minds and to prompt 'click-throughs' to their main site. Internet florists use 'Virtual Bouquets' to encourage visitors and to generate 'pick-ups' from their website by providing users with the opportunity to send a real bouquet as an alternative. E-mails can also be used to mass-mail in the same way that postal or fax mailings are used. Thus, e-mail address lists can be purchased and used in a similar fashion. In extremes, these become Spam; unsolicited bulk e-mails to addresses usually obtained through dubious means or trawls of publically available sources. Something approaching 90 per cent of all e-mail traffic is reckoned to be spam; the costs of which are borne by the internet service providers and the end users.

Once a potential purchaser is on a website, there are a number of challenges. Where the website is acting as a virtual shop and visitors are there because they have chosen you as the place to make a purchase, the challenges are relatively simple and are about: ease of navigation around the site; ease of placing an order; and ease and security in making the payment. The skills required are similar to those of a retail operations specialist who understands how to organize physical retail premises to optimize the customer experience and the revenue obtained from a shopper. More difficult are the challenges of attracting people in browsing mode and then persuading them to stay, return and/or repeat purchase. Even more challenging is managing a site that has a social or information purpose such as the various Wiki sites, and the generation of income to support that activity. Underneath all this are the expectations that people tend to have when using the web: that information should be free.

This expectation of free information emphasizes the importance for all users wishing to benefit from a web presence to provide free user value, usually in the form of content. Site visitors now expect to be able to find information that in the past had to be paid for. If a user wishes to purchase, for example, a replacement part for a washing machine, they also expect video demonstrations of how to install that part. At the time of writing, newspapers are still struggling with this dilemma. This illustrates the potential for the internet to catalyse complete restructuring of whole industries.

In spite of this, the use of the internet as a commercial channel still requires adherence to the established principles of marketing. Customers have to be understood, competitive advantage has to be established and an appropriate marketing mix has to be developed. Thus, for example, the 'AIDA' framework is as relevant to internet commerce as it is to other commercial media where sellers must generate Awareness, Interest and Desire, culminating in Action, as a result of effective marketing activities.

Benefits of the internet for marketing

The internet provides a number of advantages as follows:

Integration

In order to manage customer relationships, organizations need information about the customer purchase cycle from initial contact through pre-sales, order placement and delivery, to post-sales service. Such data must be available across the various communication mechanisms used by an organization (telephone enquiries, a sales person's visit, direct mail, website visits, and so on) but also updateable from these multiple sources. Without this, customer experiences will be variable across the different channels, important information may be lost, or opportunities to improve information will be squandered. Managing customer data in this way is referred to as data integration.

Although many organizations have websites, they often fail to integrate data from their sites in this way. Instead, sites are used simply to provide details of the products or services, purchase facilities and/or the collection of e-mail addresses for direct mail purposes. In doing so, they miss the opportunities to provide customers with insight into their purchase history, relevant special offers, their search history and a wealth of other data that could be of interest or help develop a relationship. Led by organizations such as Hewlett Packard and Google, more are using the internet's facilities in this way, although care needs to be taken to ensure people's privacy is protected and that customers do not feel they are at the mercy of 'Big Brother'.

Individualization

Advances in information technology have enabled increased individualization of products, ie the ability to deal directly with individual members of a mass market from one central source. Thus, builders can use simple software packages to provide alternative designs for extensions or conservatories. Previously, customers would have been offered standard products or would have had to incur the expense of a specialist architect.

Amazon has taken this further. Although they started as a simple book retail service, over time they began to offer customers information about books that other readers of similar purchasing patterns had found interesting; and then information about other booksellers who could also supply the book on a cheaper and/or second hand basis. As their market reach expanded so has their product range, so that today they are almost a reference site for many different product lines. Further, individualization is achieved when, for instance, a customer returns a product because of a particular issue (eg a vacuum cleaner proves too heavy to use), and they then e-mail you with a selection of lighter weight models.

Interactivity

The potential of the web to provide instantaneous interactivity enables personalized or individualized provision to be taken one step further. UK boiler manufacturers and suppliers, for instance, now provide consumers with a facility that takes them through a series of questions to lead them to identify the correct boiler configuration for their premises. Information may also be provided about pricing, availability and order tracking. Beyond this, many websites now have provision for customers to write product reviews or to pose public questions about a product or service that will be answered by both the company and other users. Some also provide 'live chat' facilities in the form of instant messaging that allow a customer to pose questions directly to a 'technical' expert.

Independence of location

The internet also enables independence of location, which allows individualization to be achieved alongside economies of scale and a reduced need for expensive premises and multiple branches. Similarly, niche products such as speciality foods can serve their target markets even if they are spread far and wide.

Being able to reach customers wherever they are may also have the effect of widening consumer choice and extending consumer power. The growth of comparison sites that search the web for specific items and the range of prices available effectively out-sources a time-consuming activity while levelling prices. One survey found that 22 per cent of US car buyers who bought conventionally paid the asking price, against only 9.3 per cent of online buyers. Computer support in the areas of pricing individually tailored services or providing information services has the added benefit of freeing up expensive sales people for the tasks for which they are best suited; building relationships with individuals and key accounts at senior levels.

Top ten considerations in internet marketing

1 Search engine optimization

Search engines such as Google, Bing and Yahoo! use different and variable criteria to present the browser with suggestions of sites they might visit. It is recognized that appearing in the first page or so of search results is significant in attracting potential customers. Configuring a site in a way that promotes its positioning in an engine's search results is an important consideration for internet commerce or services. Since the criteria that search engines use vary over time, this becomes a constant task.

2 Price

The internet has made price comparisons very easy for potential customers and has forced internet traders to pay more attention to being within price bands that have become narrower over time. This has also forced a hard look at operating costs and acceptable levels of profitability for many businesses and created a more 'perfect market' as referred to by economists. Information about price bands is now so widely available that anything significantly lower than market price is a good indicator of fraud.

3 Click-through and pay-per-click

The need to find ways of attracting people to a website has encouraged organizations to look for ways of getting referrals, or click-throughs, from other sites. The most common method is banner or other forms of advertisement on a site that will lead to the advertiser's site if clicked. It is usual for the advertiser to pay the site owner on a 'pay-per click' basis. Payment on a 'pay-per-view' basis is when a browser clicks an advert and gets more information in the form of a pop-up.

4 Substance

The virtual nature of a website can hide the true nature of an internet trader, giving rise to the suspicion that a business is being run from someone's bedroom. Web-based businesses therefore need to provide evidence that there is more to them. Trading history data, customer testimonials and photographs are helpful here, as is having physical retail premises and/or a showroom that can be displayed or visited.

5 Independent or peer reviews of service

As internet provided products cannot be sampled, tried on or tested before purchase, the interactive nature of the web is often used to allow or even encourage customer reviews so that products can be compared before a choice is made. The ability to compare offerings and to benefit from the experience of others becomes particularly important when marketing over the internet.

6 Storms

Bad news traditionally travels fast and on the internet, it travels even faster. The multi-channel nature of the web makes such 'storms' of protest or condemnation difficult to counteract or mitigate. Internet suppliers need to be aware of the potential for this and if possible have contingency plans in place.

The upside of this is, of course, that good news will also travel fast; sometimes referred to as 'going viral'. Unfortunately, it is hard to identify which adverts or pieces of information will go viral, and which are the majority that won't.

7 Personal contact

The impersonal nature of the web and the inflexibility of some of the information sources on it can lead to frustration and the need for personal contact with an internet-based supplier. Although organizations readily provide 'Frequently Asked Questions' pages, many people observe that it is rare to find the answer to their question among them. Internet marketing therefore needs to consider how the human element can be brought back into cyber interactions to avoid alienating their customers in the same way that press-button telephone answering systems have frustrated many callers to customer service centres.

8 Security

Payment by credit or debit cards over the internet still raises issues of security for customers, who sometimes shy away from lodging their details on an anonymous website. The banks have responded by introducing greater security hurdles, and businesses such as Sage Pay, WorldPay and PayPal provide online alternatives, but the base fear that details will be stolen and used fraudulently remain. Similarly, having made a payment, there is always the concern that the purchase will not arrive. Marketing on the internet needs to include measures to mitigate these concerns.

9 Communities

The internet provides the opportunity to create communities among users through the development of 'social media'. These are the equivalent of the 'user groups' that many technology businesses sponsored to help them develop their products. The provision of forums or blog opportunities on a website helps promote the development of such communities, which in turn will promote brand loyalty.

10 Engagement

The internet provides the opportunity to engage people beyond the traditional means of competitions, quizzes and self-exploration distributed via direct mail or on packaging. The opportunities are only limited by organizations' imaginations and can include photo uploads, cartoons, educational material, new product information, technical help and so on.

Conclusion

Overall, market research suggests that the dominant factors affecting internet use remain the traditional concerns: price; convenience; service levels; product availability, and so on. Within this, however, the internet generates other challenges that marketing organizations need to take into account.

Social media marketing

The increased access to the internet provided by the spread of broadband has enabled the proliferation of social media websites. For the purposes of this topic, a social media website is defined as one that enables interaction both between site visitors and between site visitors and the host on a real-time basis. Other sites such as Wikipedia, news media, or dating sites are seen as information sites as they do not allow social interaction; or if they do, it is only limited interaction through associated e-mail or chat lines. At the time of writing, social media sites are probably in the growth phase of their product lifecycle with large numbers of new entrants to the market. One site that tries to provide an up-to-date list of all social media websites shows new entrants and drop-outs from the market on a daily basis.

Different social media sites have different emphases in what they provide and different 'tonal qualities' for the content and interactions they support. As an example, some sites are more female in orientation in that members share views on fashion, make-up, weddings, food and kids. Others function as online photo albums for sharing pictures or travel experiences and comments with friends. Still others have a professional, technical or topic-specific focus. To be effective, contributors need to adopt the appropriate tone for that site if they are to be taken seriously. For organizations seeking to exploit social media for marketing purposes, this is no different from public relations submissions that similarly needed to be written in the style appropriate to the publications being targeted.

The five most popular social media sites (popularity here is measured by each site's average traffic ranking of a number of monitoring organizations) at the time of writing are: Facebook (about which a feature film has now been made); Twitter; LinkedIn; MySpace and Google+. These are all open sites that any member of the public can register with, join and create their own online identity or page. The range of applications or different emphases is almost unlimited. As an example, Reddit, stylized as reddit, is a social media website based around news. Members upload text, videos or links to other sites related to a particular news item that they feel is worth sharing. Other members then vote submissions either 'up' or 'down', and the votes are then used to rank them. Submissions considered favourably by a majority of other users eventually make the 'front page' of the site.

Reddit also makes provision for members to post comments about an item on the site, which can lead to several pages of exchanges and commentary on a particular topic. 'Sub-reddits' can be created for particular interests; although the site did get itself into trouble through hosting what some considered inappropriate content. However, the ability for members to create special interest groups, to exchange views and to share content perfectly illustrates the key features that distinguish social media sites from other types of internet activities.

Marketing objectives

From a marketing perspective, social media websites form two distinct groups: those that offer the chance to target individual consumers (B to C marketing) and those that are part of business-to-business marketing (B to B marketing). The former tends to be conducted through the popular open sites such as Facebook, while the latter tends to be through the creation of specialist sites to which interested professionals are attracted.

The first objective that can be fulfilled via social media is that of **awareness**. Large membership public sites are attractive in that they provide access to the general public in the same way as other media. The first marketing task is therefore to participate on the site in a way that raises awareness or to encourage significant opinion leaders to participate in a way that promotes the spread of information about you or your products. The idea is similar to that of lending cars to motoring journalists.

The second objective will be to create or reinforce **brand values or reputation**, which creates a similar marketing task; that of finding ways in which these can be promoted. As an example, by March 2012, Coca-Cola had 40 million 'fans' on Facebook. It had sought to develop and leverage this fan-base through a number of 'playful' interactions that would keep fans engaged and reinforce the fun element of the brand's values. It requested fans to post 'Coca-Cola stories' about good times to drink Coke etc, which provided a human interest element. It also posted riddles, which, if solved, provided a click through to a 'sitelet' that held an image supposed to 'provoke small moments of happiness'.

The interesting thing about the Coca-Cola Facebook page that it was in fact created by two hardcore fans, Dusty and Michael, after they failed to find one that felt official enough! Having then employed the originators to manage the site officially, part of Coca-Cola's strategy is to let fans express themselves freely and to allow the community to police the content. This emphasizes one of the critical elements in social media marketing – that it is community-based, not supplier-based, and needs to allow the community to develop and flourish outside its direct control to be successful.

Dell have also fared well to date using social media. Their main focus is product news, deals and company information. While they are less community driven, they do provide scope for members to post both positive and negative comments about them, their products and other members' comments, and will engage in dialogue. In this way, they claim to be 'listening' to their public and learning as they go. As part of this, they have segmented their presence by having a number of different pages or sites to provide for the different interests people have, whether that be purchase, support or geographical location. They have also tried to engage with the small business community by creating a guide for small businesses that will help them develop a social media strategy for themselves. In this way, they are reinforcing the 'helpful' element of Dell's brand.

Dell's approach illustrates a further marketing objective that can be fulfilled through social media: the generation and collection of customer and market information. Freely provided commentary from users and other stakeholders provide invaluable data for a marketing company that normally costs a fortune to collect. Here, a Twitter account that can provide a continuous stream of commentary and feedback from followers can add to this fund. Dell's claim to 'learn' and the large number of people they employ to monitor and participate in social media testify to their commitment.

Another relevant marketing objective is the **development of relationships**. Social media, better than any other apart from personal contact, offers the opportunity to develop relationships with customers and stakeholders, both existing and potential. If relationships are developed through having similar values or outlooks, shared experiences and some form of rapport, then social media clearly has the potential to work on all three. The marketing task is to ensure a business's presence has the right mix of activities and interactions to develop the 'right' sort of relationship. More than ever, this will require a clear sense of the business's values, purpose, personality and objectives.

One further marketing objective is of course **sales**. Opportunities should always be provided to link to the supplier website or to generate leads that can be followed up using established sales processes. Indeed, a core objective for participation in social media should be traffic to your website. This is a virtuous circle as the more traffic a site receives, the higher it appears on search lists. A company website is therefore a core requisite so that traffic and enquiries have somewhere to 'land' to access more information or even an opportunity to purchase. This is not to say that a social media site has to be independent of a supplier but that simply using them for awareness raising may leave customers/users 'hanging in the air'. At the point of landing, it is important to grab people and to stop them 'running away'. The key here is good web design and the role of social media will have been to provide a vehicle that captures prospective customers.

B to B marketing more usually uses dedicated social websites that suppliers have created for themselves; although there are some generic sites where a business can upload slide shows or technical information in the hope of catching browsers. There are also a number that try to provide a facility for businesses to share ideas with other businesses or professionals; but on a general networking rather than marketing basis. For marketing purposes, it will probably be more effective to create a site where people are drawn together by a mutual technical or product interest. A social media site that enables product or service users and suppliers to share comments, solutions to problems, wish lists and experiences is therefore likely to have greater marketing impact. In many ways, these are the virtual equivalents of 'user groups' that computer and other high tech companies have created in the past.

The associated marketing objectives, however, remain the same for B to B marketing organizations as for B to C marketing. The key difference is likely to be that the host is also the supplier and they will be trying to impress members with their expertise as well as their values, purpose and personality. A good example would be Microsoft's website where both users and Microsoft technical personnel answer technical queries and Microsoft products are promoted.

Key marketing considerations

Consistency

Given that social media provide a dynamic environment with numerous contributions, it is vital that marketing organizations are consistent in the image they portray. Lack of clarity about the organization's values, purpose, objectives or personality will allow variability of message and a potential dilution of their brand.

Enrol staff

Social media sites, particularly B to B sites, often involve wider than usual numbers of staff in direct contact with customers and other stakeholders. It is consequently more important than usual to ensure staff are 'on message' in their interactions, apply common sense and are respectful of the community as well as their employer.

Transparency

The power of the internet and the possibility of dishonesty or underhand dealings going 'viral' promote the importance of transparency for participants in social media.

Frequency

Content, whether it be a blog, announcements, responses or whatever, need to be done on a frequent basis. Content or other activities designed to engage stakeholders have to be renewed constantly to make it worthwhile people returning to the site or sites in which you are maintaining a presence.

Spread

It is important to be present on a number of different social media sites to gain better chances of capturing traffic. Even if you host your own social media site, a presence on Twitter, LinkedIn and competitor sites can be useful.

Response

Since the key to effective social media is interaction, a marketing organization has to ensure that it responds to queries or significant adverse comments. In addition, the 'real time' interaction enabled by broadband means that responses are expected to be fast as well as relevant.

Community

Effective social media marketing will actively do things that promote the idea and/or feeling of community. Since membership of a site is an 'opt-in' decision, feelings of affinity become important.

Blogs and apps

Links to regular blogs plus apps that can be downloaded to smartphones are an important adjunct for businesses marketing through social media. They enable both the development of image and keep the business front-of-mind outside the immediacy of the social media site.

Trust over sales

Since social media are about communities and sharing, it is inadvisable to use sites to engage in too many selling activities. The danger is that community members come to regard the supplier as cynical or exploitative, ie only interested in sales rather than the best interests of the members. Better to use sites to create trust, which is usually regarded as a far more powerful commercial asset.

Expertise

The interactive nature and sharing ethos of social media enable individuals and businesses to establish themselves as experts. For marketing purposes, they then become 'movers and shakers' or 'gurus' in their areas to be wooed by marketing organizations for their support.

Mobile marketing

The concept

Mobile marketing is simply marketing activities conducted over the medium of mobile telecommunications devices. The use of cellular and satellite mobile devices has increased rapidly since the 1990s, and in some parts of the world has leapfrogged the use of cable-based communications media. Advances in the technology have included miniaturization; incorporation of cameras; Bluetooth for short-range messaging at 'hot-spots'; touch sensitive screens; and location identification. At the time of writing, the advent of smartphones, the introduction of 3G and 4G technologies, plus the potential for 5G (non-zonal, limitless download capacity) in a further 10-15 years, are all opening up more and more possibilities for the sophisticated marketing organization.

Marketing over mobile devices can involve many different activities including the transmission of text, graphics, video or sound via wireless networks. These use long-range or short-range radio frequencies and rely on cells formed by radio masts or satellites. Higher speeds and increased bandwidth have also enabled access to the internet, which has opened up even more possibilities. The recent addition of cloud computing accessible via mobile devices has meant a reduction in the need for large data storage on the device itself, making them even more versatile from a marketing perspective. For many commentators, mobile technology represents the key media for the future of marketing communications.

The simplest marketing activity via mobile devices is the use of SMS messages or texts. Many banks now routinely alert their customers via texts to their mobiles of account balances, warnings of limits being breached, special offers, and so on. Similarly, rail operators will text if your train is going to be late and financial service providers will text virtual and real-time information about price changes. In addition, friends will text purchase experiences and comments about the world around them as well as just engaging in virtual conversations. As an indication of the extent of SMS usage, in 2011 6.9 billion SMS messages were sent and received; this is expected to increase exponentially over the next few years.

More sophisticated activities include the development of 'apps' that either replicate an organization's website or provide a particular aspect of service, individual and social games for mobile devices, and more recently, payment mechanisms. There are some estimates that 2011 saw $86.1 billion move around the world in about 141 million exchanges via mobile devices. In some places in Africa, mobile satellite technology has become the norm for communications and trade having skipped landline and cellular infrastructure because of the distances and expense involved.

One significant development for mobile marketing is the introduction of technology that enables the use of augmented reality; the interaction of superimposed graphics, audio and other sense enhancements over a real-world environment that is displayed in real-time. Originally developed as a heads-up digital display for aircraft navigation, the technology is now available for commercial applications. Thus, Hallmark has incorporated augmented reality into many of their greeting cards, whereby one can place a mobile phone camera over an area of the greeting card to witness an animation for that card. This may be cartoon characters or a scene of some kind. Similarly, Starbucks incorporated augmented reality into a Valentine's Day marketing campaign whereby pointing a mobile phone camera over a special Valentine's Day cup would create some very interactive animations.

Over the next few years augmented reality technology will introduce a vast array of possibilities. As an example, pointing the camera in a mobile device at an object, say a hotel, could bring up room availability, locations of those rooms, pictures of the rooms, plus the hotel facilities and the current price. In other words, it will be possible to manipulate the full gamut of the marketing mix on a continuous and real-time basis.

What is unique about mobile marketing is a supplier's ability for highly targeted, direct, personal, and immediate communication and exchanges, ie the ability to connect with the consumer at the very heart of their personal space, location and even their consumption context. Thus, like no other media, the consumer can be reached when they are closest to buying. Take the example of an individual, tired after a long day in which he or she has missed or had an unsatisfactory lunch and who is on their way home thinking about a nice relaxing meal. If their phone recognizes where the person is and their past purchase behaviours, and now presents them with the option of a freshly prepared ready meal of their favourite ingredients being broadcast from their local delicatessen that they can pick up on their way home – and at 20 per cent off the normal price – it would take a truly dedicated self-caterer (or financially disadvantaged person) to pass on buying.

However, marketing is not just about making a sale; it's about creating the possibility of sales now and into the future. The above example is driven by the mobile device's ability to track its owners' behaviour. Mobile marketing requires that interaction to be captured and to open the possibility of recruiting people to the delicatessen's community; which also implies a functioning mobile website with social media facilities where you can link consumers to your organization and other members of the community. Links to, and the use of, social networking sites will increase in significance as they are expected to get more exposure on mobile phones over the next few years and indeed it is expected that more than half of social networking will be done using mobile devices by 2015.

As an example of how organizations can use mobile marketing and social media, in 2011 Weight Watchers improved revenues and earnings by approximately 60 per cent through embracing the internet and using social media as a key part of their marketing. Their three key activities were:

1 providing expertise and knowledge to their community – with a subscription fee – demonstrating that if you provide something of value, people will pay;

2 encouraging members to share experiences and talk about them via Facebook, Twitter or YouTube;

3 using platforms such as Twitter and Facebook to publish promotional offers and discount coupon codes.

Marketing enhancements from mobiles

Mobile marketing offers a number of ways in which relationships can be enhanced (see Figure 19.1). First and as demonstrated above, contact with customers is *direct* – allowing the marketer to cut through a saturated media landscape with highly targeted communications and services for the user. It offers a valuable channel to reach consumer segments that have become difficult to reach through other means. Initially, this included highly mobile

FIGURE 19.1 M-Marketing enhancements

younger groups but is now extending to house-bound individuals and those in remote locations. As penetration of mobile devices increases, this will incorporate vast tracts of consumers and purchases in both individual and organizational settings.

As contact is at a *personal* level it becomes possible to link with people in their physical and psychological context. Mobile devices are usually customized to individual preferences and applications, are often with the owner 24/7, and are thus intricately integrated into their daily lifestyle and routine. Organizations that can become part of this environment will gain significant advantage over competitors. The provider of a consumer's travel app will give valuable information (late trains, platforms etc) and remain as part of the evoked set of potential suppliers beyond most rivals.

Mobile devices also offer *immediacy*, ie organizations can respond to an individual's movements or to changes that might be of interest to them almost immediately. News feeds would be one example; Twitter-type messaging and new-product availability could be another. Such immediacy also offers the possibility of interaction on the move, which in turn opens up the potential for a more continuous relationship with consumers.

Mobile campaigns can also strengthen brand associations through *entertaining* via multimedia content that can be personalized through preference, context and location. As such, it will facilitate *frequent* interaction and dialogue between consumers and marketing organizations.

Mobile marketers can additionally develop and enhance *communities* and through increased interaction have a much greater presence that will enhance brand *affiliations*. Such activities will also, therefore, strengthen *relationships* between organizations and consumers as they identify with the activities and outlook implied by the organization's activities and use of the opportunities offered by mobile devices.

Challenges for mobile marketing

While mobile marketing offers potential enhancements to a brand, there are challenges that could, if not managed effectively, negatively affect an organization's marketing efforts.

At a base level, wireless communications are notoriously less secure than communication over fixed lines, and this potentially opens the door for security and privacy breaches and the transfer of unwanted viruses. The 2012 scandals involving some journalists hacking into people's mobiles and voicemails illustrate the dangers here. Because mobile communications strike at the heart of the consumer's personal environment, consumers could perceive a virus or unsolicited messaging as far more intrusive and threatening than if received through a PC. Some countries are clamping down on unwanted commercial advertising through mobile phones and, to avoid consumer backlash, organizations will increasingly need to deploy permission-based opt-in marketing programmes.

A key challenge for organizations using mobile marketing is to achieve a level of interaction with consumers that adds value to the relationship but that does not threaten privacy. In addition, marketers must avoid alienating customers with multiple or untimely messaging, and particularly uncoordinated messaging from different parts of the organization. In relation to mobile financial transactions, organizations need to bolster consumer confidence by employing highly secure connections. Businesses and consumers need to feel safe transmitting personal details, profiles and passwords, and marketers must provide for appropriate authentication, privacy, integrity and information to reassure consumers.

The technology itself also remains a challenge. Screen sizes limit the visual impact of activities and applications, and the unpredictability of breaks in wireless connections can be a source of considerable frustration for consumers. Device compatibility is another issue since devices vary widely in their display capabilities; input options, processing power, memory and battery life, and constantly emerging technologies can make it difficult to determine the best technical platform for a new marketing campaign.

Alliances are also a major strategic issue for marketers seeking to access mobile channels. Achieving access and exploiting the potential may well require relationships with hardware manufacturers, network providers, agencies that design the interactive software, content providers and aggregators, advertising agencies for the creative message, and even partner brands. The challenges include both aligning and co-ordinating the various inputs for the development of effective and timely strategies.

The immediacy of mobile communications and the potential for ideas 'going viral' also mean that dissatisfaction can be transmitted more rapidly than an organization can counter or compensate for. Since the propensity to communicate frustration or poor experiences is, in general, greater than the propensity to communicate positive experiences, mobile communications can be as much a danger as an opportunity.

Databases for marketing

Technological advances and reducing costs have made databases a much more versatile and cost-effective tool for the support of marketing activities. Indeed, some would argue that they are now a vital component of any competent marketing organization and their relationships with customers and suppliers. Where an organization's customer base numbers a few hundred up to several thousand, databases are relatively easy to construct and keep up to date. For FMCG companies, the task is greater. However, the introduction of loyalty cards, the proliferation of organization-specific credit cards, and the increasing volume of online purchases have all created the potential for much larger databases built on information captured through monitoring spending and activity patterns.

The increased importance of internet marketing, direct marketing, telemarketing, sales performance management (using laptop computers), and delivery performance (using handheld point-of-sale or point-of-delivery computing), are factors that have encouraged the development of good databases. Clearly, these provide important opportunities to enhance the quality of an organization's relationship with its customers. Good databases will enable: the personalization of communications; performance analysis; faster notification of changing consumption patterns; and comprehensive customer records to be available at the 'touch of a button'. In addition, good databases can allow for micro segmentation based on such criteria as buying patterns, customer-initiated communications, fine-tuned demographics and other, normally difficult-to-discern, characteristics.

Most organizations of any substance now operate some form of customer relationship management (CRM) system, which are effectively databases that organizational members can access quickly to view a personalized record of the organization's exchanges with that customer. Call centres will often refer to these records in their conversations with an enquirer. Sophisticated online organizations will make similar records available to customers so that they can develop their own understanding of their relationship with the supplier or track the progress of a particular transaction.

Problems with databases

One drawback to using databases is that managers sometimes fail to recognize that some of the rhetoric of databases is in fact myths that need to be viewed from a very critical perspective. A number of these are illustrated in Table 20.1. The consequence of this is that databases often hold data that is not 'fit for purpose' either at an operational level or for the needs of strategic planners. The attempt to develop databases that serve both strategic and tactical purposes is at the heart of database marketing.

One of the most acute problems is that of reconciling internal and external views of markets. The usual problem is that data retrieved from the sales ledger rarely possesses the details needed to link customer records to market segments. Some of the problems are described in Table 20.2 against the key issues involved in identifying a market segment: what is bought; by whom; and for what reason?

TABLE 20.1   Myths and realities about databases

Myth	Reality
The database collects what we need.	We collect what is easily available.
The database measures what matters.	We measure what is least embarrassing.
Database users understand what data they need.	We know what we used last, what the textbooks say and what might be interesting on a rainy day.
The database needs to hold more and more data.	We feel safer with 'loadsadata', even when we haven't a clue how to use it.
The database must integrate the data physically.	We like neat solutions, whatever the cost.
The database will save staff time.	We need more and more staff to input and analyse data.
The database will harmonize marketing, finance and sales.	We all compete for scarce resources, and this involves fighting.
The database is the key source for our market intelligence.	We haven't thought through what information is needed to make strategic or tactical decisions.

TABLE 20.2   Problems of reconciling internal and external market audits

External audit variable	Problem with internal audit
What is bought	Internal systems have rich detail on accounts and stock-keeping units. However, information about products such as colour, style, etc, can often be missing. Information on the outlets or channels through which they were sold is also very often lacking.
Who buys	Internal systems record who paid the invoice and who received delivery of the goods. They rarely record who made the buying decision or who influenced it. Even when buyer details are on the system, it is rarely easy to determine their characteristics such as age, sex and so on.
Why products are brought	Internal sources of information on why people purchase is scarce. Enquiries can be qualified, using survey techniques, to provide some clues about why people respond to an advertising campaign. Customer satisfaction surveys may also yield clues. Call reports from field sales and telesales can also provide valuable clues, especially if survey disciplines can be observed by the sales staff.
Reconciling variables	Reconciling external with internal variables involves: <ul><li>matching accounts to customers</li><li>matching stock-keeping units to products</li><li>matching external variables to internal records</li><li>collecting data from sources other than the sales ledger (eg from surveys of sales representatives)</li></ul>

Fusing together data from external sources and internal data is becoming increasingly common as a solution to this problem and is often referred to as data fusion. Where large volumes of data are involved, computer programs, known as deduplication routines, are used to automate the matching of the data. However, automation rarely achieves more than 80 per cent accuracy in matching, and manual matching has to be applied to the remaining data.

The cost of matching external and internal market coding schemes is driving some companies to collect customer profiles at source. This occurs either when they first enquire, or when their sales ledger records are first created. However, the cost of making changes to the sales ledger, and the fact that it is 'owned' by the finance department, are often barriers to success. In the future, marketing will need to work much more closely with finance and IT departments if it is to develop databases successfully.

Avoiding badly constructed databases

Information in the minds of most marketing managers lies in a strange 'no man's land', part way between the 'nitty-gritty' stuff of marketing management and the abstractions of technologists, cyberneticists and 'boffins'. Widely misunderstood, or equated to 'computer literacy' or 'technology awareness', the management of marketing information often ends up neglected or delegated to the most junior member of the marketing team. In reality, this should be a responsibility addressed by senior marketing managers (ie those who have a good view of the decision areas a database will be required to support).

In addition, it must be remembered that information is not all hard, objective data, and organizations will not necessarily become better informed by collecting more and more raw data and storing it until they end up knowing 'everything'. The belief tends to be that accounting systems are a source of hard facts, since most accounting transactions have to be audited and therefore must be reasonably accurate. Constructing good marketing databases must take into consideration the fact that most accounting data has little direct relevance for marketing strategy.

Information needed to support a marketing strategy

The information needed depends upon the marketing objectives for which a strategy is developed and the tactical decisions that have to be made on an ongoing basis. If strategic marketing objectives are changed, then different kinds of information are needed to support the new strategy that will have to be developed. Table 20.3 illustrates how different objectives require different supporting information. At this point, the sales or marketing director might feel that, because the situation changes so radically every year, there can be no hope of developing an effective system or procedure for obtaining marketing information. However, without seriously addressing the problem, marketing managers will end up ill-informed when they come to develop their marketing strategies or make tactical decisions.

TABLE 20.3 Examples of business objectives and segmentation methods

Business objective	Segmentation method	Information source
Market extension:		
• new locations	Geodemographics	Electoral roll (consumer)
• new channels	Prospect profiles	Companies House (business)
• new segments	Survey analysis	Prospect lists and surveys
Market development	Customer profiling	Sales ledger and added profile data
	Behavioural scoring	Models from internal data source
Product development	Factor analysis Surveys Qualitative methods Panels/discussion groups	

For all the problems, there are, in practice, a limited number of basic underlying marketing issues with which all companies have to contend. Furthermore, the solutions usually adopted can be seen as variations on relatively few themes. The basic model of information flows to support a marketing system can, therefore, be visualized as shown in Figure 20.1. The main components of this system are explained in Table 20.4.

The critical issue, then, when building such a system is that it is not self-contained within marketing. It requires interface programs that will alter the systems used by finance, sales and other internal departments, so that information can be produced that will be of direct relevance to marketing management. In addition, it will need to capture appropriate data feeds from external sources to provide other supporting information. The secrets of success in developing such systems for marketing are:

1 understanding the information needs of marketing and particularly how internal and external views of a market will be reconciled;

2 developing a strong cost–benefit case for the development of information systems, given that other systems, including financial

FIGURE 20.1   Information flows in a marketing system

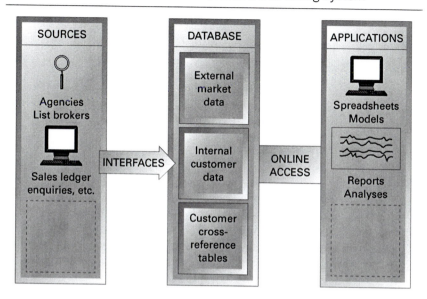

ones, will have to be altered to accommodate the needs of marketing;

3 working continuously with internal IT staff until the system is built while recognizing that they are/will be under pressure from other sources, especially finance, and that unless marketing maintains momentum and direction, then other priorities will inevitably win.

To be effective, marketing planners need to become far less insular and parochial if they are to obtain the information they require to do their job. Cross-functional understanding and co-operation must be secured by the marketing department if it is to develop the systems it needs. In many companies, marketing staff are, at best, tolerated by their colleagues in finance, operations, IT and on the Board. Building the interdepartmental bridges to secure data, information and knowledge is possibly one of the greatest challenges facing marketing today.

TABLE 20.4   The main components of a marketing database system

External market data: which is purchased from external agencies. These include governmental agencies, market research firms, list brokers and so on.

Internal customer data: which is collected from the sales ledger and other internal sources such as customer service, field sales, telesales, etc. It is coded and segmented in such a way that market-share figures can be created by comparison with external data.

Customer reference table: which is needed to make the system work effectively. It identifies customers (as defined by Marketing) and provides a cross-reference to sales ledger accounts. Whenever a new sales ledger account is created, the cross-reference table is used to determine the customer associated with that account. This avoids the need for costly manual matching or deduplication after the account is created. It is also used by marketing applications as a standard reference table for customers.

Databases: refer to all three of the above data types. They need to be structured using a technique known as *data modelling* which organizes the data into the component types that Marketing wants, and not the structure that Finance or anyone else provides. Usually, the data is held using *relational database* software, since this provides for maximum flexibility and choice of analysis tools.

Interfaces: refers to the computer programs that grab the data from the source systems and restructure it into the components to go onto the marketing database. These programs have to be written by the in-house IT staff, since they obtain and restructure data from the in-house sales ledger, and other in-house systems.

Applications: are the software programs that the planners use to analyse the data and develop their plans. They include data-grabbing tools that grab the items of data from their storage locations; reporting tools that summarize the data according to categories that Marketing defines; spreadsheets that carry out calculations; and 'what-if' analyses on the reported summary data.

NOTE: Tables 20.1 to 20.3 and Figure 20.1 are reproduced with the kind permission of Dr Robert Shaw of Shaw Consulting, London.

PART FOUR
Understanding customers

Consumer buying behaviour

Organizations supplying goods and services need to have an appreciation of the way customers *think* when coming to a specific purchase decision, and how they *behave* when making that purchase. Understanding thinking is, however, not easy as it is hidden from view. In fact, what goes on in people's minds is always a bit of a 'black box', so we can only ever look for clues as to what's going on. Behaviour is one such clue, and as what we do can be observed, it is usually a better basis for analysing customers. Indeed, an understanding of how behaviour varies between different groups of customers is often a good starting point for segmenting a market. Without this, suppliers will find it difficult to construct a marketing mix and value proposition that will find favour with those customers it has decided to target.

Components of a purchase decision

The basic process by which a purchase decision is made is an interaction between a number of factors external to a potential purchaser plus their 'black box'. The outcomes are the different components of a purchase decision (see Figure 21.1).

External factors

The external factors that may affect a potential buyer consist of the marketing mix offered by a supplier plus various elements of the market environment such as:

- the economic situation;
- technological developments;
- the media;
- political and legal influences;
- cultural differences;
- competitor marketing mixes.

FIGURE 21.1   Components of a consumer's purchase decision

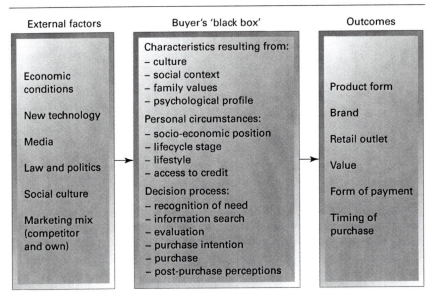

External factors	Buyer's 'black box'	Outcomes
Economic conditions	**Characteristics resulting from:** – culture – social context – family values – psychological profile	Product form
New technology	**Personal circumstances:**	Brand
Media	– socio-economic position – lifecycle stage	Retail outlet
Law and politics	– lifestyle – access to credit	Value
Social culture	**Decision process:** – recognition of need	Form of payment
Marketing mix (competitor and own)	– information search – evaluation – purchase intention – purchase – post-purchase perceptions	Timing of purchase

The 'black box'

A buyer's 'black box' is a combination of thoughts stimulated by each of the stages through which an individual passes on their way to a purchase decision. These thoughts will be influenced by a number of psychological factors such as a person's personality traits plus their responses to life's experiences. Thus, someone with a personality preference for order who has had some bad experiences from being late for appointments may think more positively about a time-management system than someone with a preference for spontaneity who knows they can get away with missing deadlines. Other influences include their social context, such as their social groups, or family values, plus personal circumstances such as socio-economic position, life cycle stage, lifestyle, access to credit facilities and so on. A person's psychological make-up is more complicated and will involve factors such as their motivations, perceptions and values. The interaction of these factors is complex and variable making it difficult to predict the outcome.

The buyer's response

The outcome of a purchase decision will consist of:

- the type of product chosen;
- the particular brand or supplier picked from the range of choices within a product type;

- the retail or dealer channel used;
- issues such as the timing of the purchase or the volumes bought.

Together, these components make for difficult marketing decisions. As an example, it is reckoned that only 15 per cent of West Europeans who could benefit from a hearing aid actually use one. This is thought to result from a number of influences including, among others:

- self-image;
- the social stigma associated with incapacity;
- non-recognition of the onset of deafness;
- ignorance of the range of aids available;
- the high cost of hearing aids.

For hearing aid manufacturers, the marketing choices this leads to are:

- alert people to their need;
- change attitudes towards hearing aids;
- concentrate on those who are actively seeking a hearing aid.

Each alternative has its drawbacks and does not exclude action in other areas. The choices, however, do illustrate the problems inherent in making sense of, and responding to, a consumer's propensity to purchase.

Personal involvement

In understanding consumer's buying behaviour, it is also usual to distinguish between **high involvement** and **low involvement** purchases. The degree to which purchasers find themselves spending time, effort and thought on a purchase will depend on the frequency of the purchase, plus the level of perceived **risk** they experience. Feelings of risk will be driven by four main 'need' areas:

- the importance of the function the product or service performs for them;
- the proportion of disposable income it requires;
- the emotions aroused by the product;
- the extent to which the product reflects their self-image, or causes others to view them in a certain light.

Thus, for a young executive with high aspirations, but with income constraints due to a large mortgage, the purchase of a new 'smartphone' might be influenced by:

- its functionality in areas such as battery life, screen visibility, range of information sources, data transferability, and so on;

- the extent to which it signifies status;
- the cost of a good/reliable product;
- the significance of the brand;
- the way others would view possession of such a device.

Under these circumstances, the purchaser is likely to be concerned to make the 'right' decision and engage in some highly complex purchase behaviour. If the purchaser were a young person in full-time education, behaviour is likely to be less complex and driven more by brand, price or availability, rather than by weightier issues of functionality and social status.

The decision-making process

The process by which the final decision is made during a purchase tends to follow a number of stages. The extent to which each stage is included will depend on the nature of the purchase and the complexity implied. Fundamental to all purchases is **need recognition** or **arousal**, which may come in the natural course of events, or which may require effort on the part of a supplying organization. The latter will be especially true for new products or product categories with low market penetration.

Once a need has been acknowledged, people will either start an **information search** or, in the case of low-involvement habitual purchases, move straight to a purchase. If seeking variety, this might then involve a cursory review of alternative brands. The information search may be informal and take the form of becoming open to information about the product type, or it may be active and involve talking to friends, browsing websites, consulting reports and experts, or actually visiting outlets to try out different offerings. This can be described as a **cognitive** stage in which beliefs and knowledge are developed about the range of alternatives available. Suppliers without high market shares, therefore, have to work hard if they wish to be included in the list from which a final choice is made.

The next stage in this process will be some form of **evaluation**, during which a customer is likely to develop a preference for a particular brand or small group of brands. At some point, a customer will become **convinced** of the value of a particular offering, at which moment they can be characterized as having a **purchase intention**. This is known as an **affective** stage, during which potential buyers develop an emotional response to different offerings, which will be a reflection of their personality, social context, values and beliefs, and their psychological make-up. It will also be a reflection of the influences exerted by the different aspects of the market environment and the ways products have been positioned in the market by their suppliers.

Purchase intention, however, can still be altered by the **intervention** of others or by some unanticipated factor. If a buyer's intentions conflict with the attitudes of peer groups or some strong social/cultural values, they will have to work hard to maintain their intention, but could easily be persuaded not to buy if their emotional convictions are not well-grounded. Thus, an Italian male who had decided to buy a French car might find his conviction crumbling in the face of strong nationalistic views combined with others' attitudes that such cars were designed for more 'effeminate' drivers.

Unanticipated factors might include the arrival of new information, a change in priorities, or a change in personal circumstances. For the supplier, the implications are that clear positioning and unambiguous communications are of vital importance, and that they should plan to reduce the impact of unanticipated factors, especially those not within their control. These could range from availability, ease of contacting a supplier, point-of-sale information, or the actions of a sales person. For high-risk purchases, customers will be more vulnerable to such deflection as a result of their heightened anxiety.

Once a purchase has been made, the final stage in the process is customers' **post-purchase perceptions** of their acquisition. High involvement purchases, where a choice has been made between several carefully considered alternatives, often lead to feelings of discomfort, or **cognitive dissonance**, since they will be well aware of the advantages of other offerings and the possible existence of disadvantages. Dissonance will be magnified by:

- the extent to which perceived performance is below pre-purchase expectations;
- receiving fewer validating messages through communications such as advertising;
- any shortfalls in after-sales service.

Customers will naturally seek to reduce their dissonance, either by confirming the wisdom of their choice, or through seeking some form of redress such as instant upgrade or refund, publicizing their misfortune, or taking legal action. For suppliers, the instant nature of the web makes this a dangerous time. Whatever the result, it will have a significant impact on repeat purchase decisions if the outcome is felt to be unsatisfactory.

Together, these factors combine to make consumers' buying behaviour a complex process, and consequently difficult to research and predict. Apart from the models used above, there are a number of other models, more or less mathematically based, that seek to explain the formation of preferences in different ways. Thus, there is no clear picture or universal theory that encapsulates all aspects of consumer behaviour. What *is* clear, however, is the need to develop the best possible understanding of the dynamics and variations of the ways that customers approach a purchase. The more this is understood, the easier it is to see how continued sales could be jeopardized without constant attention to the careful manipulation of the marketing mix.

Organizational buying behaviour

When a business wishes to sell its products to other organizations rather than to individuals, it faces a rather more complex marketing situation. This complexity is a result of the number of people involved in the decision to purchase, the situation in which those people operate and the activities which, together, form the stages of the decision-making process.

These processes are not entirely dissimilar to those followed by consumer purchasers, but tend to be characterized in different ways as a result of the contexts in which an organization buys. For example, organizations have more formalized purchasing procedures as a consequence of the need to monitor and control purchasing activities, and they will often appraise a product in more technical terms because of the impact that a wrong purchase may have on the organization's operations.

Organizational buying stages

The major stages, or 'buy phases', of an organizational purchase are usually listed as:

- problem recognition;
- general need determination;
- supply specification;
- identification of suppliers;
- solicitation of proposals;
- evaluation and selection of a supplier/suppliers;
- establishment of order routines;
- performance review.

These stages will not necessarily be followed sequentially and not every stage will be included for all purchases. In general, though, they indicate the way in which an organization will approach a purchasing problem, which will involve different people and processes at alternative stages and in different situational contexts. The interaction of these factors will determine the information required by a purchaser and the purchase outcome (see Figure 22.1).

FIGURE 22.1   Organizational buying behaviour model

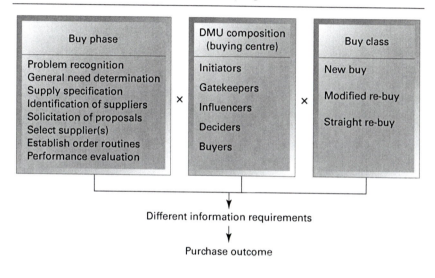

Organizational buyer situations

To help unravel the complexities of such purchasing, it is useful to isolate the situations in which purchases generally are made. These are frequently referred to as 'buy classes' and cover: **new buys; modified re-buys** and **straight re-buys**.

New buy

When purchasing for the first time or making a complete reappraisal of a particular requirement, there will be little experience in the organization of purchasing that type of product. As a consequence, the organization and the individuals within it will experience high levels of uncertainty and risk, which are likely to produce a number of behaviours less in evidence when purchasing within the other two 'buy classes'.

Behaviours that will be of particular interest to potential suppliers will be associated with the need to reduce perceived risk. Buyers are likely to attempt risk reduction by requiring much more information about a purchase, not just in terms of the product itself, but also the ability of the supplier to meet specifications, quality levels and supply continuity requirements. In addition, they will tend to seek outside opinions and recommendations about both the products and suppliers. This can incorporate the use of paid advisers such as product experts and consultants; the collection of assessments and appraisals in technical journals; talking to existing users or customers of particular suppliers; and the use of other referees such as bankers and credit reference agencies. Risk reduction is also likely to be sought through visits to suppliers' premises, inserting penalty clauses in the terms of the contract and by soliciting quotes or offers from a large number of potential suppliers to ensure that they have not missed the least risky purchase. In some industries, **pre-qualification** is used to ensure the suitability of suppliers.

As a consequence, purchase decisions often take a long time and will probably be taken at a fairly high level in the organization. In addition, individuals will try to reduce their own vulnerability by involving a wider range of people in the decision and passing responsibility upwards, thereby spreading the risk. A further response will be a tendency to purchase from the market leaders, or the higher priced suppliers, since these will be perceived as lower risk solutions.

Modified re-buys

Modified re-buys will occur when a purchasing organization becomes dissatisfied with existing suppliers, or modifies its requirements in some way. Since the organization will already have experience of sourcing the product, less risk will be perceived by higher management and the decision is likely to involve fewer people and focus on those at lower levels in the business. Those at the lower levels, however, are likely to experience greater personal risk in the absence of the involvement of their superiors. The main risk factor is the possibility of changing to an unknown supplier. The purchaser will then probably require 'out-suppliers' to demonstrate a significant advantage to break the inertia of an existing relationship.

Straight re-buys

'Straight re-buys' refers to purchasing on a routine re-order basis with little risk being perceived by the purchaser. Individuals will either select a product of their choice from the offerings of 'approved suppliers' or will place orders in strict adherence to company-established specifications and relationships. Where choice can exist, it will be exercised by either the user or the purchasing department. As long as 'in-suppliers' maintain both product and service quality, this is a difficult situation for 'out-suppliers' to penetrate. One drawback for the purchaser in this respect can be that price loses its visibility in the purchase process, which helps explain why annual purchase reviews are often institutionalized as part of supply-chain management processes.

The organizational decision-making unit

The risk associated with a purchase, plus the complex way in which the product will be viewed and used, means that a number of people will have the opportunity to influence the outcome of a purchase decision. As indicated, the greater the risk, the more people likely to be involved, with as many as 40 for an expensive, first time, purchase. Together, these constitute a decision-making unit (DMU) or 'buying centre' with individual members playing one or a number of different roles. While there have been several approaches proposed for classifying these roles, there is general agreement that they will cover:

- **Initiators**, who will first propose a purchase and who could be anyone from the chief executive to an operational employee, depending on the nature of the product.

- **Policy-makers**, who will set the overall context for a purchase, or who may even initiate a purchase; policies could refer to dual sourcing, just-in-time manufacturing, preferring domestically produced products, quality requirements and so on.

- **Users**, who will actually consume the product or service as part of their job. Where such people have expert knowledge, they can significantly influence the choice of supplier. For less risky purchases, they may also have significant influence, both positive and negative.

- **Other influencers**, who may include: technical experts; the media; referral markets; financial personnel; the organization's own customers; and so on. Exactly who influencers are will vary from one organization to another, but the notion is important to spur suppliers to view any purchasing relationship in its wider context.

- **Deciders**, who will have the power to approve or veto a purchase decision and who will ultimately reconcile conflicting opinions within the DMU. They often rely on the presentational power of the people requesting the acquisition, but may also be driven by personal preference.

- **Gatekeepers**, through whom information is passed into the organization. These can sit at many points in a business and can range from receptionists and secretaries to purchasing officials, product experts and general technocrats.

Since sales people or account managers are usually the most significant external influence on organizational purchasing, it is vitally important for them to work with the appropriate gatekeepers within the organization. Once 'in', they then have to recognize the different information needs that each member of the DMU will have and the general orientations or perspectives they bring to the decision-making process. As examples: users will be concerned about ease of use, consistency and continuity of supply; influencers such as finance people will be concerned with cost, while influencers such as design engineers will more likely be interested in quality; and deciders such as the chief executive may be concerned with reputation or status. As an example of different needs, one French supplier to hospitals segmented the market by age of purchasing officer, since those with low levels of experience required much more support to be able to satisfy the information requirements of the various hospital administrators involved in the decision.

An outline of the complex interactions of the organizational purchasing process is shown in Figure 22.1.

It is clear that organizations do not, in themselves, exhibit behaviour. It is the collective interactions between individuals from supplier and buyer organizations that are at the heart of the process, plus the buyer's interactions with their external environment. These will include:

- state of the economy;
- regulatory changes;
- technology advances;
- competition;
- social developments;
- culture and structure of the organization itself.

Often, internal politics and the nature of the personalities involved will be as much a determinant of a purchase decision as anything else.

Organizational buyer behaviour, then, emphasizes the notions of relationship marketing and the need to understand both the organization as a whole and the buying styles of the individuals within the buying organization. A continuing trend is the 'outsourcing' of requirements by establishing supplier partners. Within this, many organizations now prefer total solutions or systems purchasing where suppliers provide 'turnkey solutions' either on their own or as a prime contractor. In addition, purchasing is progressively a professional activity incorporating the concept of supply chain management. Together, these are promoting the tendency for organizational buyers to become more demanding and even more complex in their behaviour, which in turn leads to a greater requirement to understand organizational buying behaviour.

Market segmentation

No organization can be all things to all people. The danger of trying to do so is that they end up satisfying no one. The trick is to concentrate on those who will experience the biggest benefits from your offering and for whom you have a competitive advantage. Identifying these targets requires organizations to segment their market into those whose needs they can really satisfy well and those where the benefits are less obvious.

Suppliers need to be engaged in a continuous dialogue with target segments so that their needs are understood in depth, and specific offerings that have a differential advantage over the offers of competitors can be developed. Only when this has been done should an organization consider the array of communication and other marketing communications possibilities they have at their disposal. Market segmentation, then, is a process that identifies different requirements in the people who buy, and as such is the key to successful marketing.

Market segmentation, however, remains one of the most misunderstood and elusive of marketing skills and is often taught incorrectly in business schools and written about incorrectly in marketing books. Indeed, after over 70 years of marketing, according to a recent *Harvard Business Review* article, poor segmentation is at the core of most business failures. At its heart are a number of judgements or insights that an organization makes about it customers, which rely on the skill, experience and creativity of the individuals involved. Too often, managers see markets as a series of fixed segments that are described in terms of the products they use, such as the family car segment, *Guardian* newspaper readers or soft cheese eaters. While these are useful ways of referring to a market, they can disguise the reasons behind a particular product preference and suppliers can lose sight of customer needs.

Starting the process

Although no two customers are the same, except in very special circumstances, it is not commercially viable to make exclusive products for single customers. Organizations thus need to find commonalities between customers so that they can group them in a way that enables them to deal with such groups in a cost-effective way. Thus, the principal criteria for identifying a commercially useful segment are that:

- segments have to be large enough to make it worthwhile developing products or services especially for them;
- segments must be sufficiently different from other segments to warrant creating a different strategy for them;
- there has to be some way of identifying members of a segment so that they can be communicated with in a cost-effective way.

There are basically four steps in performing a market segmentation analysis:

1 analysis of customer responses, preferences or behaviour;
2 analysis of customer characteristics or attributes;
3 analysis of benefits sought;
4 clustering of groups with similar needs.

Analysis of customer behaviour

This is essentially a manifestation of the way customers actually behave in the market place. In respect of *what* is bought, suppliers should look for buying behaviour in terms of:

- the physical characteristics of products;
- how they are used;
- where they are bought;
- how they are bought;
- the price paid.

These can indicate if there are any groups of products, outlets or price categories of potential interest to a supplier (ie where the opportunities and problems might be). These natural groupings, while obvious, do at least provide clues as to what is happening in the market, since they represent the different purchase combinations that actually take place. They are known as micro segments.

Look, for example, at the complexity of the cooking appliances market (see Figure 23.1). A method for finding a way through this complexity is shown in Figure 23.2, which shows how different purchasing patterns can be broken down into micro segments (more about this below).

FIGURE 23.1 Cooking appliances market

Cooking appliances

Is it a single market or several separate markets?

- Volume   (units)
- Value
- Domestic/commercial
- Fuels   (gas, electricity, coal, oil, etc.)
- Cooking methods   (heat, radiation, convection)
- Cooking function   (surface heating, baking, roasting, charcoal, etc.)
- Design   (free standing, built-in, combination)
- Prices
- Product features
- OEM/replacement
- Geography
- Channels   (direct, shops, wholesalers, mail order)
- Why bought
- Others   (promotional response, lifestyle, demographics)
- Usage

FIGURE 23.2 Micro-segments

Micro-segment	1	2	3	4	5	6	7	8	9	10
What is bought										
Where										
When										
How										
Who										
Why (benefits sought)										

Analysis of customer attributes

Suppliers also need to know *who* these customers in the micro segments are, so that they can communicate with them. In this respect **demographic** descriptors have always been found to be the most useful method. For consumer markets, important variables include age, sex, stage in the family life cycle and socio-economic groupings, which describe people by their social status in life as defined by their jobs.

Demographic descriptors are useful for describing consumer and industrial segments. It is easy to understand how demographics can be related to purchase behaviour, since people have specific needs at certain times in their lives. There is also a useful relationship between readership habits, viewing patterns and socio-economic groupings, which is very helpful in deciding what media to use to communicate with customers. Additionally, analyses such as A Classification Of Regional Neighbourhoods (ACORN), which classifies all households according to 40 variables drawn from population census data, can be particularly useful for retail businesses in terms of outlet location or direct marketing. In the UK, ACORN classifies neighbourhoods into 54 types with similar characteristics that are closely related to specific consumption patterns for different categories of goods and services.

For industrial markets, Standard Industrial Classification (SIC) categories, number of employees, turnovers, production processes, and so on, are also examples of demographic descriptors.

The problem, however, is that many organizations describe a sector as a segment, while others describe a socio-economic group as a segment. But these are *not* segments because, for example, all members do not behave in the same way; nor do all women between the ages of 18 and 24; nor does everyone in my street. Such descriptors are only useful at a very high level of aggregation, such as, for example, new couples, who clearly provide a big potential market for manufacturers of carpets, beds and the like. But, as all organizations are aware of these opportunities, there is no differential advantage in them for suppliers. In order to gain differential advantage, suppliers need to delve deeper and get into proper market segmentation.

Analysis of benefits sought

The third step is to try to understand *why* customers behave in these ways, so that suppliers will then be in a better position to sell to them. In this respect, it will be important to look at what *benefits* customers derive from their purchases. These benefits will obviously be closely related to customers' attitudes, perceptions and preferences. This needs to be done for each micro segment.

Clustering of groups

The fourth step is to search for clusters or groups of micro segments with similar needs. While this can be done manually, it is preferable to use one of many computerized clustering packages, as there can often be as many as 50 micro segments identified during the preliminary segmentation process.

A finished market segmentation example from the consumer market is given in Figure 23.3. (This has been amended for confidentiality reasons, but it illustrates how the process described above results in market segments.)

FIGURE 23.3 Example of segmentation of consumer market for toothpaste

	Segment Name	Worrier	Sociable	Sensory	Independent
Who buys	Socio-economic	C1 C2	B C1 C2	C1 C2 D	A B
	Demo-graphics	Large families 25 – 40	Teens; young smokers	Children	Males 35 – 50
	Psycho-graphics	conservative hypochon-driacs	high sociability; active	high self involvement; hedonists	high autonomy; value oriented
What is bought	% of total market	50%	30%	15%	5%
	Product examples	Crest	Maclean's Ultra Brite	Colgate (stripe)	Own label
	Product physics	Large canisters	Large tubes	medium tubes	small tubes
	Price paid	low	high	medium	low
	Outlet	super-market	super-market	super-market	Independent
	Purchase frequency	weekly	monthly	monthly	quarterly
Why	Benefits sought	stop decay	attract attention	flavour	functionality
Potential for growth		nil	high	medium	nill

Exactly the same principles can be followed in respect of industrial markets. An example of the segmentation of a particular industrial market based on purchase behaviour is shown in Figure 23.4.

FIGURE 23.4   Example of segmentation of the industrial market for a technical service product

Koala Bears	Uses an extended warranty to give them cover. Won't do anything themselves; prefer to curl up and wait for someone to come and fix it.	
	Small offices (in small and big companies).	28% of market
Teddy Bears	Lots of account management and love required from a single preferred supplier. Will pay a premium for training and attention. If multi-site will require supplier to effectively cover these sites. (Protect me).	
	Larger companies	17% of market
Polar Bears	Like Teddy Bears except colder! Will shop around for cheapest service supplier, whoever that may be. Full 3rd-party approach. Train me but don't expect to be paid. Will review annually (seriously). If multi-site will require supplier to effectively cover these sites.	
	Larger companies	29% of market
Yogi Bears	A 'wise' Teddy or Polar Bear working long hours. Will use trained staff to fix if possible. Needs skilled product specialist at end of phone, not a bookings clerk. Wants different service levels to match the criticality of the product to their business process.	
	Large and small companies	11% of market
Grizzly Bears	Trash them! Cheaper to replace than maintain. Besides, they're so reliable that they are probably obsolete when they bust. Expensive items will be fixed on a pay-as-when basis – if worth it. Won't pay for training.	
	Not small companies	5% of market
Andropov Big Bears	My business is totally dependent on your products. I know more about your products than you do! You will do as you are told. You will be here now! I will pay for the extra cover, but you will . . . !	
	Not small or very large companies.	9% of market

Figure 23.5 shows a segmentation map of buyers of information technology (the result of interviews with 5,000 buyers on three continents).

FIGURE 23.5 Understand the different category buyers

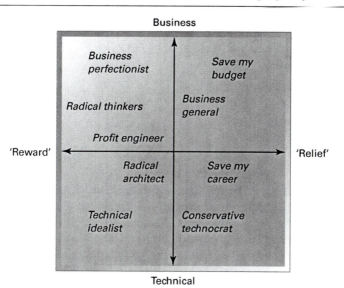

From this and from the earlier examples it will be seen that the resulting segments can be translated into typical members or caricatures that can be displayed for all members of an organization to become familiar with.

Summary

In summary, the objectives of market segmentation are:

- to help determine and to focus the direction of marketing resources through the analysis and understanding of trends and buyer behaviour;
- to help determine realistic and obtainable marketing objectives;
- to create a basis for developing sustainable competitive advantage.

International market segmentation

The purpose of a segmentation exercise is to identify groups of purchasers that are sufficiently large, different and reachable to make them a worthwhile investment of marketing effort. The identification of a new segment whose needs are either unserved or poorly served by existing suppliers can provide an opportunity for significant competitive advantage. Unfortunately, segmentation models in international marketing tend to consist of geographical groups, such as Western Europe, Eastern Europe, North America, ASEAN, Australasia and so on. Such groupings, however, are of very limited value as actionable marketing propositions, since they bear little relationship to the benefits sought, consumption or usage patterns.

Using Europe as an illustration, a distinction is often drawn between EU and Non-EU countries or those within or outside the eurozone. However, although these countries are linked economically and politically, there are many differences within and between EU countries that require different marketing strategies. It is therefore a mistake to assume that just because countries or regions are clustered together geographically, they will respond to similar marketing activities. While there may be some similarities, there are significant differences arising from other phenomena. For example, Scandinavia has short summers and long winters; Greece, Portugal, Italy and Spain have long summers and short winters; The Netherlands has low plains; and Austria has mountains. The per capita gross domestic product of Switzerland is seven times that of Portugal and, at the same time, there are significant communication and distribution differences. As an example, Denmark is the only country in Europe in which public channels, operated by the two public broadcasters, DR and TV2, still attract more than half of average daily audiences. Elsewhere, channel proliferation has been rapid and public broadcasters have suffered. Similarly, retail channel concentration is very dense in Northern Europe, whereas there is a preponderance of small, independent outlets in Southern Europe; and there are also significant cultural and linguistic differences.

If, therefore, geography is to be relevant, it is more sensible to think in terms of the Anglo Saxon North; the Latin South; North-east France, Benelux and North-west Germany; and so on. Even this, however, is simplistic, in the sense that there are basically three kinds of 'products' that have to be considered when looking at such segmentations.

Types of international products

Truly global products

These are either products or services that are inherently global, such as international services, world-standard industrial products, high-technology products and so on, or they are fashion or national products that have become global, such as Chivas Regal, Coca-Cola, Rolls-Royce, McDonald's, Marlboro cigarettes, and so on. These have become global because their national appeal is replicated in other countries.

National products

These typically exist where the market thrives on supplier responsiveness, client relationships, national preferences, and where global efficiencies are less critical.

Hybrid products

Here, adaptation across countries is possible and this requires a rethinking of simple geographical segmentation bases to ones based on customer groups with similar needs across national boundaries. In advertising, for example, it has been found that there:

- are three broad breakfast types across Europe;
- is a fashion lager market that spans Europe;
- are similar Facebook membership rates across Europe.

There are, thus, significant legal, regulatory, linguistic, communication media and distribution channel differences across Western Europe and even throughout the world. There are, consequently, few truly global products and many traditional habits remain deep-rooted, militating against international segmentation. On the other hand (and this applies particularly to Western Europe), there are a number of growing trends that suggest that the need for international market segmentation will become increasingly important. These include:

- the desire for monetary union, social affairs union, foreign affairs union and defence policy unions;

- increasing product and technical standardization;
- deregulation of transportation, telecommunications, pharmaceuticals and others;
- attitude convergence towards work, individuality, materialism, the environment, and so on;
- pan-global buying;
- international mergers, acquisitions and joint ventures;
- increased international travel, education, media exposure, fashion, and so on.

International market segmentation therefore requires the introduction of market variables that would not be normally used when segmenting a national market. For example, differing legal regimes will be found in different countries and may make a difference to product configuration, safety requirements or importing conditions. In some countries, political circumstances will play a role in creating different consumption or distribution circumstances that might provide a basis for segmentation. The bases for international market segmentation are, therefore, likely to be specific groupings of countries, such as the new 'Euro regions' outlined earlier, or customer groups across selected countries.

Thereafter, the normal rules of market segmentation apply (see Topic 23, 'Market segmentation'), although trying to obtain data for this may be harder internationally. The collection of statistics will be harder in some countries than others and the way in which information is collated may also vary, making it difficult to compare countries on similar bases. Similarly, people respond differently to market research in Spain, France and Germany making it difficult to get meaningful data to compare markets.

Implementation

For companies trading in numerous countries around the world, finding a single global segmentation model that can be applied to every country is clearly an attractive proposition. However, the experience of 'globalization' has highlighted for many companies that they have to 'act local' in order to succeed in their markets. This does not mean that every country is completely unique in respect of the segments found within it. What the international company may find is that the global picture for their market can be captured by one of the following:

1 to all intents and purposes there is a single global segmentation model that at the local level simply requires a series of small changes to the segment details to make the global model applicable; or,

2 although different segmentation structures exist in many countries, individual segments are found in more than one country, the total of which can be brought together into a global model consisting of a manageable pool of segments; or,

3 a combination of 1 and 2 with not every segment found in each country, as in 2, and various segments requiring small changes to their details to make them applicable at the local level, as in 1.

Getting to this point will require a progressive series of segmentation projects with each project based on a sensible geographic boundary. As experience builds with each project it is likely that a point will be reached where no additional segments are being uncovered and patterns emerge that associate external dimensions, such as the stage of market development and socio-economic factors, with specific segments. Once this occurs, subsequent projects can be reliably scaled back to exercises that simply test the existence of various segments.

As a guide to predetermining which countries can be included in a single segmentation project, companies need to ensure that in each of these countries the stage of market development, the available routes to market and the pattern of marketing activity are the same, or at least very similar.

The advent of e-commerce has added another dimension to this discussion both for those companies who once only served a local market but now, thanks to the internet, serve a global customer base, and for start-up companies looking to the internet for a wide geographic reach. It is unlikely that many (if any) of these companies will be able to afford a global segmentation project, so the most sensible starting point is the geographic area that is key to the business with a progressive roll-out of the project as already described. Guidelines as to which geographic areas the segmentation project should be extended into could, of course, be based on the areas from where enquiries to the company website originate and where sales are made.

PART FIVE
Understanding markets

Marketing information and research

Decision-making in organizations requires relevant information if the outcomes are not to be based on those often-used management support tools – 'gut feel' or rationalized personal preference. Within this, marketing information is of vital significance. Indeed, one of the key roles of marketing professionals should be the supply of market and marketing performance information that will enable the rest of the organization to make decisions about the market-related areas of their responsibilities. As examples, corporate or strategic managers need good market environment and competitor information to be able to set the overall strategic direction of the organization, and operational managers need to understand the critical success factors associated with the delivery of their product or service, since these should form the basis for the design of their operating systems.

These examples illustrate that marketing research is not an activity to be performed in isolation, but one where the results will contribute to many managerial or policy decisions. The implication of this is that the collection, collation and reporting of marketing information needs to be structured in ways appropriate to the decisions it will support. Managers requesting marketing information and research must, therefore, have a clear understanding of exactly what they need to know in order to make the judgements for which they are responsible. This is often one of the biggest problems in drafting a market research brief or in specifying a marketing information system: distinguishing between what it would be 'nice to know' and what is actually needed for management purposes. Tables 25.1 and 25.2 illustrate the areas that commonly form the focus of marketing research.

TABLE 25.1   Main areas of market research

• Customers	Behaviour
	Needs
	Responses
	Beliefs
	Characteristics
• Markets	Size
	Structure
	Dynamics
	Relationships
	Trends
• Competition	Share
	Positioning
	Aims
	Strengths/weaknesses
• Environment	PEST*
	Institutions
	Trends
• Our impact	Share
	Penetration
	Coverage
	Image
	Service levels

*PEST = Political, Economic, Social and Technological factors of the environment.

TABLE 25.2   Top ten marketing research topics*

• Market-share analysis	• Economic forecasting
• Market potential	• Competitor products
• Market characteristics	• Pricing studies
• Sales performance	• Product testing
• Business trends	• Information systems

*Note that these cover both internal and external topics investigated to enhance marketing performance.

The activities involved in marketing research can be described in a number of different ways, but together indicate the major issues in conducting marketing research or creating marketing information systems.

Reactive versus passive research

This is sometimes used to distinguish between the different forms or styles of research and is a useful way of classifying the various types of marketing research activities. **Reactive research** implies an interaction between the researcher and the subject(s). It can, therefore, take the form of asking questions as part of a postal or e-mail survey, an interview or a group discussion. In each case, the researcher will be prompting the subject(s) to provide their views, state their intentions or recall their experiences. Reactive research can also take the form of experiments, such as test marketing a product, altering an aspect of the marketing mix to establish variations in response, or 'laboratory' studies such as simulated shopping environments.

Passive research concerns the pure observation of subjects, or the collection of data. These could include:

- consumer panels who simply report their activities on a regular basis so that patterns of behaviour can be established;

- retail audits, where stock levels and shelf-space allocations are observed on a sample basis to ascertain market share, market penetration, etc;

- surveys of publicly available reports to identify market trends, market scope or competitor positioning;

- internally generated data that will provide indications of organizational performance.

Passive research limits the researcher's understanding to his or her own interpretations of observed phenomena or data. Reactive research provides more scope for prompting subjects or for seeking clarification.

Primary versus secondary research

These distinguish between the various sources of data available to the researcher. **Secondary sources** refer to data already available in some form or another and may include the results of previously performed research or other publicly available material such as newspaper reports or government statistics. **Primary research** involves gathering data directly from the market through the collection of opinions, the observation of behaviour, or through tapping into sources within the organization. The advantage of primary research is that it will probably provide information that is unique, whereas secondary sources are likely to be available to everyone else in a market.

Desk versus field research

These are another way of describing the sources that can be used to provide marketing information. **Desk research** usually involves a search of existing data sources, whereas **field research** involves going 'out into the field' or market place to collect, usually primary, data. It is normal to engage in desk research first to establish what information needs to be obtained from field research because it is unavailable elsewhere.

Internal versus external research

This distinction draws attention to the range of information sources that often exist within an organization without having to look outside or commission specific market research projects. **Internal sources** can include sales records, shipping documentation and invoices, as well as reports generated by sales people, service engineers or delivery and installation personnel. Customer correspondence can also be a useful source of data on the way that the market is responding to an organization's offering. Sadly, it is not unusual for organizations to commission, for example, competitor analysis research when they themselves employ people who previously worked for those competitors and whom their current employers had ignored in their search for information.

When considering marketing research, it is also useful to distinguish between **marketing data, information** and **intelligence** when discussing any activity or system. In this context, data can best be thought of as the raw facts, figures or descriptions of the topic being researched. Information is ordered data, or data that has been selected to describe a particular market or performance feature. Intelligence can best be regarded as information from which conclusions have been drawn. As an example, an 80:20, or **Pareto analysis** of an industrial company's customers based on sales invoices (the data) would yield information (a list of their best customers in revenue terms) that could then be interpreted and/or explained to provide intelligence.

Marketing information systems

A comprehensive marketing information system requires attention to four main areas of activity. The first area concerns **performance monitoring over time** and relies heavily on information drawn from internal sources. Such information can include profitability analyses, which can cover customer, segment and product profitability. Also important are sales volumes across different sectors, product mixes and the effectiveness of discount structures. Other points of interest might be trends pertaining to delivery performance, complaints and product returns. Advances in software and the introduction of **Enterprise Resource Planning** systems (ERPs) that concentrate on the efficiency of a firm's internal production, distribution and financial processing provide a good opportunity for the regular generation of timely reports on performance effectiveness. ERPs are management information systems that integrate and automate many of the business practices associated with the operations or production and distribution aspects of a business.

The second area, **market monitoring,** refers to the regular collection of externally generated materials about developments in the marketing environment. This activity could be performed by an organization's library, if they have one, an outside agency, or by individuals in marketing or marketing associated roles. Whatever the mechanism used, it should be able to deliver steady flows of newspaper, journal and other published matter that will alert managers to changes in their areas of interest. It should also act as a repository from which information required on an occasional basis can be drawn. Market monitoring could also involve the generation of information from employees who operate in the field, from regular surveys, or from panel reports generated at specific intervals. Topics for market monitoring might embrace:

- competitor activity;
- publications from standards bodies;
- legislative activities;
- technological advances;
- pressure group campaigns;
- fashion trends.

The third aspect of an integrated marketing information system is a **market investigation facility** for specific questions or *ad hoc* projects. This would involve expert researchers administering questionnaires (postal or telephone), conducting interviews, or engaging in desk research of some form or another. The popular conception of market research usually focuses on this type of activity, but requires careful management if it is to be useful. Critical is the process of problem definition, from which a research plan is developed. The plan will focus on two main elements: the population to be researched and the methodology to be employed. Such projects, however, are very expensive and need to be used carefully for the best effect.

The fourth feature of a system would be a **decision support** mechanism so that marketing personnel can manipulate information and intelligence using the analytical tools of marketing. These may be various statistical techniques such as correlation, cluster or conjoint analysis, or may be based on analytical models of different kinds. Such models could include:

- 'what if' facilities;
- portfolio modelling;
- complete planning systems.

Just as the increased use of computers for administrative systems has enabled much more data to become available for analysis, so the leaps made in information technology towards expert systems and virtual reality will provide ever-increasing sophistication in this type of activity.

Marketing information is now recognized as a source of competitive power and increasing amounts of effort are being spent on the development of marketing information systems. Systems, however, cannot substitute for personal judgement and the creativity required to develop innovative marketing strategies. Such attributes are needed to identify the 'golden nuggets' often hidden by systematic approaches, and to generate the unique positioning or segmentation programmes essential for competitive advantage. In addition, it must be remembered that data, information or intelligence is only ever as good as the specifications from which it was produced, and much information is either too general, or the result of poorly conducted research, to be relied upon. Finally, it must also be remembered that any market research or marketing information systems invariably throw up more questions than they answer. There is no such phenomenon as perfect information.

Preparing a marketing research brief

Regardless of who carries out the work involved in a market research project, it is important that a clear brief is produced against which the subsequent work will be undertaken and judged. The research brief, which should be produced in both written and verbal form, is a key document and the starting point for any significant research project. In its preparation it is important that the following questions are addressed:

- What actions will we take as a consequence of the research information?
- What do we need to know in order to decide which course of action to take?
- How much are we prepared to spend to get this information?

Contents of a brief

First, the commissioning organization should think very carefully about what, and how much, it wishes to reveal in the brief. Ideally, the brief should be open, precise and factual, but there may be particular points, such as the exact budget, which are best omitted. A good briefing document, preferably accompanied by product literature, may span 1–5 pages.

If the meeting is part of a tendering process for the research contract, it will be important for the agency to demonstrate competence and commitment to the project, but also for the commissioning organization to ensure they have tested the agency sufficiently to feel that they will be able to work comfortably with them.

Once an agency has been chosen to perform the research, it is important that the brief is presented face to face or at least in interactive discussion. No matter how clearly the commissioning organization believes that it has specified the project, there is always the potential for misunderstanding. Interactive discussion is the only way to check an agency's interpretation of the brief. This is particularly important if the research is qualitative and involves interviewers or observers where the line of questioning or focus of observation will have a significant effect on the quality of the information collected.

A good research brief should contain:

- background information on the market, the company, its products/services, market standing, and so on;
- the objectives of the research, which may include both primary and secondary objectives and, if possible, the precise questions for which answers are required;
- the desired timescales such as the completion date required together with any interim report times or key decision dates;
- preferred report and presentation formats;
- the main point of contact and information to be made available in support of the research;
- the degree of confidentiality required when conducting the research.

It is not suggested that the briefing document be seen as a 'straitjacket' but as a series of well-thought-out guidelines. As such, the expertise of the agency/consultancy should be sought in the briefing meeting in terms of both the information being sought and the parameters set out in the brief. A good agency should be able to talk about the population being surveyed with respect to:

- what will encourage them to co-operate;
- the ease with which they can be accessed;
- the information required from the commissioning organization;
- realistic timescales;
- appropriate research methodologies;
- costs and cost differentials.

A brief that is also an invitation to tender should specifically state the form of proposal required and for anything large or complex, it is fair to ask for a written proposal offering best solutions. This should include the recommended methodologies, the expected timeframes and the costs involved. Commissioning organizations should also include a deadline for a proposal or a tender submission date.

At the discretion of the commissioning organization, information may also be given about the competitive quoting levels involved without necessarily defining or naming these precisely. Normally, the costs involved in the briefing meeting and preparation of the research proposal are seen by consultants/ agencies as part of their prospecting and business development costs.

The research proposal

The proposal, usually a written document supported with a personal presentation, represents an agency's ability to communicate and is a good indication of the quality of the research output to be expected.

As such, this should be a selection factor given that the organization commissioned to carry out the research is providing an indication or preview of its listening, communication and presentation skills. The proposal is therefore an opportunity to provide additional clues as to the likely quality of the final product. This assessment opportunity for the client should not be overlooked!

The research proposal also needs to provide a specification of what the research organization will do, how it will carry out the work and what it will cost. It is important that it conveys its understanding of what is expected and its competence to provide the work most efficiently. A good research proposal should, therefore, include:

- background information, to convey a clear understanding of the project and the issues involved;
- objectives, which should be clearly listed and very precisely defined against the specification of the problem;
- work programme and methodology, covering both the way that the objectives will be achieved and the way that the work programme would be completed; it should detail sample size, research stages and questionnaire methods;
- fees/payment terms and timescales, which should be clearly stated and classified showing expenses, tax and so on, set against the work schedule;
- company details and research personnel involved, including research company competence and brief biographies of personnel, plus, if relevant, any business terms;
- summary of research project benefits and agency's confidence in its competence to 'deliver' what is required.

The sponsoring organization's response

Acceptance of the proposal should be in writing. It should authorize the work and confirm the points of agreement and costs involved. This should provide a binding agreement as to what is to be done and at what cost, so as to eliminate any subsequent disagreement between the sponsoring organization and the agency/consultancy.

Auditing a market

Basically, a marketing audit is the means by which a company can understand how it relates to the environment in which it operates. It is also the means by which a company can identify its own strengths and weaknesses as they relate to external opportunities and threats. It is thus a way of helping management select a position in that environment based on known factors and is the basis of a marketing plan and a key input to any longer term strategic or business plan.

In its simplest form, the purpose of a marketing plan is to answer three central questions in relation to its markets and its competitors within those markets:

- where is the organization now?
- where does the organization want to go?
- how should the organization organize its resources to get there?

The audit provides the information from which the first of these questions is answered. Just like a financial audit, a marketing audit is a systematic, critical and unbiased appraisal of an organization's position; but in this case its position with respect to its market environment and its marketing operations.

Unfortunately, the need for an audit is not always recognized until things start to go wrong. Typically, it is not until there is a decline in sales, a fall in margins, reduced market share, under-utilization of production capacity, and so on, that an organization decides to take a long hard look at its position. At this point the marketing audit becomes a last-ditch, end-of-the-road attempt to understand the exact nature of the marketing problem. Since marketing is a complex function and at the heart of an organization's relationships with its customers, it is better to build an audit into the regular planning cycles of an organization in much the same way that organizations will perform annual audits of their financial position before setting a budget. Indeed, there is much evidence that many highly successful companies, as well as using normal information and control procedures plus marketing research throughout the year, also start their planning cycle each year with a formal review, through an audit-type process, of everything that has had an important influence on marketing activities that year. Certainly in many leading consumer goods companies the annual self-audit approach is a tried and tested discipline. Where they are integrated into their management process, audits become easier to perform the more regularly they are conducted.

Performed on a regular basis and covering similar set of variables on each occasion, the audit becomes a structured approach to the collection and analysis of information and data in the complex business environment that is an essential prerequisite to business planning and problem-solving.

Marketing audit variables

Organizations that perform marketing audits are faced with two kinds of variables. First, there are variables over which the company has no direct control. These usually take the form of environmental, market and competitive variables. Second, there are variables over which the company has complete control, often referred to as operational variables. These provide the basis for the two critical elements of any audit:

- external variables;
- internal variables.

An audit starts with an examination of information on the general economy and then moves on to the outlook for the health and growth of the markets served by the company. The purpose of the internal audit is to assess the organization's resources as they relate to the environment and vis-à-vis the resources of competitors. Table 27.1 contains a checklist of areas that should be investigated as part of both the internal and external marketing audit.

Each of the headings shown in Table 27.1 should be examined with a view to isolating those factors that are considered critical to the company's performance. Initially, the auditor's task is to screen the enormous amount of information and data for validity and relevance. Some of the data and information obtained for an audit will have to be reorganized into a more easily usable form, and judgement will have to be applied to decide what further data and information are necessary for a proper definition of the problem. Behind the summary headings, however, more detailed questions should be asked. Thus there are basically two phases that comprise the auditing process:

1 identification, measurement, collection and analysis of all the relevant facts and opinions that impinge on a company's operations;

2 the application of judgement to the areas of uncertainty remaining after this analysis.

TABLE 27.1   The marketing audit checklist

EXTERNAL AUDIT	
Business and economic environment	Economic
	Political/Fiscal/Legal
	Social/Cultural
	Technological
	Inter-company
The market	Total market, size, growth and trends (value/volume)
	Market characteristics
	Developments and trends in marketing mix variables as follows:
	• products
	• prices
	• physical distribution
	• channels
	• customers/consumers
	• communication
	• industry practices
Competition	Major competitors
	Size
	Market shares/coverage
	Market standing/reputation
	Production capabilities
	Distribution policies
	Marketing methods
	Extent of diversification
	Personnel issues
	International links
	Profitability
	Key strengths and weaknesses
INTERNAL AUDIT	
Marketing operational variables	Sales (by geographical location, industrial type, customer, and product)
	Market shares
	Profit margins/costs
	Marketing information/research
	Marketing mix variables as follows:
	• product management
	• price
	• distribution
	• promotion
	• operations and resources

Occasionally it may be justified to hire outside consultants to carry out a marketing audit to check that an organization is getting the most out of its resources. However, it seems an unnecessary expense to have this done every year. The answer, therefore, is to have an audit carried out annually by the organization's line managers on their individual areas of responsibility.

Objections to this usually centre on the problems of time and objectivity. In practice, these problems are overcome, first, by institutionalizing procedures in as much detail as possible so that all managers have to conform to a disciplined approach, and second, by thorough training in the use of the procedures themselves. However, even this will not achieve the purpose of an audit unless a rigorous discipline is applied from the highest down to the lowest levels of management involved in the audit. Such a discipline is usually successful in helping managers to avoid the sort of tunnel vision that often results from a lack of critical appraisal.

Alternative structures for a marketing audit include PEST (Political, Economic, Sociological and Technical) analysis and variations on this mnemonic such as STEP, but since these do not cover competitor or internal analyses, they are only a part of the fuller audit referred to here.

A useful framework for presenting the findings of an audit is an adaptation of Michael Porter's Five Forces Analysis under the headings:

- market influence of suppliers;
- market influence of buyers;
- potential for new entrants;
- threats from alternative technologies;
- intensity of competition in the market (see Topic 29, 'Competitor analysis').

Once completed, the information gained from a marketing audit forms the basis for many decision-making activities in the organization. For marketing, a summary is required that highlights the key market situations and trends that will impact on the organization's marketing strategy and programmes. The best summary is in the form of a SWOT analysis, which displays the organization's key Strengths, Weaknesses, Opportunities and Threats. Regularization of the marketing audit will allow for annually updated SWOTs from which developments in an organization's strategic and tactical approaches to marketing can be made. For further details, see Topic 28 'Constructing a SWOT'.

Constructing a SWOT

A SWOT analysis, covering an organization's strengths, weaknesses, opportunities and threats, is often included as part of an organization's policy and decision-making process. A well-constructed SWOT can provide powerful insights into the situation facing an organization and can demonstrate, in a clear fashion, the direction an organization needs to take. Poorly constructed SWOTs will, at best, provide only a bland interpretation of an organization's position. At worst, they can be misleading and will lead to wrong conclusions and misguided policy. It is, therefore, important for managers to be well versed in the issues involved in developing a good SWOT; particularly as it is their interpretation of the market and the organization's position within it that will form the basis of a SWOT, no matter where the data are drawn from.

A SWOT analysis only makes sense if it is performed against an organization's competitors in a market and is usually derived from a marketing audit. In conducting an audit, it is important to remember that the results will be used to identify points that will appear in the SWOT. In this way, an audit can be given focus, and when the time comes to create the SWOT, the chances of relevant information being absent will be reduced. Poor SWOTs tend to be based on opinion or are constructed without reference to market and marketing information.

It is also important to understand that a SWOT is constructed for a specific market, segment or customer. While it is possible to perform a SWOT for an organization that relates to the whole range of its activities, it is unlikely that the strengths and weaknesses identified will be relevant to all the markets in which it operates. Thus, a hotel might rate its high-class restaurant facilities, which provide meals freshly cooked to order, as a strength for the 'special occasion eating-out market', but would be wrong in thinking this feature was also a strength for the 'business conference market', which requires fast throughput at meal times in order to cover their agendas.

Strengths and weaknesses

Strengths and weaknesses thus refer to the conclusions of the internal marketing audit in relation to customer requirements. They also refer to the organization's performance against those requirements relative to its competitors. In this way, a strength is only a strength if it is something that is of value to customers and is also something that an organization does better than its competitors. For instance, having the ability to deliver against the placement of an order within 48 hours is not a strength if customers require 24 hours' delivery and its major competitors are all able to fulfil this requirement. The converse situation would, of course, be a strength. Also, if a 24 hours' delivery service is the norm and all competitors fulfil this requirement, it is what is known as a 'qualifying' strength and should be omitted from the SWOT.

It is also important to distinguish between a marketing strength and a marketing asset. An asset is something that an organization possesses that could, potentially, become a strength. A useful means of developing strengths from assets is to apply the question 'which means that...?' or 'so what...?' until something about the asset that delivers a competitive advantage is found. Thus, high-level engineering skills are an asset from which a strength – which might, for instance, be the ability to supply against a tight specification – can be derived. In a similar fashion, weaknesses will be derived from the absence of an asset of some form, or an asset that underperforms when compared with customer requirements and competitors' abilities.

A useful means of differentiating between strengths, weaknesses and assets is to identify order-winning as opposed to order-qualifying criteria. Qualifying criteria will be those features or benefits of goods or services that have to be present for a supplier to be a contender for a sale. Thus a holiday company might need to offer packages in Greece to qualify for consideration by a potential customer. Order-winning criteria will be related to those characteristics that it offers as unique or that outperform competitor offerings. Strengths can only refer to order-winning features and benefits, whereas weaknesses can encompass both order-qualifying and order-winning factors.

A similar methodology is to use the concept of critical success factors (CSFs). These relate to those factors that a supplier in a market must possess if they are to compete successfully. There are usually relatively few factors that can be deemed 'critical'. Factors such as product performance, breadth of offering, speed of service, low prices, reputation, and so on, are often the most important here. A layout such as that shown in Figure 28.1 can be useful when comparing overall competitive positions using CSFs. Having identified the main CSFs for a market segment, each factor should be weighted out of 100, according to its importance to customers. Total weightings should add up to 100. It is then possible to score each major competitor out of 10 on their performance against each CSF. Multiplying each score by its weight will provide a quantitative assessment of the relative strengths of each competitor within a segment. Figure 28.2 illustrates a typical calculation based on this method.

FIGURE 28.1   Establishing competitive positions using critical success factors

Competitors / Critical success factors	Weighting factor	Your organization	Competitor A	Competitor B	Competitor C
CSF 1					
CSF 2					
CSF 3					
CSF 4					
Total weighted score	100				

FIGURE 28.2   Strengths and weaknesses analysis

Critical success factor	Weighting %	Strengths/weaknesses analysis
The few elements of the marketing mix in which any competitor has to perform well to succeed	The relative importance of each CSF scored out of 100	Performance against each CSF is scored out of 10 and multiplied by the weighting

			Competitors			
			You	Comp A	Comp B	Comp C
1	Product	20%	1 9 = 1.8	6 = 1.2	5 = 1.0	4 = 0.8
2	Price	10%	2 8 = 0.8	5 = 0.5	6 = 0.6	10 = 1.0
3	Service	50%	3 5 = 2.5	9 = 4.5	7 = 3.5	6 = 3.0
4	Image	20%	4 8 = 1.6	8 = 1.6	5 = 1.0	3 = 0.6
	Totals	100%	6.7	7.8	6.1	5.4

Opportunities and threats

Opportunities and threats refer to external issues and are identified as a result of the external marketing audit. Thus, improving quality or creating a brand name are not opportunities and low stock turnover or poor industrial relations are not threats, since they all relate to internal issues for an organization.

Apart from the problem of definition, it is also often difficult to identify relevant opportunities and threats. In theory, an organization is faced with limitless opportunities and myriads of threats. These can range from the opportunities created by new markets, new products and poor performance by competitors, to the threats of war, earthquakes and competitor activities. What makes an opportunity or a threat relevant is its significance for the organization and its likelihood of occurring. The opportunities and threats matrices depicted in Figures 28.3 and 28.4 provide a useful means of prioritizing opportunities and threats for the purposes of inclusion in a SWOT analysis.

FIGURE 28.3   Opportunities matrix

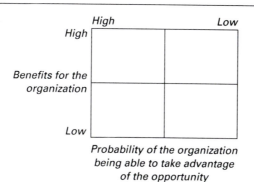

FIGURE 28.4   Threats matrix

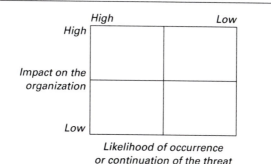

A further means of identifying opportunities is to concentrate on those that result from one of two different situations. The first concerns changes that are occurring in the market place. These changes can take the form of legislative developments, a competitor leaving a market, infrastructural changes, market growth, and so on, and can yield some very attractive opportunities. Although such developments may also yield threats, it is important to consider them in light of the organization's marketing asset base. As an example, the current increase in e-tailing is a threat to major retailers who rely on expensive High Street stores, but has been an opportunity for an organization with well-developed household delivery facilities. Similarly, the present trend towards healthier eating was a threat to McDonald's whose core asset was pre-produced processed foods. It has been very costly for McDonald's to re-engineer its supply chain and menus to regain market position on the back of 'healthier' menus.

Other opportunities derive from situations where an existing need is poorly served by current suppliers. If a supplier services the CSFs for its customers to a high degree of satisfaction, there is unlikely to be an opportunity of any value to competitors. If, on the other hand, a supplier performs poorly against one CSF when compared with customer needs, then an opportunity will exist as long as the organization has the potential to service that need more effectively than the existing supplier. As a simple example, if a reader is entirely satisfied with their newspaper, there is little opportunity for other newspapers to entice them away. However, if a reader's main interest is soft pornography and celebrity gossip, a lack of good pictures and stories in their traditional paper provide a real opportunity for other journals. Probably the most enduring example of the last 25 years is the launch of First Direct who offered 24-hour access to banking initially through the telephone and latterly via the internet thereby exploiting a customer need for convenience banking poorly fulfilled by branches.

A good SWOT, then, provides a clear presentation of an organization's platform and position within a particular market. The issues it contains will have been refined for relevance and meaning. Each issue will have been the subject of a 'so what?' or 'which means that...?' analysis, so that the true implications of each of the features included are reached. Following the presentation of a good SWOT, it should be easy to understand where an organization's priorities should lie.

Competitor analysis

An important aspect of a market that needs to be understood and characterized for the development of marketing policies is the substance and nature of the competition within it. In recent years, the work of Michael Porter has become synonymous with the process of such competitive analysis. His 'five forces' analytical framework provided a systematic method for exploring the competitive context of a market. Good analysis of these forces will help identify where power lies in the market, who can influence market trends, how the market is likely to develop, where to concentrate when seeking new market opportunities and the basic platforms from which it is possible to compete.

Components of Porter's five forces framework

The threat of new entrants

In analysing markets, one of the factors to be appraised is the existence, or absence, of 'barriers to entry'. In other words, how easy is it for new entrants to enter the market? Typically, barriers might be provided by high market share or economies of scale, so that without a minimum market share, unit costs will be uncompetitive. Similarly, heavy start-up costs, whether through the need for capital investment or high levels of marketing expenditure, can also provide a barrier. Conversely, markets may be easy for new competitors to enter where product differentiation is low, where technology changes can overcome cost barriers or where there is the potential for high levels of market fragmentation. For many competitive organizations, the advent of the internet has significantly reduced the barriers to entry and the trend towards deregulation has encouraged more competition in other areas.

Substitute products or services

One factor that can considerably alter the strategic balance in a market place is the development of products that meet underlying customer needs more cost-effectively than existing products. As an example, the development of oil-based film had a major impact upon the demand for wood-based film. In the past, the advent of fax machines virtually killed off the demand for telex, while fax machines have been made redundant by the developments of electronic communications and the legal acceptance of such communications in contractual exchanges.

The bargaining power of buyers

The competitive climate of a market will clearly be influenced by the extent to which customers wield power through purchasing strength. Thus, a market that is dominated by a limited number of buyers, or a situation where a buyer takes a large proportion of the seller's output, will substantially limit the seller's opportunities for individual action or development. The UK and US grocery market illustrates this situation well, with a handful of major retail chains being able to exert considerable influence over manufacturing suppliers' marketing policies, and thus their profitability. A further source of competitive threat from buyers will exist when opportunities arise for backward integration by buyers taking control of greater proportions of the value chain.

The bargaining power of suppliers

Many of the threats that potentially exist from buyers can also be posed by suppliers to an industry. If the supply of critical materials is controlled by a few suppliers, or if an individual company's purchases from a supplier constitute only a small part of that supplier's output, then freedom of manoeuvre may be limited. Again, if opportunities exist for forward integration by suppliers, this constitutes a further source of potential competitive pressure.

The degree of market competition

Obviously, the more numerous or equally balanced the competitors, the more intense will be the rivalry within the market. If this is combined with a slow industry growth rate, and if fixed costs relative to variable costs are high, then the prognosis is for a high level of aggressive competition, probably accompanied by severe price-cutting. A further influencing factor will be the extent to which competing products are seen as substitutes by the market place, especially if there are few switching penalties for buyers. Of key importance in this will be the relative cost structures of the major players in the market. These will be determined not just by market share, but by capacity utilization and production technology.

What has become increasingly obvious during the severe shakeouts that regularly occurred since the late 1990s is that the most meticulous analysis of an organization's competitors is no longer an option – it is an absolute necessity in order to survive.

Performing a competitor analysis

A good starting point is a summary of the findings of a market audit in respect of major competitors. An organization should understand the sales of each of their competitors within the particular product/market segment under consideration – their share now, and their expected share three years from now. The greater a competitor's influence over others, the greater its ability to implement its own independent strategies and the more successful it will be. It is suggested that organizations should also identify each of their main competitors according to one of the classifications in the guide to competitive position given in Table 29.1, based on their influence in the market and their ability to pursue alternative strategies within their markets.

The format shown in Figure 29.1 provides a useful framework for comparing competitors. In this, organizations need first to list their principal products or services; each major competitor's business intention and current strategies (see guidelines in Table 29.2); and their major strengths and weaknesses.

TABLE 29.1 Guide to market competitive position classifications

- *Leadership*
  Has a major influence on the performance or behaviour of others.
- *Strong*
  Has a wide choice of strategies. Can adopt an independent strategy without endangering their short-term position. Has low vulnerability to competitors' actions.
- *Favourable*
  Exploits specific competitive strengths, often in a product-market niche. Has more than average opportunity to improve their position; several strategies are available.
- *Tenable*
  Performance justifies continuation in business.
- *Weak*
  Currently unsatisfactory performance; a significant competitive weakness. Inherently a short-term condition; must improve or withdraw.

FIGURE 29.1   Competitor analysis framework

Products/ markets	Main competitor	Business direction, current objectives and strategies	Strengths	Weaknesses	Competitive position

TABLE 29.2   Alternative business directions

- *Enter*
  Allocate resources to a new business area. Consideration should include building from prevailing company or division strength, exploiting related opportunities and defending against perceived threats. May involve creating a new division

- *Improve*
  Apply strategies that will significantly improve the competitive position of the business. Often requires thoughtful product/market segmentation

- *Maintain*
  Maintain one's competitive position. Aggressive strategies may be required, although a defensive posture may also be assumed. Product/market position is maintained, often in a niche

- *Harvest*
  Intentionally relinquish competitive position, emphasizing short-term profit and cash flow but not necessarily at the risk of losing the business in the short term. Often entails consolidating or reducing various aspects of the business to create higher performance for that which remains

- *Exit*
  Abandon a business because of its weak competitive position. The cost of staying in is prohibitive and the risk associated with improving its position is too high

At a more detailed level, it is also important to develop a profile of each major competitor in terms of their contribution to the market in which an organization is interested, plus their basic capabilities. Most organizations will position themselves in terms of one or two of these capabilities. Thus Maytag positions itself as innovative and dependable while Dexion (international storage equipment manufacturer) competes in the 'small user' market on the basis of local retailers with local knowledge and fast ex-stock supply. Table 29.3 illustrates some of the key ways in which competitors might position themselves in an effort to influence customers' purchase decisions.

To collect, analyse and disseminate this information, some kind of organized, systematic intelligence system is necessary. It is essential to specify in advance the precise information that is needed by the organization about its competitors.

TABLE 29.3 Individual competitor analysis

- Segment shares (biggest in the market)
- Product line position
- Brand-based strategies
- Price positioning
- Channel strategies
- Customer service strategies
- Management skills and philosophies (the sort of business we are)
- Technological capabilities and position
- Financial strength
- Sales capabilities and strategies

The Boston Matrix

The Boston Matrix is a vehicle for classifying and characterizing an organization's activities in relation to the markets in which it operates. It can be used to plot strategic business units (SBUs), or product portfolios, which are then located on the matrix for analytical purposes. The matrix will provide a 'big picture' view of a business's position and a basis for thinking about how to manage each aspect of a portfolio. In addition, it can highlight strategic imbalances in a portfolio such as gaps or areas which may prove problematic as markets grow, mature or decline.

The matrix focuses on two key aspects of markets: their growth rates and a product or SBU's relative market share by value (see Figure 30.1). Market growth rates are ranged on the vertical axis and were originally rated between

FIGURE 30.1   The Boston Matrix

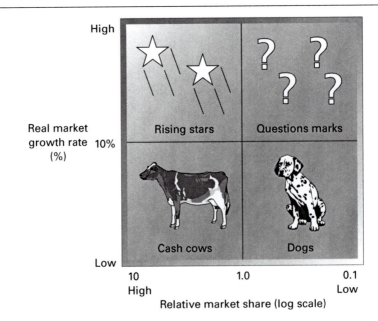

0 per cent and 30 per cent, with a growth rate of over 10 per cent being high, and under 10 per cent low. In fact, what is considered a high or low growth rate will vary from industry to industry, market to market or time to time, and practitioners need to make their own judgements about where the break-points between high and low should fall. Market share is depicted on the horizontal axis on a log scale and shows a product or SBU's share relative to that of the largest competitor in the market. A relative market share of 1.0 means that its share is equal to that of the largest competitor; 10 will mean that it is ten times larger and 0.1 will mean that it has one tenth the share of the largest supplier. The log scale is used so that equal distances on the axis represent the same percentage increases or reductions.

The rationale behind the matrix is that growth rates will significantly affect the attractiveness of a market to an organization for investment purposes and relative market share is a good indicator of a business's strength in that market. Growth rates are also of interest because they relate to the stages of a product life cycle. High growth rates are associated with markets where the customer base is expanding rapidly and in which businesses have to match or exceed the growth rate to maintain their market share position. Low growth rates indicate that the market is maturing and implies that a business does not have to compete with other suppliers for new customers entering a market, in order to maintain its share of the market.

The importance of market share is derived from the concept of the experience curve (see Figure 30.2). If a business can maintain the position of market share leader, it will, by definition, have produced and sold more products than any of its competitors. This will enable it to achieve greater economies of experience and, thus, lower costs and better knowledge than

FIGURE 30.2 The experience curve

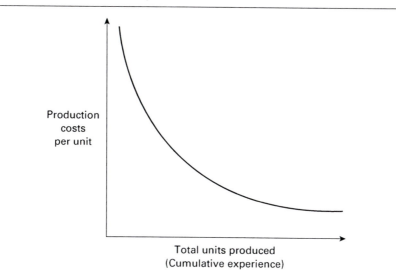

Production
costs
per unit

Total units produced
(Cumulative experience)

competitors. Such economies and knowledge are not achieved automatically, but must be actively pursued by an organization's management. If gained, such economies should yield cash that can be used for reinvestment in other products/SBUs; protection against price wars or other marketing efforts of competitors, or profit distribution. The knowledge gained from the experience should yield market intelligence, which should, in turn, make competitive activities more effective. High market share can also reduce the relative expenditure required for competitive marketing activities and can often provide a business with the power to influence a market in terms of price, technical standards, product development and the way competitive activities are conducted.

The products/SBUs in each quadrant of the matrix are, therefore, faced with different marketing tasks. Those in high-growth markets, but with a low market share (referred to as Question Marks or Problem Children) need to seek market leadership so that when the market matures, they will be a long way down the experience curve and in a position of strength in the market. This will require investment to challenge the existing leaders and may force a business to prioritize between a number of products/SBUs if they are not to spread their resources too thinly.

A Star is a business or product that has attained market leadership in high growth markets. Here, the priority will be to invest to maintain leadership against challenges from the Question Marks of other organizations. As a market's growth slows, Stars will become Cash Cows if they have protected their leadership. Cash Cows still require some investment to keep their leadership position, but not to the same extent as Stars or Question Marks. Thus, they can potentially generate cash that can be used to support Question Marks seeking to become Stars in other markets. If a business has a low relative market share in a mature market, the matrix classifies it as a Dog, since it is unlikely to generate cash to the same extent as the market leader. Recently, the concept of Cash Dogs has been introduced to indicate products/SBUs that have a reasonable market share and which can generate useful cash flows in spite of not being the market leaders. Sometimes, Dog products can be very profitable, which is usually a result of holding a position in a niche market that has been subsumed into a larger market for analysis purposes.

An unbalanced portfolio can, therefore, have significant cash flow implications for a business either now or for the future. As an example, an absence of Stars could mean no Cash Cows in the future. Alternatively, the absence of Cash Cows will imply a need for external funding if it is to be in a cash-generating position in the future. Too many Question Marks may drain a business of cash if it has ambitions for leadership in each of the markets in which they are launched. Dogs consume management time and a business must consider whether they are holding them for good reasons, since they are unlikely to be contributing much to the bottom line on their own, and so on. Figure 30.3 illustrates the cash situation faced by products/SBUs in different parts of the matrix.

FIGURE 30.3   The Boston Matrix – cash flow implications

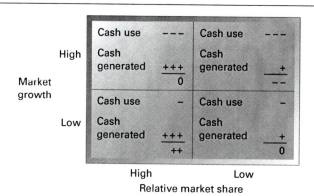

The implications of the matrix are that organizations need to invest heavily in Question Marks and Stars, which are potential Cash Cows, and only moderately in Cash Cows and Dogs. Thus, each category of product will have different cash-flow requirements and will need attention to different marketing priorities. In this way, a more rational basis for strategy development is possible and the 'health' of an organization can be more easily assessed from a marketing viewpoint.

Like all simplifications, there are a few drawbacks to using the Boston Matrix as a diagnostic and strategic tool:

- the now-popularized labels given to different quadrants may act as demotivators for managers, especially if they feel that the organization views them as only suitable to manage Dogs;

- growth and market share are not the only factors that make markets attractive and that give companies strength in markets;

- the data to position products/SBUs accurately on the matrix are not always available;

- a clear and common definition of the market must be agreed so that growth and share positions are not distorted.

As an extreme illustration, it would be quite easy for a business to claim a 100 per cent share of the market if it defined the market as all those customers it supplied! In a similar way, maintaining a Cash Cow assumes that other organizations recognize the position and do not invest heavily in their Dogs and attack the Cash Cows of other organizations, thereby requiring them to spend money to defend their position. Overall, though, the tool can be extremely useful as a means of depicting an organization's situation or market position and as a basis for internal managerial debate.

The Directional Policy Matrix

The Directional Policy Matrix (DPM) is a framework that can be used to classify and categorize an organization's business activities in terms of its strengths, capabilities or market position, together with the way it perceives markets to be attractive. The basic structure of a DPM is illustrated in Figure 31.1. The purpose of the matrix is to diagnose an organization's strategic options in relation to the two composite dimensions of business strengths and market attractiveness. The DPM enables organizations to conduct an analysis of their portfolio of products or areas of activity.

The analysis is performed according to the potential each product area or business unit has to achieve the organization's objectives (market attractiveness) and then, according to the organization's ability to take advantage of the range of opportunities it faces (organizational strengths). The matrix requires its users to identify a number of factors that will act as indicators of the attractiveness of a market or opportunity and, similarly, those factors

FIGURE 31.1 The Directional Policy Matrix (DPM)

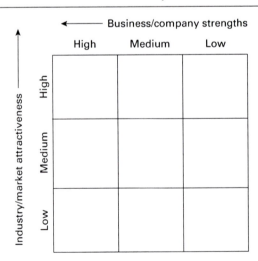

that will act as indicators of organizational strengths. These factors will obviously vary from one product or business area to another since what will be attractive in one area may not be attractive in another. Similarly, a strength or capability in one area may not be a strength in another.

The big advantage of the DPM is that, compared with other portfolio analysis tools such as the Boston Matrix, it is a much more sophisticated analytical tool. Like its forerunner, the Boston Matrix, it can be used to derive quantitative comparisons between areas of activity, but can also take into account a wider range of decisional influences. In fact, the DPM was originally conceived by General Electric, developed by McKinsey and later by Shell, as a means of overcoming some of the limitations of the Boston Matrix. It is usually drawn as a 3 × 3 box matrix, rather than the more standard 2 × 2 format, in order to encompass the range of strategic options it covers. In the end, the number of lines drawn is irrelevant. What is more important is defining the substance of the matrix and its axes, and adopting a rigorous methodology for its application.

Strategic business units

Since the purpose of a DPM analysis is to help develop strategy and the allocation of organizational resources for the alternative products or business within an organization's portfolio, it is important to consider the organizational level at which the analysis should be conducted. Usually, this is taken to be at 'strategic business unit' (SBU) level, but can also be used to plot any portfolio of activity where significant choices between alternative products or markets have to be made. The most common definition of a SBU is that it will:

- have common segments and competitors for most of its products;
- operate in external markets;
- be identifiable as a discrete and separate unit;
- be managed by people who will have control over most of the areas critical to success.

It is usually felt that there should be at least three and up to ten areas for analysis if the DPM is to be of value.

Market attractiveness

The vertical axis of a DPM represents the degree to which a market is attractive to an organization. The key determinant of market attractiveness is its potential to yield growth in sales and profits. Although what constitutes a market for the purposes of DPM analysis will vary, a useful definition is:

TABLE 31.1 Criteria which might make a market attractive*

- Growth rate
- Accessible market size
- Competitive intensity
- Profit margins
- Differences between competitive offerings
- Existence of technical standards
- Compatible infrastructure
- Ease of obtaining payment
- Sensitivity to interest rates
- General volatility
- Degree of regulation
- Barriers to entry
- Rate of technological change
- Likelihood of political stability
- Potential for supply 'partnerships'
- Availability of market intelligence

* List non-exclusive

'an identifiable group of customers with requirements in common that are, or may become, significant in that they will require a separate strategy.'

Thus, there is a large element of judgement required at an early stage in the construction of a DPM, which will be critical to the quality of the analysis. To avoid unnecessary bias, it is vital that market definition and the identification of market attractiveness criteria are done in as objective a way as possible. It is also the case that both these judgements need to be made in isolation from the organization's position in its markets. This is difficult to achieve since most of the managers involved in such an exercise will have views about the organization's position, which will potentially influence their judgements. To make the exercise worthwhile, however, as much objectivity as possible should be sought.

For some examples of what might constitute market attractiveness criteria, see Table 31.1. The most important are usually the first four.

Business strength or position

The horizontal axis of a DPM is a measure of an organization's strengths, or potential strengths, in the market place. The criteria used to judge strengths

TABLE 31.2   Factors that might be considered, or which may yield, business strengths*

- Relative quality
- Production capacity
- Production flexibility
- Product adaptability
- Unit cost of production
- Price position
- R&D capabilities
- Brands owned

- Company image
- Market share
- Range of commercial contracts
- Influence on regulatory bodies
- Delivery performance
- Service facilities
- Channel access or distribution network
- Size/quality of sales force

* List non-exclusive

must be related to customer requirements if they are to have any meaning. The criteria will vary between markets and will need to be assessed against the performance of competitors. The purpose of identifying these criteria is to evaluate the degree to which the organization can take advantage of a market opportunity. Similar to market attractiveness, business strengths or position need to be judged in as objective a way as possible to avoid all products or business areas falling within the same sector of the matrix. Ideally, such judgements should be validated by independent market research.

A list of factors that might be considered when assessing business strengths is shown in Table 31.2. It is usual, however, to translate these into capability to deliver what the market or segment requires. For guidelines on how to do this, see Topic 28 on SWOT analyses.

Constructing a DPM portfolio

Having identified the criteria that will make a market attractive and that will yield business strengths, objective judgements about attractiveness can be made by weighting each factor and then scoring each of them in terms of relative performance or attractiveness. By multiplying each factor's weight by its rating, a numerical value can be obtained. When the values for each factor are totalled, the product or activity can be positioned on the Matrix.

The use of a 2 × 2 form of the matrix yields four strategic categories as shown in Figure 31.2. Each category will have a strategy choice associated with it, which managers will have to translate into specific objectives and marketing programmes for that area. Illustrations of what these might be for each quadrant are shown in Figure 31.3. In addition, the steps required for the creation of a DPM are summarized in Table 31.3.

FIGURE 31.2   Four strategic categories

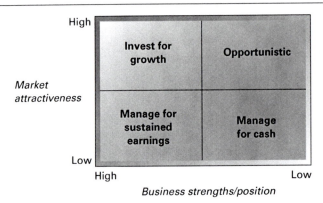

Note:

Invest for growth – businesses that are relatively high in business strengths and market attractiveness.

Manage for substained earnings – businesses with medium strengths in markets of medium to low attractiveness. Maintain strong position in moderately attractive markets, but do not invest to increase market share.

Manage for cash – businesses with a relatively weak position in a relatively unattractive market. Harvest for current profitability or divest.

Opportunistic – businesses with low business strength, but high market attractiveness.

To avoid all products ending up on the left-hand side of a 2 × 2 form of the matrix, scores for performance can be expressed as a ratio where the value is set against a similar value for the best-performing organization in the market. If a log scale is used for this axis, ranging from, say, 3 to 1 to 0.3, this tendency can be overcome.

FIGURE 31.3 Programme guidelines suggested for different positioning on the DPM

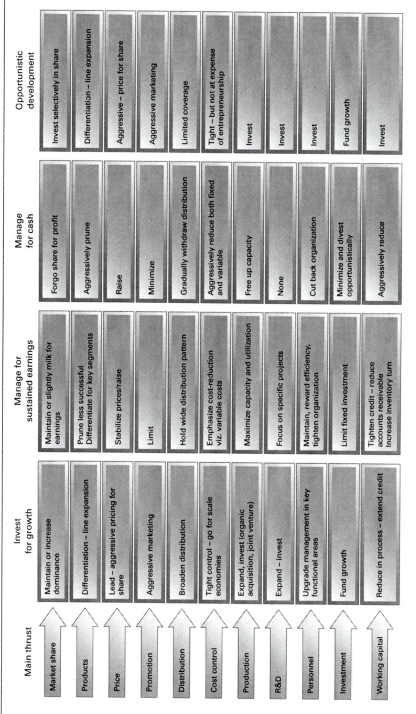

Main thrust	Invest for growth	Manage for sustained earnings	Manage for cash	Opportunistic development
Market share	Maintain or increase dominance	Maintain or slightly milk for earnings	Forgo share for profit	Invest selectively in share
Products	Differentiation – line expansion	Prune less successful. Differentiate for key segments	Aggressively prune	Differentiation – line expansion
Price	Lead – aggressive pricing for share	Stabilize prices/raise	Raise	Aggressive – price for share
Promotion	Aggressive marketing	Limit	Minimize	Aggressive marketing
Distribution	Broaden distribution	Hold wide distribution pattern	Gradually withdraw distribution	Limited coverage
Cost control	Tight control – go for scale economies	Emphasize cost-reduction viz. variable costs	Aggressively reduce both fixed and variable	Tight – but not at expense of entrepreneurship
Production	Expand, invest (organic acquisition, joint venture)	Maximize capacity and utilization	Free up capacity	Invest
R&D	Expand – invest	Focus on specific projects	None	Invest
Personnel	Upgrade management in key functional areas	Maintain, reward efficiency, tighten organization	Cut back organization	Invest
Investment	Fund growth	Limit fixed investment	Minimize and divest opportunistically	Fund growth
Working capital	Reduce in process – extend credit	Tighten credit – reduce accounts receivable. Increase inventory turn	Aggressively reduce	Invest

TABLE 31.3   The ten steps involved in producing a DPM

Step 1	Define the products/services for markets that are to be used during the analysis.
Step 2	Define the criteria for market attractiveness.
Step 3	Score the relevant product/services for market.
Step 4	Define the organization's relative strengths for each product/service for market.
Step 5	Analyse and draw conclusions from the relative position of each product/service for market.
Step 6	Draw conclusions from the analysis with a view to generating objectives and strategies.
Step 7	(Optional) Position the circles on the box assuming no change to current policies. That is to say, a *forecast* should be made of the future position of the circles.
Step 8	Redraw the portfolio to position the circles where the organization wants them to be. That is to say, the *objectives* they wish to achieve for each product/service for market.
Step 9	Detail the strategies to be implemented to achieve the objectives.
Step 10	Calculate the appropriate financial consequences of changes by product.

The Ansoff Matrix

The Ansoff Matrix is a 2 × 2 depiction of the options open to organizations if they wish to improve revenue or profitability. The matrix was first described by Igor Ansoff in 'Strategies for Diversification' (*Harvard Business Review*, September–October 1957, p. 114). Although 'old', it remains a very powerful model because it provides a simple framework that encapsulates all the strategic directions an organization can pursue in one analytical tool.

Unlike some of the other analytical tools used in marketing, the matrix is not diagnostic; rather it is a method for structuring thinking or a means of classifying objectives.

The axes of the matrix focus on the essential relationship an organization has to manage: the provision of products for customers. Whatever an organization's position or industry, the product will be either an existing offering or a product that is new to the organization. Customers, similarly, will be either part of an existing market or members of a market not yet addressed by the organization and, therefore, new to them. An organization is thus faced with four options for commercial action:

- concentrating on existing products for existing markets;
- looking for new products for existing markets;
- seeking new markets for existing products;
- diversifying into new products for new markets. (See Figure 32.1.)

FIGURE 32.1 The Ansoff Matrix

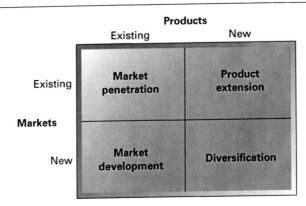

Existing products for existing markets

In developing a strategy, the first area for attention should always be existing product/market relationships. Increased revenue in this option can be gained in a number of ways:

- The easiest method is to attract non-consumers who share the same needs as existing purchasers, but who have not yet become regular users. This is particularly important in growth markets where new customers are appearing all the time. Strategies will concentrate on persuading such people or organizations to test a product and then, if they like it, to use your offering rather than those of direct competitors.

- In mature markets, increased sales will have to come from competitors by persuading customers to use a different supplier or brand. This will usually involve manipulating elements of the marketing mix such as lowering price, broadening a brand's appeal, or initiating sales promotion campaigns. In fact, it is more beneficial to focus on customer service since price wars can be damaging to all concerned and product differentiation is often difficult to achieve.

- Improved sales can also come from persuading the market to increase usage of the products. For consumer products, this may be very appropriate, especially during periods of economic growth and increasing levels of disposable income. Thus, the notions of two-car families, different mobile phones for different purposes and more frequent replacement of consumer durables have an appeal during times of prosperity. In industrial markets, such strategies may be more difficult to implement as purchasers are likely to be seeking better value per purchase; unless they can see competitive value from increased usage or shortened replacement cycles.

- Higher sales revenue can also be achieved through improved productivity, such as: a better mix of products and customers; price increases, or reductions in discounts; charging for deliveries; and so on.

- An alternative to revenue growth is to reduce costs. This, however, may only yield short-term benefits since there is a limit to the scope for cost-reduction. Nonetheless, all good organizations are continuously seeking the benefits of value engineering, process effectiveness and supply chain efficiencies. All of these can provide useful breathing spaces during which an organization can explore other, longer-term areas, for enhancing revenue.

New products for existing markets

The second option for growth is to introduce new products targeted at existing customers with whom the organization already has a relationship. Within this, the better approach is to build on some aspect of the relationship that already exists. This can take a number of different forms:

- One option is to supply new products closely associated with the products that customers already purchase from a supplier. Thus, a computer manufacturer could add computer peripherals, such as printers, plotters and service contracts, or consumables such as paper, ink and discs, to its range in order to provide a 'one-stop shopping' service.

- A similar approach particularly appropriate for organizational customers would be to identify the way in which they categorize their purchases and endeavour to supply products that meet a customer's purchasing management structures. For instance, a retailer might include shampoo as a personal care item, as a fashion accessory or as a bathroom product. Each classificationwould provide different opportunities for the shampoo producer to expand the range of associated products they supply.

- An alternative would be to concentrate on the technology base used to supply existing products and to identify other product needs customers might have that could be produced using current facilities and know-how. A good example is Amazon's expansion from books and CDs into a huge range of household goods and more recently as a representative of other suppliers.

- The other main approach is to build on the way in which existing customers use a supplier. Some relationships might be based on a partnership approach with joint problem-solving, while others might use a supplier for convenience or for a particular attribute of their product or service. Each type of relationship will provide different opportunities for the addition of new products to an organization's range.

New markets for existing products

A third option in the matrix is to look for new markets for existing products requiring the identification of users in different markets with similar needs, or new customers who would use a product in a different way. The most obvious example would be to expand from a domestic market into foreign markets (ie a geographical market extension). Although such a move would probably require some product adaptation, and maybe some different positioning or selling methods, the experience required to supply the product would be essentially the same. A similar example would be an expansion from, say, the public sector into the private sector, or from financial services to the leisure industry. Again, while product modification and adaptation may be required, the core technologies of the product are unlikely to be unaltered.

The same would be true for new markets where the product would be used in a different way. Raw materials, standard components and many service products would be quite easy to adapt, whereas bespoke products, or consumer goods, would be more difficult to transfer. As examples, expanded polystyrene can be used for noise insulation, heat retention in hot water tanks, as a packaging or protection material and as a floor-cushion filler. Similarly, a floor cushion manufacturer could look to expand into cushions for pets, for cars, for beds and for the garden.

New products for new markets

The fourth option, new products for new markets, is the most risky diversification since it utilizes little of an organization's existing expertise or capabilities. It is also the type of expansion that has the highest failure rate. Where organizations have been successful in this domain, it is usually possible to identify some synergy in sales, distribution or product technology. The expansion by BIC, for instance, from pens into disposable razors, utilized both their understanding of the technology of mass production of cheap plastic items and their ability to sell to, and to service, multiple retail organizations. Where no synergies exist, attention to risk management becomes very important.

The Ansoff Matrix can therefore be seen as a framework for describing the range of strategic options open to an organization for expansion. It is also a means of conceptualizing the development of a product over its market life by providing a useful conceptual approach to diversification. However, rather than moving straight to new products for new markets, organizations should see if it is possible to get there via new products or via new markets first, since these will provide experience that will reduce the risk of managing both new products and new markets simultaneously.

Whether it is preferable to expand into either new products or new markets first is a matter for debate. Some would argue for new products on the grounds that customers are more difficult to manage. Others would prefer new markets, since unfamiliar technologies are fraught with hidden problems. In the end, it is probably the option with the least degree of complexity that will determine the choice.

Overall, the Ansoff Matrix has a certain beauty in its simplicity because it strips marketing down to its basics: getting products to market. Having said this, it does perhaps over-simplify marketing in that there are different kinds of new products and different kinds of new markets. It is important to be clear about what these are, as illustrated in Table 32.1.

The Ansoff Matrix is good at reminding us that marketing does not need to be complicated, but its inference that things are either old or new overlooks those middling shades of grey. One way of clarifying this is to re-draw the Ansoff Matrix as depicted in Figure 32.2.

TABLE 32.1   Kinds of new products and markets

Degrees of newness of the product:
- It can stay the same
- It can be extended in some way
- It can be re-designed, modified or improved
- It can be a new product or concept entirely

Different forms of new markets:
- They can be the same
- They can be broader in terms of how they are defined
- They can include new coverage, but on related areas
- They can be totally new

FIGURE 32.2 An extended product/market matrix

	Newness of product			
Product / Market	Same product	Extended product	Modified or improved product	New product
Same market				
Broader market coverage				
New coverage but in related areas				
New market				

Newness of market (vertical axis label)

PART SIX
Managing the marketing mix

Branding

When making a purchase, a customer is influenced by a whole range of factors associated with the complete product offer. One of these may be the product's brand name. In spite of its intangibility, a well-developed brand can be a powerful influence on both customers and competitors alike, and will be a key contributor to the way a product, company, or whatever the brand represents, is positioned in the market place. It consequently becomes important to understand the scope of branding, the difference between major brands, lesser brands and commodities, the specific components of a brand name and the differences between successful and unsuccessful brands.

The scope of branding

When considering brands, it should be stressed that the term 'brand' is used to encompass not only consumer products such as Flora, Persil or Nescafé, but a host of offerings including places (such as Paris), transport (such as the Orient Express or DHL), companies (such as Microsoft, Google and BMW), industrial products (such as Caterpillar), service products, and even individual people. In addition, a distinction should be drawn between a 'brand' and a 'commodity'.

Typically, commodity markets are characterized by a lack of perceived differentiation by customers between competing offerings. While there may be quality differences, the suggestion is that within a given specification, this carton of milk, for example, is just the same as any other carton of milk. In situations such as these, one finds that purchase decisions tend to be taken on the basis of price, promotions or availability, and not on the basis of the brand or the manufacturer's name. As an example, petrol clearly falls into the commodity category. As a result, petrol companies try to promote 'image'. In the long run, however, they inevitably end up relying on promotions such as loyalty cards, extra services (coffee, groceries etc) and special offers to attract the vast majority of the public who see little real value in the brand.

There are examples, however, of taking a commodity and making it a brand. A good example is provided by Perrier Water: the contents are naturally occurring spring water which, while possessing certain distinctive characteristics, at the end of the day is still spring water. Yet through packaging and, more particularly, promotion, an international brand has been created with high brand loyalty. Consequently, it sells for a price well in excess of the costs of the ingredients. A similar approach is nowadays evident for Evian, Badoit and San Pellegrino.

The difference between a brand and a commodity can be summed up by the phrase 'added values'. A brand is more than just the sum of its component parts. It embodies for the purchaser or user additional attributes that, while they might be considered by some to be 'intangible', are still very real to a significant portion of the market. To illustrate the power of these added values, it is only necessary to consider the preference given by consumers to successful brands by dint of the brand name, rather than because of any functional superiority that can be discerned in objective comparisons.

Successful and unsuccessful brands

Successful brand building aids profitability by helping to create stable, long-term demand and by adding values that entice customers to buy. They also provide a firm base for expansion into product improvements, variants, added services, new countries, and so on, and can help to protect organizations against the growing power of intermediaries. A strong brand name may also help organizations transform themselves from faceless bureaucracies into firms that are attractive both as employers and as businesses with which to associate.

It is important, then, not to make the mistake of confusing successful and unsuccessful brands. The world is full of products and services that have brand names, but are not successful brands. Successful brands tend to:

- have a unique identity that is widely recognized by members of the target market;
- provide sustainable competitive advantage by being more attractive than most other identities or positions in the market;
- add significantly to the asset value of an organization as demonstrated when the organization is sold or acquired;
- require continuous investment to avoid the diminution experienced by some previously powerful brands, such as Hoover, Singer, Biro, and so on.

The components of a brand

The first component of a brand is its brand positioning. This is concerned with what the brand actually does and with what it competes. In other words, brand positioning starts with the physical, or functional, aspects of the product. For instance, Schweppes is positioned in the United Kingdom as a mixer for spirits, rather than as a soft drink competing with Coca-Cola, Pepsi-Cola and 7UP. Similarly, Tide is presented as a tough, general-purpose detergent, rather than as a powder for woollens. Marks & Spencer goes to great lengths to support its image as a high-quality multiple rather than a low price chain store, and easyJet is positioned as a low-cost carrier. In fact, easyJet illustrates how a powerful brand can be used to create identity for other product areas such as car hire.

Positioning is usually performed against identifiable motivators in any market – only one or two of which are of real importance when developing a brand. These dimensions are best seen as bipolar scales along which brands can be positioned. Examples of these are provided in Table 33.1.

TABLE 33.1 Bipolar scales for brand positioning

Expensive ———————	Inexpensive
Strong ———————	Mild
Big ———————	Small
Hot ———————	Cold
Fast ———————	Slow
Male ———————	Female

The second component of a brand is its personality. This is a useful descriptor for the total impression that consumers have of brands and indicates that in many ways brands are like people in that they have their own physical, emotional and attitudinal characteristics. Thus, they are a complex blend of different characteristics, which together create a brand identity. In this way, two brands can be very similar in terms of their functions, yet have very different personalities. As an example, the Ford Fiesta, the VW Polo and the Renault Clio all perform about the same along the functional dimensions of size, speed and price. Yet each one has a totally different personality, which is the result of a blend of three sorts of appeal: sensual, rational and emotional.

Sensual appeal: refers to the way the product or service looks, sounds or feels. It is easy to imagine how this appeal can differ in the case of, say, smart-phones or cars. A Mercedes is said to have a classic styling and to provide a very comfortable ride.

Rational appeal: concerns the way the product or service performs (what they contain, their relative costs and so on). Many people, for example, rationalize their preference for a Mercedes on the grounds that it holds its resale value better.

Emotional appeal: is perhaps the most important aspect of a brand, and has a lot to do with the psychological rewards it offers, the

moods it conjures up, the associations it evokes and so on. It is easy
to see the overt appeal of certain products as being, for instance,
particularly masculine, feminine, chic, workmanlike, or 'flashy'.
Many people prefer a Mercedes because of the status it implies.

Brand personality is also the result of a whole gamut of influences, such as:
the places where it is sold; the price that is charged; other brands from the
same manufacturer; how it is used; the kind of people who buy and use it;
after-sales service; the name of the brand; advertising; point of sale material;
PR; sponsorship; and many others. However, for any brand to be successful,
all of these elements have to be consistent. Since they will all affect the
brand's personality, and it is this personality above all else that represents
the brand's totality and that makes one brand more desirable than another
it is vital that consistency is maintained. Thus Apple is careful about who
it lets retail its products to ensure there is no brand contamination from
inappropriate retailers. At its simplest, it is a brand's personality that con-
verts a commodity into something unique and enables a higher price to be
charged for it.

Overall, then, a good brand is an identifiable product, service, company,
person, or place, augmented in such a way that buyers or users perceive
a personality that incorporates relevant and unique added values, which
closely match their needs. A brand's success results from being able to sustain
these added values against competitors over time.

The product life cycle

This topic complements Topic 35, Diffusion of innovation, which provides an explanation for the shape of the product life cycle curve.

The product life cycle is a conceptual tool that provides a means of describing the sales patterns of products over their time in a market. If absolute sales are plotted on a period-by-period basis (usually annually), the ideal-type life cycle approximates to an S-curve (see Figure 34.1). In reality, product life cycles adopt a number of different shapes and are never smooth. However, a good understanding of the concept, its variations, and the determinants of its shape are a powerful aid to the development of marketing strategies. A product life cycle differs from a market life cycle in that a market consists of those who share a common problem or need while a product is merely a means of satisfying that need.

FIGURE 34.1   Standard product life cycle curve

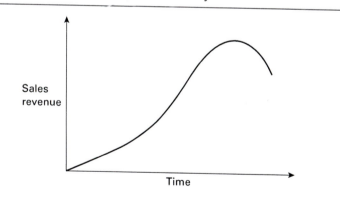

Life cycles and product categories

Understanding product life cycles requires an appreciation of the different categories of product they can plot: product class, form or brand. Because a market is based on a need that will be satisfied by alternative technologies over time, each successive technology will provide a new product class and enhanced performance. The need to store information, for instance, has been satisfied by many product classes including: stone tablets; papyrus; string; ledgers; microfilm; cards; tapes; discs; and, more recently, CDs, SDs, DVDs and now Clouds. These form the basis for most product life cycles. Specific needs may, in the end, disappear, such as the need for protection against smallpox, or are greatly reduced, such as the need for radio and television rental facilities. At this point, a market life cycle comes to an end. More generic needs are likely to remain current for a long time, as is the case for personal security, home entertainment, personal and mass communications, and people's social and physiological needs. More specific needs such as the need to send paper-based confirmation fast will be superseded by electronic communications, making the need for telegrams and faxes redundant.

More focused examples of product classes include: mobile phones; bicycles; internal combustion engines; and personal computers. Each of these classes will have its own life cycle. Within each class, there are likely to be a number of product forms, or families, which will also experience a life cycle. Thus, the product class 'personal computer' has included several product forms such as: desktops; portables; laptops; notebooks; and now tablets.

In a similar way, each product form will include a number of brands or models that may be on the market for a very short time (say, 6–18 months), or which may last for longer (say, 3–9 years). If a brand can become a 'brand name' with a significant customer franchise, or a 'super brand' such as Mercedes, Coca-Cola or Rolex, then it will probably be used to cover a number of successive models, forms and even classes over a number of decades. This has been the case for product brands such as Tide and Persil, and company brands such as McDonald's, Hitachi and IBM.

For marketing analysis, the most useful life cycle is usually that of the product form. Product class life cycles are often too macro to be of use, except for very long-range planning such as the 50-year strategies common among the larger Japanese corporations. This remains true even for the powerful brands that encompass a number of successive generations of a product. Sales of a particular form, such as colour televisions or neon lights, will track the activities of all suppliers to the market and will, therefore, enable judgements to be made in the context of a market as a whole. It is, nonetheless, extremely useful to compare a product or brand's performance against the projected life cycle of the product form in order to ensure that nothing untoward is happening to it.

Stages in the product life cycle

Product life cycles will usually experience a number of successive stages (see Figure 34.2). The introductory stage will cover the launch of a new product form into the market to the point at which sales begin to accelerate rapidly. During this stage, sales will be relatively slow while customers get used to the new ideas it incorporates. If the form is to be a successful innovation, the product will move into its growth phase, during which sales volumes will increase rapidly from one time period to the next. At some point, sales growth will slow as the number of potential new purchasers reduces, at which time the life cycle will be in its maturity stage.

FIGURE 34.2 Phases in the product life cycle

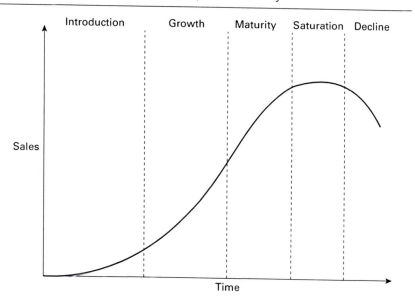

Once sales growth has levelled off, the life cycle has reached its saturation phase where sales are either replacements or to latecomers to this particular product form. Since these will probably be replacing the innovators who were the first to try a new product, and who have probably moved on to replacement product forms, they will add little to the growth of the market. The final stage therefore is decline, either as more people migrate to a new product form or the need disappears. As an example, at the current time it is to be wondered whether cable-based telecommunications has a future in Western Europe or the US.

Life cycles will move into the decline phase for one of two main reasons. The first, as indicated, will be that a replacement technology, usually delivering enhanced performance, will have been developed. In this way, LCD and plasma televisions replaced those utilizing cathode ray tubes versions and e-mail has effectively replaced facsimile transmission. The second will be a change in another aspect of the marketing environment such as: fashion;

legislation; standards; the development of a new industry structure; or a social trend of some form.

Deviant product life cycles

Deviations from the shape associated with a 'standard' product life cycle (see Figure 34.3) will be caused by the nature of a product and its patterns of consumption. Some products will experience growth followed by a sharp slump before levelling out into maturity (Figure 34.3a). This is typical of the sales patterns for small kitchen appliances and will occur because saturation is achieved before replacement purchases come into play. Scalloped life cycles (Figure 34.3b), where sales continually level off and then grow again, will be associated with products that are constantly finding new markets and new applications. Bar coding and nylon are good examples of this. Rapid growth followed by rapid decline, with sales levelling out at a low level (Figure 34.3c), describes the life cycle of memorabilia associated with a particular event (World Cup, royal weddings etc), or fads such as the hardly-remembered Clackers, the infamous pet rocks or children's toys. A double-humped life cycle (Figure 34.3d) will be typical of products that come in and out of style, such as mountain bikes or fashions, or will be products in markets that respond well to communications so that usage will follow media or industry patterns of promotional activity.

FIGURE 34.3   Alternative product life cycles

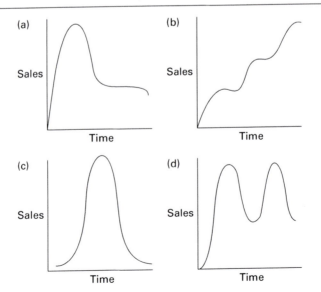

Using the product life cycle

While it is never possible to identify accurately which point a product has reached on its life cycle, or exactly what shape the life cycle will follow, the concept does enable organizations to consider the future – how strategies will need to alter, and what their market information needs will be. At the introductory stage, competitors will typically be limited and the focus of a marketing strategy will be educating the market. During growth, organizations are likely to face more numerous competitors and will be seeking to establish a strong position in terms of market share, niches, brands and/or reputation, while at the same time, looking for product range extension and market development. As a market matures and becomes saturated, marketing strategy will tend to concentrate on price, brand protection and customer service. When decline begins to bite, competition will eventually reduce and the organization will tend to concentrate on the next product form or on reducing costs, while maintaining price (see Table 34.1).

The problems associated with using the concept of product life cycle occur either from its misuse or from its misinterpretation. Misuse would result from confusing the life cycles of product forms with organizational sales or brands, or by trying to use them as predictive tools. Misinterpretation can arise if an organization interprets a 'glitch' in sales for the onset of decline, and pulls out of a market too early. Economic recession can have this effect, when in reality it is more likely to cause a postponement of purchasing rather than an end to it. If used sensibly, however, it can raise questions of importance such as:

- how fast will growth be?
- what will limit growth?
- what could cause the onset of decline?
- what trading conditions can be expected over the next few years?

If better decisions are made as a consequence, the life cycle will be a valuable marketing tool.

TABLE 34.1 Typical marketing-mix strategies for different life-cycle stages

Stage in product life-cycle	Product strategy	Price strategy	Place strategy	Promotion strategy
Introductory	Limited range for specialist applications	Skim or penetration	Limited to specialized outlets with service often provided by manufacturer	Educate the market and aggressive selling
Growth	Product range expansion	Competitive pricing for market share	Seek wide market coverage	Actively establish image or brand with competitive selling
Maturity	Improve quality and consolidate range	Stabilise prices	Use service for competitive differentiation	Protect brand and market position
Saturation	Reduce costs and range	Push price to limits	Transfer costs to distributors and automate service	Maintain brand or image at low cost
Decline	Further reduce costs and range	Maintain as high as possible	Reduce costs	Focused low cost communications

Diffusion of innovation

The shape of the standard product life cycle implies that purchasers for a new class of product become customers at different times, at different rates and with different motivations following its introduction. This has been described by Everett Rogers as the diffusion of innovation or the adoption process (Rogers, Everett M (1962) *Diffusion of Innovations*. Glencoe: Free Press). Adoption is concerned with the way that a consumer becomes a regular customer for a new product concept. Diffusion refers to the way in which the product penetrates its potential market, which in turn suggests that there will be different stages of adoption. Variations between the shapes of product life cycles for different products indicate that the rate of diffusion may also vary from one product to another. Effective marketing requires a good understanding of these processes and the causes of any variations.

New product adoption

The adoption process for a product new to a particular consumer will tend to follow a five-stage pattern. The first stage is *awareness*, whereby a consumer learns of the existence of a product. This may happen by accident, or it may be the result of a deliberate communications campaign on the part of the supplier, or of a deliberate search on the part of the consumer. Awareness becomes *interest* if the product is perceived to offer benefits appropriate to the needs of the consumer. At this point, the consumer will actively search for information about the new product. As information is gathered, consumers will go through a process of *evaluation* as they decide whether or not to try the innovation. The next stage is therefore *trial*, where consumers will extend their evaluation by an experimental consumption. The fifth and final stage is *adoption*, whereby either the trial or the appeal of the concept is good enough, or sufficiently strong, to convince consumers to buy again on a regular basis, although not necessarily from the same supplier.

Not all stages will be involved for all new products; consumers could move straight from awareness to adoption if the offer matched their particular need closely enough. More important, however, is the recognition that new purchasers will not necessarily pass from one stage to the next, and could get stuck at any one of the five stages.

New product diffusion

When plotted over time, the adoption process for a population of consumers or market tends to follow a normal distribution. The mid-point of the distribution will represent the average amount of time (months or years) it took members of a market to adopt a product. Most consumers will come to a new product within plus or minus one standard deviation of the average time. A minority of people, however, will either be among the first to become users of a product, or will be behind the rest of the market in the adoption of the innovation (see Figure 35.1). The various categories of adopters can be described as:

- innovators;
- early adopters;
- the early majority;
- the late majority;
- laggards.

Innovators are usually characterized as being 2.5 per cent of a market and are the first to become regular users. Innovators are usually venturesome, or

FIGURE 35.1 The diffusion of innovation curve

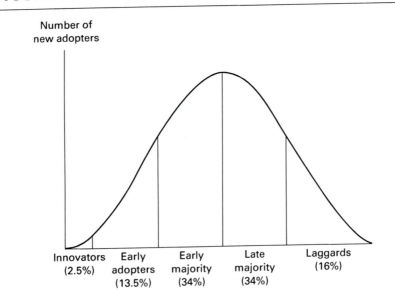

find value in being at the forefront of consumption. In industrial markets, innovators will either be technology-orientated and keen on seeking competitive advantage from new products, or will be forced into innovating as a 'distress purchase'. In consumer markets, innovators are usually hard to identify by their demographic, psychographic or media characteristics. It is also the case that an innovator in one product area could easily be a laggard in another; an internet games hobbyist may be the first to try a new computer game, but the last to adopt a new fashion in clothes. Without knowing the individual involved, it is hard to tell who is what.

Early adopters, who comprise 13.5 per cent of a market, will be keen to take up a particular innovation, but will treat it with caution. However, they will often see themselves as being significant community members and therefore at the forefront of opinion in terms of the particular product area. Consequently, they will usually enjoy the attention early consumption brings.

The early majority will cover 34 per cent of the market and will consolidate a new product's success. They will probably see themselves as early adopters, but will tend to be more risk-averse than the early adopters. Their purchase will, therefore, be a statement of their willingness to try something new, but will be tempered by a natural conservatism.

The late majority, again 34 per cent of all adopters, will be even more conservative in their approach to the purchase of this product type, possibly even to the extent of being sceptical about the value of the innovation. Thus, as the innovation becomes more widely used, as its price falls, or as the traditional alternatives become less available, they will move to the new, increasingly acceptable, alternative.

Laggards, as the name suggests, will be the last to come to an innovation and will be the remaining 16 per cent of a market. They will occupy this position for a number of reasons, including: education level; focus of activities; degree of isolation; attitude towards tradition; level of disposable income; lack of any alternative; and so on. For laggards, the innovation will need to have lost its 'new product' status before they will adopt its consumption.

There will always be some non-consumers. Even today, there are some West European and US households without a television, computer or mobile phone.

Rate of diffusion

The rate at which a new product class will penetrate a market will depend on the characteristics of both the market and the product. Market factors that will provide hurdles to penetration include:

- the absence of appropriate communications media, distribution channels or physical infrastructure (such as regular electricity supply);

- the slow speed of the decision-making process;
- the existence of complicated regulatory or procedural requirements;
- adverse economic conditions;
- socio-cultural factors that militate against the product's adoption.

Product factors that can hamper adoption include:

- little relative performance or cost advantage over the present solutions to the problem that the product is designed to solve;
- low product compatibility with existing structures in the market, which can be physical, social, regulatory, and so on;
- high complexity, which will make it hard for adopters to evaluate or understand the benefits on offer;
- few possibilities to try the product before purchase, making it difficult for consumers to judge its value in advance, which is especially true of expensive goods and services;
- features that are hard to describe, as is often the case for products delivering abstract or intangible benefits such as service products; or products that are hard to conceptualize or demonstrate, such as software consultancy or insurance services.

Within this, it should also be noted that word of mouth has often been identified as one of the key features in aiding the diffusion of an innovation throughout its potential market. Unfortunately, this is one of the most difficult aspects of promotion for an organization to influence.

These variations help to explain the different shapes of product life cycles, and the possible hurdles to adoption mean that not all new products will fulfil their market potential. Diffusion and adoption are not inevitable and marketing organizations have to develop strategies that will overcome the blockages they are likely to encounter.

Developing new products

A significant proportion of most organizations' revenue is derived from products introduced in the recent past. While their origins may go back a long way, such as Microsoft's Windows operating systems, current versions are usually very different from the early versions. Other products and services may be very different from an organization's original offerings and can have been derived from a number of different external and internal sources. Rentokil Initial started selling insecticides and is now a major industrial services conglomerate. The development or acquisition of new products, however, is costly and there is a great danger of failure. This danger can be reduced if marketing principles underpin every stage of the acquisition, development and launch of new products.

Types of new products

New products that are not just the acquisition of another organization's established products will have different degrees of 'newness' associated with them. A common way of classifying new products is:

- revolutionary new products: products the like of which have never been seen before and that create entirely new markets;
- improved products: existing products that have been enhanced to provide better performance or greater perceived value; often referred to as the 'next generation';
- modified products: where current models are replaced by new ones that combine features from a number of older models;
- adapted products: products that have been changed to address needs in other markets or market segments, but whose key functionality remains the same;
- new brands: successful new products often stimulate the launch of similar competitive products by other organizations under different brand names or with alternative positions.

FIGURE 36.1 New product classification

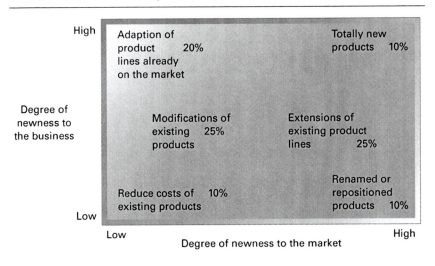

An alternative classification based on 'newness' to markets and the businesses launching them is shown in Figure 36.1. The percentages shown for each category demonstrate that only a small proportion (10 per cent) of all new product launches are totally new concepts or in any way revolutionary. This suggests that new product management must cover a wide range of different new product situations.

Sources of new product ideas

Organizations that are open to new ideas and that actively pursue new product opportunities are usually systematic in their search. They recognize that there are a number of different sources that can generate good ideas and that sometimes a proactive approach needs to be adopted. Appropriate sources, however, will vary from industry to industry, although all ideas must be closely linked with customer needs and wants if they are to be successful commercially.

For many organizations, customers are, in fact, the most profitable source of new ideas. This is certainly true in industrial markets where they often produce the highest percentage of new ideas, particularly if they are lead users (ie organizations that make the most use of a new product). Lead users are also, therefore, likely to see the limitations of a product first and can recommend improvements ahead of later purchasers. Establishing close development partnerships with such organizations can provide a valuable source of new product ideas, modifications or extensions of existing product lines. Indeed, establishing user groups for an organization's products is a good way of ensuring this happens, which has been made much easier via the use of social media. In the UK, Walkers Crisps (owned by PepsiCo at the time of writing) regularly invites all consumers to help determine new flavours and product variations.

In more highly populated markets, organizations can use different forms of customer research as sources of ideas, such as:

- social media dialogue;
- monitoring social media chat sites, user reviews and blogs via the internet;
- customer shadowing;
- High Street, telephone, mail and e-mail surveys;
- focus group discussions;
- competitions among users;
- analyses of letters of complaint.

As an example of digging deep into customer preferences to determine the positioning for a new product launch, when Toyota decided it wished to enter the US car market it decided to use the VW Beetle as its benchmark product. Using focus groups and surveys, it closely questioned existing users about the problems they experienced with Beetles. The result was a car positioned as a 'fun' product for drivers who were prepared to buy foreign cars, with none of the drawbacks of a Beetle, but all the advantages. Their subsequent success has led to a market share approaching 20 per cent.

Non-customer external sources of new product ideas include:

- competitors;
- patent offices;
- intermediaries;
- universities;
- commercial laboratories;
- consultants;
- market research firms.

In some areas this process is made easier by publications for advertisers seeking ideas or inventors searching for a business willing to exploit their discoveries.

In the past, Japan was known to deconstruct competitor products (a process known as reverse engineering) as a source of new ideas and was a net importer of licenses for various technologies, which they often improved for their own commercial purposes. Today, they register more patents than most advanced Western economies and China, Korea and India have replaced Japan as 'copycat' economies. Taking advantage of lower labour costs, they often produce improved versions of products at a fraction of the original's cost.

Internal sources can be equally valuable and can include: research laboratories; sales representatives; and other employees. Sometimes, the chief executive, as the founder or key technical force within the business, is the main source of innovation. Whatever the source, the organization must be willing to explore new ideas. In too many enterprises, organizational culture can act as a damper and stifle initiatives that could be the future life-blood of the business (see Figure 36.2).

FIGURE 36.2 Cultural blockages to new product initiatives

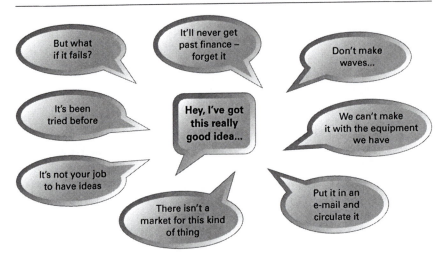

Stages in product development

Once an idea for a new product has been conceived, the process of development and placing it on the market needs to be carefully managed to reduce the risk and costs of failure. The initial stage is a preliminary market and technical assessment of the concept to judge whether its creation and sale seem feasible. This should be performed fairly quickly and be at minimal cost. The next step is a detailed technical product analysis and the creation of prototypes in parallel with some more detailed market research to test the assumptions made during the initial feasibility or concept test.

Once an organization is satisfied that a new idea has sufficient potential, the technical side of the business should move towards a pilot production stage while marketing begins to establish the product's launch pad. This may involve preparing the media, identifying appropriate channels of distribution, understanding the target-market buyer behaviour, and establishing a market position. These are followed by some pilot production and a test marketing exercise to confirm or deny the potential before full investment is made in production facilities and the market as a whole.

The cost of developing a new product for commercialization will increase dramatically as an organization moves towards full commercialization. The task of marketing is to reduce the risk by pursuing market knowledge that will enable a project to be dropped before expenditure becomes too high. For mass market consumer products, the cumulative expenditure at the point of full launch can be well into the millions. Of this, 50 per cent can be accounted for by the national rollout of the product. The importance of rigorous procedures to prevent the inappropriate launch of a new product by moving from Curve A to Curve B is therefore vital (see Figure 36.3).

It has also been estimated that for every successful new product, between 50 and 70 new ideas have to be considered and that only one in four products that are test-marketed prove successful once launched nationally. When products are successful, they tend to be ones that:

- deliver a significant differentiated benefit;
- have a good technological fit with the supplying organization;
- stem from businesses that have 'done their marketing well'.

These features are more likely to be achieved where new product teams are set up that consist of representatives from the major functional disciplines in the organization: operations; engineering; finance; human resources; marketing, and so on. In addition, where development is managed as a parallel process between engineering, production and marketing, as opposed to a linear development process, success is even more likely. Whatever the process, however, without good marketing input, new products become a game of Russian roulette rather than a disciplined management contribution to the organization.

FIGURE 36.3   Risk and new product development

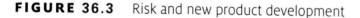

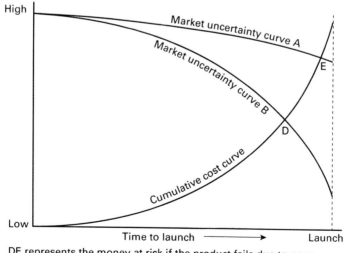

DE represents the money at risk if the product fails due to poor market information.

Pricing strategies

A customer's response to an offering from a supplier is affected by all aspects of the marketing mix, which together constitute the whole of that offer. Among these variables, price is always an important feature since it is one of the key determinants of a product's value. Price is thus one of the evaluative criteria used by potential customers, as are the costs incurred in both making the purchase and owning or utilizing the product. Price and associated costs are, therefore, an important adjunct to positioning.

At the same time, price is a very difficult aspect of the marketing mix to manage. This is because it is subject to many pressures that are often independent, or even at odds with, the organization's marketing objectives. These can be both internal (from financial, operations, sales and other senior managers) and external (from customers, competitors and government agencies). To maintain the integrity of prices, a sound pricing strategy is required. A strategy for pricing is also required to support an organization's overall marketing strategy and to protect profitability. The strategy adopted will vary depending on an organization's circumstances and requires managers to possess a good understanding of the alternative strategies available.

Market skimming

A market skimming strategy is one where a supplying organization positions itself at the top of the market against its competitors. If there are no competitors (as might be the case for a new product), then skimming suggests a price at which only a small number of the potential customers for a product will be prepared to buy. The implication of a skimming strategy is that an organization will be targeting a niche in the market for which the benefits of a product have a high value. A further implication is that product volumes and market share will never be high, but that margins should be good.

Skimming strategies are appropriate for products or offerings that are unique or that attract high quality ratings. Uniqueness may be derived from:

- proprietary access to materials;
- facilities or the technology a product incorporates;
- the way in which the product is produced;
- its particular formulation or construction.

Uniqueness can be protected by patents or by keeping processes and recipes a secret. Quality will be associated with the care with which a product or service is produced, the materials it incorporates or the customer service offered alongside the product. Quality can also be associated with: precision; reliability; longevity; finish; presentation; robustness; and many other features, depending on the product's application.

Maintaining a pricing-skimming strategy over the life of a product requires support from other positioning variables such as image, brand value, relationship management and the way in which a price is presented. It also requires efforts to distance a product away from competitors and a strategy for maintaining differentiation over the product life cycle. Where significant economies of scale and/or experience are potentially available, skimming and sustaining high price levels becomes difficult unless a really powerful brand has been created, there is a wide patent platform, or proprietary access to the supply of non-substitutable materials or facilities exists. The advent of the internet has made market skimming a more difficult proposition to sustain as consumers have better access to suppliers, information and substitute products.

Sliding or reducing skim

As the name implies, this strategy involves an initially high price, which is dropped either as new entrants make a market more competitive or as a market matures. While it does not imply continuing as the most expensive in a market, it does mean that the organization will seek to be towards the upper reaches of the continuum of prices that prevail in a market. In this way, an enterprise can seek to address larger sections of a market with the object of becoming one of the market-leading suppliers, if not the market leader.

A sliding or reducing skim strategy is also appropriate when it is difficult to sustain a technological advantage or where costs are sensitive to economies of scale and/or experience. Both these factors will make a product attractive to competitors and require price adjustments as the market evolves. In this case, the organization will be following the market and trying to recover product development and investment costs in as short a period as possible. At the same time, it will be seeking to position itself as a dominant player through branding or service quality while using price as a support for its ambitions.

Market penetration

A strategy of market penetration is the opposite of a skimming approach. Here a low price is used to obtain volume sales and market share. The price, however, must not be so low that it becomes indicative of poor quality or unacceptable performance. Sometimes this can be used as an entry strategy into an already established market. Alternatively, it might be used to create a market or to speed up its development by making a product accessible to a wide audience early in its life cycle. In some cases, organizations have been known to price ahead of expected cost gains from economies of experience in order to achieve this.

Such a strategy can require an organization to maintain its price advantage in the face of changes in the general market price structure. It also requires that the benefit to price ratio between supplying organizations is sufficiently different to be significant in the eyes of the consumer, ie that whatever products act as benchmarks for customers appear to them to be significantly more expensive. The developing Malaysian and Indian automobile manufacturers provide good examples of organizations adopting this type of approach.

Floor pricing

This strategy implies keeping prices right at the lower end of the price spectrum and will be used to appeal to those who are very price conscious. High sensitivity to price will be a result of the customer seeing little differential value between the various offerings in the market or having restricted disposable incomes. Alternatively, economic downturns usually see an upsurge in the fortunes of cheaper outlets such as Primark or Poundland in the UK. The perceived benefits of the offer must still match the price adopted. Such a strategy requires close attention to costs at all times and is typical of the bargain basement, no frills type of operation. Enterprises that can survive on low margins, whether because of high turnover, lower profit requirements, or insignificant overheads, are best able to pursue this type of strategy.

A recent high profile variation of floor pricing has been illustrated by budget airlines. Here the pricing model is to offer bargain-basement prices to attract highly advanced bookings and to raise the price as the time for the flight approaches. This recognizes that people's planning horizons have shortened as information is increasingly available and decisions can be left to later dates. In addition, cheap seats are supplemented by charges for luggage, 'fast' boarding, meals, and a host of other 'extras' that are standard among other airlines.

Competitor pricing

An alternative to adopting a proactive pricing strategy is to adopt a position a specific distance from a market leader's price. This distance may be large or small, and may be above or below the market leader chosen, depending on the way in which the business wishes to be perceived. Any price changes initiated by the leader will then be followed by the competitor organization, either immediately or at the next available opportunity. In the case of forecourt or retail prices, this may be the following day. Where prices are not openly stated or are part of a competitive tendering process, this can take much longer.

Such an approach is rarely operated in isolation and may be used as part of a penetration or skimming strategy. If the distance adopted is significantly below the leader, then it is likely that a product is being used as a loss leader to attract customers who would then purchase other products at prices closer to the norm. If the distance is significant, but remains constant over time, the position may be held to attract a particular segment of the market by offering a specific value proposition. Whatever the case, the overall benefits offered are likely to be similar to those offered by the leader, who will be providing a 'price umbrella' under which others in the market can 'shelter'.

Cost-based pricing

Under all the strategies discussed above, there is an implication that costs should be managed in the light of the strategy adopted rather than the other way round. In some cases, however, cost will be a significant determinant of price. As an example, where products use expensive capital equipment to be produced, skimming or floor pricing may not be possible options. In other areas, such as some types of government procurement, or where suppliers have been developed as partnerships, prices may be determined and discussed on the basis of costs.

It is also the case that, in the end, income must exceed total costs. These and other reasons, as illustrated in Table 37.1, make costs a very appealing base from which to set prices. Setting prices according to costs, however, is fraught with dangers (see Table 37.2), and can lead to sub-optimization or the absence of any clear market position.

TABLE 37.1   Appeal of a cost approach to pricing

- Managers usually feel more certain about costs than about what customers will pay.
- Prices are easier to justify in terms of cost rather than benefits.
- A cost-based approach to pricing is administratively easier than judging market-based issues.
- Prices based on cost appear socially more acceptable and are less open to accusations of exploitation.
- A cost-plus approach should ensure that an organization remains profitable.

TABLE 37.2   Problems of a cost approach to pricing

- Costs are not always easy to identify.
- It ignores the way customers use price.
- It ignores the relative value of an offering compared with competitors.
- Costs will often vary with volume.
- Market objectives are not usually related to costs.
- Costs for different products from the same facility or organization are highly dependent on the way costs are allocated.

The strategy adopted should also, clearly, be appropriate to an organization's marketing objectives, such market share, defending markets, establishing a position, managing relationships, stabilizing a market, expanding a market or whatever. Within strategies, there is also the opportunity to decide whether an organization will operate fixed prices with no discounts, or whether they will adopt a more flexible approach. As a general rule, however, no matter what strategy is adopted, in a buoyant market with rising or excess demand, a business should always seek to raise prices, since it will find it hard, or even impossible, when times are not so good.

Value based pricing (VBP)

Value based pricing (VBP) is based on a supplier's ability to deliver a superior solution to a customer's problem, or to enable them to exploit a business opportunity. The formula for VBP is: RP (reference price of competitive products) plus NRG (net revenue gain for the customer) plus NCR (net cost reduction for the customer) plus EC (emotional contribution). The VBP may be related to reducing customers' costs, to increasing their productivity, to reducing their 'hassle', or to improving their peace of mind. Most are quite easy to calculate, although it is often more difficult to put an economic value on peace of mind. The point is that once VBP has been calculated, there is at least a corridor, or leeway, for negotiating a price between the VBP and the reference price.

Micro-transaction pricing

A challenge created by the internet and smartphones is overcoming the perception that internet services and information should be free. One response has been to generate revenue by charging very small amounts for a number of different aspects of a product or service to large numbers of people. The principle is the same as a Penny Arcade where large amounts of money can be made by charging very small amounts but on a very frequent basis. The customer perception is that they are individually being conservative, but collectively are spending large amounts. Examples are provided by 'Apps' that cost £0.69 or $0.99, enhancements to games for small additional fees, premium membership of sites or text messaging to or from mobile phones.

Setting a price

Specific pricing decisions should always be made in the context of the pricing strategy an organization has opted to follow. These can vary from a skimming or penetration approach to being the cheapest in the market, or simply following the lead of a major player. Costs are also used as a basis for pricing, although care must be taken not to ignore market conditions. In the end, however, income must always exceed total costs.

As well as strategy, there are a number of situational factors that will also influence the exact price chosen. Thus, when a pricing decision is required, an organization's pricing strategy will provide the main approach to be adopted, but situational variables will determine the actual price paid.

Occasions requiring price decision

The most obvious occasion demanding a pricing decision is when a business sets a price for the first time. This can occur when a business launches a product that is either new to them and the market, which is just new to them, or when they move an existing product into a new market. In some of these situations, a price structure will already exist, and the organization's strategy will determine approximately where it will be positioned relative to competitor products on the price continuum (see Figure 38.1).

In situations where a product is completely new to a market, pricing becomes more difficult, although it is still driven by the organization's strategy. Here

FIGURE 38.1   The price continuum

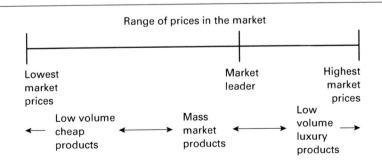

Range of prices in the market

| Lowest market prices | Market leader | Highest market prices |

Low volume cheap products   Mass market products   Low volume luxury products

it is sometimes possible to benchmark against similar but non-competing products. Alternatively, it may be possible to establish how target customers evaluate a potential purchase (payback, return on investment, upfront price, life cycle cost, etc) or how they perceive value (reliability, availability, brand, security, gaining competitive advantage, associated attitudes, social prestige, etc). In the absence of these, it may be justifiable to use costs as an indicator for price, in which case it should be acknowledged that improvements to the quality of the organization's marketing are probably required!

Costs, however, are a significant issue when they change. When costs increase, it is wise to attempt to maintain margins if the increase is likely to be permanent. This may simply require marginal changes to price lists. In more sensitive markets, it may be necessary to find ways of adding value to justify a price rise. Where costs are likely to be volatile, as is often the case for commodity raw materials or where prices are sensitive to exchange rates, it can be wise to use hedging arrangements, although these can be expensive. Whatever the cause, there is still a decision as to how margins can be maintained without alienating customers. If, on the other hand, costs drop, there is an awkward choice to be made between appearing to be exploitative, using the extra profits for investment and using the price flexibility that has become available for competitive advantage.

A price decision will also have to be made when competitors initiate a price change. If the initiator is a 'benchmark' competitor, then the response will be fairly straightforward. This will be particularly true for price followers who have adopted a set position in relation to certain key market players. If the initiator has traditionally occupied the role of a follower, then an assessment needs to be made as to their power to make the price change stick and the reasoning behind the move. Should it be felt, for example, that the competitor is trying to grab market share or penetrate new markets, a defensive response is required.

For organizations operating at either end of the price continuum, a similar judgement has to be made (ie do they need to respond or can the move can be ignored?). Crucial to this will be an understanding of the segment in which the competitor is operating, the likely response of customers and the relationship between the competitor and the responding organization in the minds of the customer.

The most difficult situation is when a customer asks for a price reduction. This may occur during regular negotiations or as a request for a discount from normal prices. Here, it is useful to establish reference points against which to negotiate, such as well-known competitors' prices and the benefits of the product under discussion. It is also useful to establish what motivated the request, since this could help to formulate a response other than a cut in price. This may be more difficult if the relationship with the customer is distant or 'transaction based'.

If such a situation leads to price negotiations, it is important for the supplier to look for trade-offs that could be made in exchange for price cuts, but that would save the supplier money or gain them advantage. These could include prompt payment, higher volumes, less frequent deliveries, joint promotions, taking a broader mix of products, and so on. This, however, does require a good understanding of operational costs on the part of the supplier to avoid reduced profitability.

Price presentation

When quoting a price to a customer, it must also be remembered that a price is not just an isolated figure, but can be presented in a number of different ways, which will make it more or less acceptable. Some prices can be made to look more acceptable if they are 'unbundled' and broken down into component parts. This can include separated delivery charges, packaging requirements, service costs, warranties, upgrades and so on. The more complex the product, the more scope there is for this type of approach. Some customers, however, may be more interested in the total cost for budgeting or comparison purposes.

Prices can also be made acceptable by providing comparisons with products that are outside a particular customer's price band. If a customer felt, for instance, that the absolute top acceptable price for a suit of clothing was £500 and a supplier was trying to sell one at £550, the supplier may help their case by referring to £1,000 high-brand suits that the customer would never purchase, but that would make £550 seem a fair price.

In some businesses, it is often worth deliberately presenting a range of models such as basic, standard and deluxe categories, in order to enhance the value of the standard model. This offers the potential to migrate deluxe features into the standard model to enhance value over time. Where a product has a tendency to move towards commodity status as customers become more familiar with it, or as a market matures, this can be a useful tactic. The present situation in the global market for PCs clearly illustrates this as suppliers offer increasing amounts of software with their products as models approach obsolescence.

Psychological elements can also be used to enhance the acceptability of a price. This can involve the use of 'attractive numbers' (although what is attractive will vary between different cultural environments) or pricing in relation to certain 'break points' in the market. The existence of such points help explain the use of £X.99 prices and the significance of keeping below certain price thresholds in a market. Again, such thresholds will vary from market to market.

Transaction price management

Pricing studies that have compared invoice pricing with the prices customers actually pay have noted that there are often 'off-invoice' concessions, which have had the effect of reducing the profitability of a customer. These can include:

- prompt payment discounts;
- promotional allowances;
- retrospective volume discounts;
- free delivery for orders over certain values;
- sales promotion campaigns;
- unofficial extended credit.

Since most customer profit calculations are based on invoices, organizations can easily overestimate the profitability of individual customers. The difference between invoice price and the price effectively paid has been shown to be as much as 30 per cent in some cases.

Advantage can be gained by monitoring such income 'leakages' and targeting those customers that incur fewer 'off-invoice' price discounts. It is sometimes possible to move particular elements of 'off-invoice' reductions on to the invoice to demonstrate to customers the real value of their purchase for comparison purposes. In addition, different customers will be sensitive to different elements of 'off-invoice' costs. As an example, one distributor or retailer may be more attracted to promotional discounts than credit allowances. In this case, it may be possible to engineer prices to achieve better results for the supplier by focusing on appropriate elements for specific tactical ends.

For all organizations, what is important is the price the customer ends up paying. However, setting a price, obtaining sales in the right volumes, and collecting the income is not a simple matter. What is important is consistency, which should be driven by adherence to a pricing strategy and which sets the context for a pricing decision. Situations, however, will vary from one customer to another, from one market to another and from one time period to another. Such situational variables will determine which tactics are appropriate and how an organization should respond to the specific circumstances it faces.

Sales promotion

The term 'above-the-line expenditure', mostly advertising, can be defined as all non-personal communication in measured media by an identifiable sponsor. This includes advertising via the internet, television, cinema, radio, print, and outdoor media. Sales promotion, often referred to as 'below-the-line expenditure', is not so easily defined. For example, Americans use the term to describe all forms of communication, including advertising and personal selling. In Europe, some use the term to describe any non-face-to-face activity concerned with the promotion of sales; some use it to describe any non-media expenditure, while others use it specifically to mean in-store merchandising. Organizations must, therefore, be clear about the nature and scope of such activities so that they can be appropriately managed and best contribute to the organization's marketing goals.

Nature and scope of sales promotion activities

In practice, sales promotion is a specific activity that can be described as the making of a featured offer to defined customers within a specific time limit. In other words, to qualify as a sales promotion, someone must be offered something that is above and beyond the core product or service, rather than just being offered something that is an everyday aspect of trade, such as delivery or normal credit terms. Furthermore, the promotional offer must include benefits not inherent in the product or service. This includes the intangible benefits offered in advertising, such as adding value through appeals to imagery. As such, sales promotions are an important tool to support positioning within the various markets an organization wishes to address.

Seen this way, every element of the marketing mix, including advertising, personal selling, point-of-sale material, pricing, after-sales service, and so on, can be used as part of a structured sales promotion campaign. Thus sales promotion is essentially a tool for solving organizational problems such as enhancing market position or persuading customers to behave more in line with the economic interests of the company. Typical objectives for sales promotion include:

- establishing or reinforcing market positioning;
- aligning demand and operational capacity;

- clearing slow moving stock;
- counteracting competitive activity;
- encouraging repeat purchase;
- securing marginal buyers;
- getting bills paid on time;
- inducing trial purchase.

From this, it will be seen that sales promotion is not just concerned with volume increases but can have both strategic and tactical outcomes. Thus, promotions can be used to assist production and distribution scheduling by persuading customers to bring forward their peak-buying from one period to another, or simply as a means of clearing outdated stock. In this way, sales promotion can seek to influence many different audiences in a number of different ways:

Salespeople	to sell	
Customers	to buy	
Customers	to sell	more, earlier, faster, etc
Users	to buy	
Users	to use	

The many and varied types of sales promotions are listed in Table 39.1. Each of these different types is appropriate for different circumstances and each has advantages and disadvantages. A typical example would be a free item for a multiple purchase, which would:

- allow cost/benefit to be easily measured;
- be fast and flexible;
- be attractive to profit-conscious customers;
- last as long as required;
- be easy to set up, administer and sell.

On the other hand:

- positioning may be adversely affected;
- it has no cumulative value to the customer;
- it is unimaginative;
- it can often be seen as a prelude to a permanent price reduction.

Among the alternatives available, points schemes in their various forms became increasingly popular in the 1990s and have continued in various formats into the 21st century as internet trading has made repeat purchase incentives easier to administer. Their advantages to the sponsoring

TABLE 39.1   Types of sales promotions

| Target market | Price promotions | | Product promotions | | Services promotions | |
	Direct	Indirect	Direct	Indirect	Direct	Indirect
Consumer	Price reduction	Coupons Vouchers Money equivalent Competitions	Free goods Premium offers (eg 13 for 12) Free gifts Trade-in offers	Stamps Coupons Vouchers Money equivalent Competitions	Guarantees Group participation events Special exhibitions and displays	Cooperative advertising Stamps Coupons Vouchers for services Events admission Competitions
Trade	Dealer loaders Loyalty schemes Incentives Full-range buying	Extended credit Delayed invoicing Sale or return Coupons Vouchers Money equivalent	Free gifts Trial offers Trade-in offers	Coupons Vouchers Money equivalent Competitions	Guarantees Group participation events Free services Risk reduction schemes Training Special exhibitions and displays Reciprocal trading schemes	Stamps Coupons Vouchers for services Competitions
Sales force	Bonus Commission	Coupons Vouchers Points system Money equivalent Competitions	Free gifts	Coupons Vouchers Points system Money equivalent Competitions	Free services Group participation events	Coupons Vouchers Points systems for services Events admission Competitions

organization include: their wide appeal; the absence of any need to hold stocks of gifts; the difficulty faced by customers who try to cross-value gifts; and their ease of administration. On the other hand, they offer no advantages in bulk buying, are difficult to budget, and lack the immediacy of dealer-loaders. Great care is necessary, therefore, in selecting a scheme appropriate to the objective sought.

In recent years, sales promotion activity has increased to such an extent that it can now exceed expenditure on above-the-line advertising. In spite of this, sales promotion will only ever support other positioning activities such as advertising, packaging, pricing and public relations.

Sales promotion strategy and tactics

Unfortunately, the tactical nature of many sales promotion activities means that they often amount to little more than a series of spasmodic gimmicks lacking in any coherence. This is very different from approaches to positioning, which usually reflect an overall strategy. This is particularly true of advertising, which has always been recognized as a means of building long-term brand franchises in a consistent manner. In contrast, the basic rationale of sales promotion is usually to help the company pursue a tactical initiative or short-term problem. In fact, there is no reason why there should not be a strategy for sales promotion so that each promotion consolidates the desired product positioning as well as achieving short-term tactical needs. In this way, tactical objectives can be linked to an overall positioning plan so that resources can be used more effectively.

One difficulty in using sales promotions strategically is in budgeting sales promotion expenditure, let alone evaluating it. Some companies include the expenditure with advertising, others as part of sales-force cost; some as a general marketing expense, others as a manufacturing expense (as in the case of extra product, special labels, or promotional packaging), while the loss of revenue from special price reductions is often not recorded at all.

Such failures can be extremely damaging, especially since sales promotion can be such an important part of a marketing strategy. Indeed, with increasing global competition, troubled economic conditions and growing pressures from distribution channels, the focused nature of sales promotion is turning into a more attractive, widespread and acceptable marketing tool. This highlights the need for organizations to set good objectives, to evaluate results after the event and to have some organizational guidelines for their sales promotion campaigns. For example, a £1 case allowance on a product with a contribution rate of £3 per case has to increase sales by 50 per cent just to maintain the same level of contribution. Failure to realize this, or to set alternative objectives for a promotion, can easily result in loss of control and a consequent reduction in profits.

Managing an organization's sales promotion expenditure effectively thus requires objectives to be established for each individual sales promotion in the same way that objectives are developed for advertising, pricing or distribution activities. The objectives for each promotion should be clearly stated in terms such as: product appropriate display positioning; image enhancement; competitor positioning at the level of strategy; or trial, repeat purchase, increased distribution, a shift in buying peaks, and so on, at the tactical level. Thereafter, the following process should apply:

- select the appropriate technique;
- pre-test;
- mount the promotion;
- evaluate in depth.

In-depth evaluation requires attitudes or product perceptions, both before and after a promotional campaign, to be analysed and spending to be categorized by type of activity (eg special packaging, special point-of-sale material, loss of revenue through price reductions, and so on). It is important, however, that the activities planned are compatible with, and complement, other activities within an organization's positioning and promotional activities.

Advertising

Advertising is one of the four major communications and promotions activities. Of these four, advertising is probably the most glamorous, although the others (sales promotions, public relations and personal selling) are nonetheless potent promotional tools. The aspect that differentiates advertising from other methods of communication is that it is: *Any paid form of non-personal presentation in a measured media by an identifiable sponsor.*

Advertising is also, probably, the most powerful aid to positioning, certainly from within the promotional mix.

Even though there are many relatively cheap forms of advertising, such as small advertisements in local newspapers, any 'serious' advertising campaign is usually an expensive undertaking. This is particularly true for major consumer goods and service companies for whom branding is a major contributor to competitive advantage, although advertising is also important for industrial suppliers, government agencies and other non-profit organizations.

For commercial organizations that see advertising as an important aspect of their promotional activities, expenditures of 5 per cent up to 30 per cent of sales are not unusual. The potential cost and contribution of advertising requires marketing managers to make careful media choices, to understand what advertising can realistically achieve, and to know how to make advertising effective.

Advertising media

The medium traditionally associated with advertising is television. In the past, it was the communications channel to which more people were exposed, although in absolute terms, more money is generally spent on newspaper advertising. More recently, television has been overtaken by the internet as the media of choice. However, television still arouses more excitement in marketing executives because of its life style, creative and entertainment associations. The range of other advertising media available include:

- mobile communications devices (smartphones etc);
- magazines;

- radio;
- outdoor displays;
- direct mail (paper and electronic);
- novelties (airships, hot-air balloons, T-shirts);
- catalogues;
- directories;
- circulars.

Marketing communications managers consequently face a wide range of media choices when putting together an advertising campaign. Their media decision should depend upon whom they wish to reach, the product they are promoting, the type of message being sent and the cost-effectiveness of the alternatives. An organization's target audience might, for example, be difficult to identify, may not spend much time reading newspapers or magazines, and may respond better to light-hearted messages. In this case, a mass media such as television, radio or popular internet sites might be required to reach them. A special interest group such as joggers or accountants, who take their interest seriously, might be better reached via targeted magazines, specialist internet sites or closely defined mail/e-mail lists.

The media chosen should also be able to support the positioning desired for a product, which again will vary between media. A complicated positioning will require bought editorial in magazines, mailings or click-through advertising on websites if it is to be communicated effectively, while simple positioning statements such as Nike's 'just do it' or BMW's 'the ultimate driving machine' can be successfully advertised on websites, over television and radio or in daily newspapers and hoardings.

Whichever media is chosen, the important financial consideration is the cost per thousand exposures, preferably to the organization's target market, and the impact the advertisement will have. Often, a combination of media is required to overcome the limitations each might have such as: clutter; fleetingness of exposure; wasted exposures; and the positioning implied by the choice of media. Some organizations, for instance, might not want their exclusively positioned Spa to be associated with mass media television advertisements or 'junk mail'.

Types of advertising objectives

There are three main types of advertising campaigns an organization can adopt, depending on the market situation it faces. The first of these is informative advertising, which is particularly important when trying to introduce new product forms or classes. The purpose of informative advertising is, normally, to build primary demand by educating a market or by encouraging the formation of attitudes. Such objectives may also be helpful for mature products to: reduce false impressions held by consumers; suggest new applications for a product; make consumers aware of upgrades, improvements, new outlets, or special events; and so on. Whatever the case, the information selected for communication, plus the way in which it is communicated, will fundamentally support a product or organization's positioning.

Positioning is more usually supported by persuasive advertising. This is commonly observed in competitive markets where a technology or product form is already established and accepted. The objective will be to create selective demand by building preferences or promoting particular attributes or benefits to differentiate an organization. As part of this, advertisers can compare their offering with those of their competitors, although competitor denigrations and criticism can reflect badly on an advertiser. In addition to positioning and brand preference, persuasive advertising may be used to: encourage immediate or early purchase; promote product enquiries or sales appointments; and stimulate a trial purchase or attendance at a demonstration. Of these, the majority of advertising used by, say, holiday timeshare firms are of this final kind. Consumer goods suppliers tend to focus on encouraging a purchase while industrial organizations usually concentrate on enquiry generation.

The third form of advertising is based on reminding consumers of a brand's values or reinforcing positioning and other messages already implanted in people's minds. This is often evident in mature markets or where reassurance is an important aspect of post-purchase evaluation for the customer. Established brand names tend to be protected by their owners with this type of advertising. The brochures that come with expensive items are equally concerned with convincing purchasers that they have made the right choice as with persuading people to buy. Where products are subject to seasonal influences, reminder advertising is also important to prevent any loss of position between seasons.

Making advertising effective

Like any other form of communication, to be effective, advertising must get people's attention, keep their interest, have a clear message and avoid distortion. In addition, advertisers must start with a good understanding of the effect they wish to achieve.

Although the obvious objective after positioning is the generation of sales, it is hard to link advertising directly with purchases. The main exception to this is direct response advertising, where it is clearly easier to identify sales resulting from advertising campaigns. Objectives are, therefore, better couched in terms of positioning-related issues such as awareness, brand recall, comparisons, knowledge and attitudes.

Once the context of a campaign is established, effective advertising requires the development of a clear message the advertisers wish to convey. This should be converted into a creative proposition that does not compromise the essentials of effective communications. Much time and effort is usually spent on this aspect to ensure the communicability of the message. Here style, time, language and presentation are important to match consumers' situations. In this, choice of media is also significant, since it will affect the possibility for distortion and the chances that the message will reach the right target group. Good advertising agencies are important contributors to decision making in these areas. Organizational managers, however, need to be careful not to get too carried away by the artistic and creative sides of advertising at the expense of the original objectives.

Advertising, of course, should never be performed in isolation and requires market research to help define and evaluate its activities. Such research should be conducted both before and after any campaign to identify the directions it should take and the effect it has had. Too often, organizations concentrate on the creation and delivery of a campaign, and whether it obtained sufficient exposure, at the expense of trying to understand what needs to be achieved. Overall, though, there is no substitute for a well-developed advertising plan that follows a logical process of decision making. The contents and structure of such a plan are illustrated in Table 40.1.

TABLE 40.1 Suggested pro-forma for an advertising plan

- **General objectives**

  What are the overall objectives we wish to achieve?

  Should they focus on conveying information, developing attitudes, giving reasons for buying or what?

  How will these affect positioning objectives?

  What other promotional activities might be needed to support these objectives?

  Are these objectives consistent with activities in other areas of the marketing mix?

  Is it possible to achieve the objectives set through advertising alone? (If not they are not an appropriate objective for advertising.)

- **Target audience**

  Who are they? How do we describe/identify them?

  What do they already know/feel about us/our competition?

  Where are they? What are their reading/viewing (etc) habits?

- **Response required**

  What response do we require from the target audience?

  What do we want them to feel/believe/know about our product?

  Is there anything we wish to avoid conveying?

  Are these responses incorporated in the *specific* objectives set for our advertising activities?

TABLE 40.1 *continued*

- **Creative platform**

  How are the key messages translated into a communicable presentation?

  Is the creative platform clearly linked with our specific objectives?

  Does the presentation link clearly with the responses required?

  What evidence is there that the presentation is acceptable and appropriate to our audiences?

- **Media platform**

  What medium or combination of media are to be utilized for the campaign?

  Why is this choice appropriate?

  What criteria have been used to determine cost-effectiveness?

  Do the media chosen match the 'quality' of our product?

- **Timings**

  When are our communications to be displayed/conveyed to our audience?

  What is the pattern of activities to be?

  Have we considered all the alternative patterns?

  What is the reasoning behind the scheduling adopted?

  How do the timings adopted coordinate with:
  - promotions of the other products we sell?
  - competitor promotional and other marketing activities?
  - seasonal trends?
  - special events in the market?

- **Budget**

  How much will the planned campaigns cost?

  When is the money going to be required?

  How is expenditure going to be monitored and controlled?

  What is the cost justification for spending this amount?

- **Measuring expected results**

  How do we intend to measure the results?

  Have we established any benchmarks required to establish change?

  Are all objectives sufficiently quantified to be measurable?

  What are our criteria for success/failure?

Public relations

As the name suggests, 'public relations' is concerned with an organization's relationships with the various groups, or 'publics', that affect its ability to achieve its goals and objectives. The aspects of these relationships that act as a focus for public relations are the image and information a market holds about an organization; in other words, its position in the market. At a simple level, this is achieved through publicity in various print and broadcast media. However, the broader views encouraged by relationship marketing require public relations activities to be more specific in their targeting and objectives. Public relations, therefore, is an important support for both positioning and relationship marketing.

Interest in public relations is also being stimulated by the reducing power and cost-effectiveness of mass media advertising. As the volume of communications aimed at the public increases and media channels proliferate, public relations offers an alternative means of reaching the audiences that an organization would like to influence. This is particularly true with the now widespread access to the internet and the proliferation of social media websites. A message received, for instance, via an editorial or a user review can be up to five times more influential than one received via an advertisement. Public relations, however, is unlikely to replace advertising or other means of communication and promotion. A more likely development is that it will increase its significance as an integral part of a communications or promotions mix.

Areas of public relations activity

News generation

One of the most widely used tools of public relations is the generation of news. News is best structured around a story, which can incorporate information about an organization or its products. Stories can be created around discoveries, achievements, personalities or changes. Often surveys or projects are commissioned to provide 'objective' reports about topics of relevance to both the sponsoring organization's products and its position. Thus, toothpaste manufacturers might support dental health research or a financial services organization might investigate people's attitudes towards saving.

News can also be used to make consumers aware of the existence of a product or service in order to stimulate enquiries from interested parties. It must also be remembered, however, that placing news where it will be accepted for publication is as important a skill as spotting and reporting newsworthy activities.

Organization-specific websites now try to do this by encouraging users to provide the 'stories' that will be 'newsworthy for other users such as the Timberland 'Good, Bad and Ugly' customer stories about their boots and shoes that they published on their website. These are currently published under the tagline 'Stories from the Timberland community about our brand, our business, our products and our passions'.

Events

Organizations can also gain people's attention through staging or sponsoring events. These can range from simple news conferences and seminars to exhibitions, competitive activities, anniversary dinners and stunts. All are likely to gain media coverage and draw attention to the sponsoring organization's name. They can also aid the achievement of credibility or establish images with which an organization would like to be associated. Events are also good opportunities to develop relationships with suppliers, opinion leaders and associates, as well as customers.

Publications

An organization's publications are another method of communication in which public relations will have a strong active interest. Sales support material is an obvious example; it can include brochures, manuals and presentations, usable by all personnel who have contact with the outside world. Annual reports, other public interest communiqués and special publications such as cookery books and children's stories also provide vehicles for influencing both customers and those who can affect customers' perceptions. Internal audiences and significant stakeholders are often addressed by organizational newsletters and magazines.

Support for good causes

Organizational support for good causes is another means of promoting an image and associating an organization with a certain set of values. This can include charity donations in return for product coupons, the sponsorship of public service activities such as festivals, and individual executives' support for local community interests such as educational establishments, hospitals or crime prevention. All these provide many opportunities for publicity elsewhere.

Expert opinion

Individuals within an organization can also act as sources of expert opinion for journalists, public enquiries or other forms of research and investigation. Public relations managers may seek to promote the expertise in their organization through the dissemination of contact lists and by grooming individuals' interviewing and presentational skills. This is a particularly important tool for knowledge-based organizations such as consultancies.

Visual identity

Organizations also often seek to establish a visual identity through either conformity of design or logos. While design can make it easier for customers to recognize an organization's products when they come across one, logos and other identification marks can be more important for internal markets as a means of signifying change or commonality of purpose.

Scope of public relations

As a support to an organization's positioning objectives, public relations activities can be used in a number of different ways. As examples, events can be used to reinforce brand values, or publications can help to draw the public's attention to features such as the stability or innovative nature of an organization. Less directly, but still importantly, public relations can be used to establish credibility for either an organization or its technologies, on the back of which a position can be established. Similarly, public relations may be used to build awareness of new products, new processes or other changes that will enhance an organization's ability to serve its customers. Public relations can thus prepare the way for more direct positioning activities such as: sales force campaigns; advertising; pricing mechanisms; and packaging.

Developing relationships with both customers and other markets also benefit from public relations activities. At one level, good relationships involve sharing information and public relations tools such as sales support materials, specialist publications and research results are useful vehicles here. At another level, relationships should involve demonstrations of commitment and, again, public relations can provide support. This can be through inviting individuals from targeted markets to events, be they customer markets, influencer markets, referral markets or third party intermediaries. Alternatively, this could be achieved by acknowledging their activities with awards, mentions in press releases or by referrals of media enquiries to them. These can be further supported by sales force and sales promotions activities.

An additional role for public relations is in dealing with special problems or disasters and limiting the damage such events can have on an organization. In this respect, the tobacco industry maintains a vigilant public relations campaign to limit the effects of adverse health publicity and government restrictions on advertising. A classic example is provided by Perrier when it became known that some of their products had become contaminated with poisonous chemicals. To limit the potential damage to their brand names, they immediately embarked on a widespread public relations campaign to show that this was an isolated event and that the public were in no danger. Coca-Cola, however, were not so lucky when they launched Dasani (bottled purified water) in the United Kingdom in 2004. First they just survived the revelation that it was simply filtered tap water plus some additives using some good defensive PR ('it goes through a sophisticated high tech filter system'). However, the death knell came a few weeks later when it was revealed that a batch of minerals had contaminated the water with a potentially carcinogenic bromate, which no amount of PR could overcome.

A more positive example is provided by Toyota who, in 2010, had a massive recall due to a 'sticky accelerator' problem that had to potential to cause driver loss of control. They successfully survived by getting executives around the world to take to the airwaves and communicate Toyota's key messages for all they are worth. Senior communicators tweeted and blogged like crazy to fill the information vacuum and take control of the escalating situation. Websites and call centres were established with information for worried Toyota customers, and US Chief Operating Officer Jim Lentz talked directly to Toyota drivers in a video posted to YouTube. In this he issued a sincere apology at the start of the clip and reiterated this message at the end. Experience of crisis management shows that this is often the best strategy, but many executives – under pressure from their lawyers – seem to find it hard to allow the word 'sorry' to pass their lips. The banking crisis, at the time of writing, appears to be no exception to this.

Public relations, then, can be a significant aspect of an organization's promotional mix and can be very influential in shaping attitudes and opinions plus overall market positioning. Relatively speaking, it is also a cheap means of gaining publicity and access to media channels. As an example, the value to Fuji of advertising on a modern airship was not the direct effect on the people it flew over, but the television coverage it gained from the novelty of the presentation. On a lesser scale, public relations are also very useful for smaller organizations with limited promotional budgets, although the exact results of public relations spending are always hard to quantify.

Sponsorship

Sponsorship has been a popular means of supporting a product or organization's position in its chosen markets since the 1980s. The impetus to seek a wider variety of communication channels to promote a name or product came mostly from the growing cost of media advertising. In addition, sponsoring the right kind of person or activity often gave global coverage that would have been difficult to achieve elsewhere, and sponsorship also offered tobacco companies exposure that was increasingly difficult to achieve as they were banned from TV advertising. Today, sponsorship in some arenas is the major income source for some activities such as major sporting events, awards or sports teams.

Sponsorship can be defined as any commercial agreement by which a sponsor, for the mutual benefit of the sponsor and sponsored party, contractually provides financing or other support in order to establish an association between the sponsor's image, brands or products and a sponsorship property in return for rights to promote this association and/or for the granting of certain agreed direct or indirect benefits.

Types of sponsorship

In general, sponsorship is most frequently found in four main areas: sport (68 per cent); social (9 per cent); arts and culture (15 per cent) and media (8 per cent). The rationales for sponsoring within these categories are shown in Figure 42.1.

Examples of sponsorship activities include:

- the Arts – Unilever and the Tate Modern;
- social and community – Tesco's Race for Life;
- educational – BT and information technology in schools;
- entertainment – T in the Park;
- broadcast – TalkTalk and X Factor, ITV1;
- sports – Emirates and Arsenal FC.

The significance of sponsorship for an individual 'personality' is illustrated by the fact that at the time of writing, Roger Federer is sponsored by: Gillette; JURA; Mercedes-Benz; Nationale Suisse; NetJets; Nike; Rolex; Credit Suisse and Wilson.

FIGURE 42.1   Sponsorship types

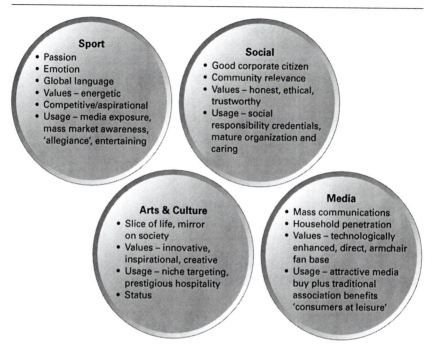

Sport
- Passion
- Emotion
- Global language
- Values – energetic
- Competitive/aspirational
- Usage – media exposure, mass market awareness, 'allegiance', entertaining

Social
- Good corporate citizen
- Community relevance
- Values – honest, ethical, trustworthy
- Usage – social responsibility credentials, mature organization and caring

Arts & Culture
- Slice of life, mirror on society
- Values – innovative, inspirational, creative
- Usage – niche targeting, prestigious hospitality
- Status

Media
- Mass communications
- Household penetration
- Values – technologically enhanced, direct, armchair fan base
- Usage – attractive media buy plus traditional association benefits 'consumers at leisure'

SOURCE: *Sponsorship, strategies for maximising the return on investment*, Ardi Kolah (2006)

Sponsorship can be on a local, regional, national, international or global level, ranging from as little as under £100 to over £1 billion and more. In 2011 PepsiCo spent between $340 million and $345 million on sponsorships and several million pounds are required to sponsor a high profile football team for a year.

Growth of sponsorship

As the 21st century unfolds, sponsorship continues to be one of the fastest developing areas of marketing practice in the world. The global sponsorship market is currently worth nearly $50 billion (2012) with the US spending circa $18 billion and in the UK is set to grow to over £2 billion, largely because of the sponsorship activities around the London 2012 Olympic Games.

For many organizations, sponsorship has established itself as an essential part of the marketing mix as a result of its perceived ability to make a difference, not only to brand awareness but also, more significantly, to a sponsor's 'bottom line'.

Objectives of sponsorship

To use sponsorship well, organizations have to be clear about the outcomes they desire. Simply targeting a better 'bottom line' is inappropriate since there are few occasions where increased business or acceptance of a price increase can be directly traced to sponsorship. More realistic and potentially more measurable objectives include:

- competitive advantage from association or exclusivity;
- alteration or reinforcement of public perception of the sponsor;
- associating a business with particular market segments;
- involving the company's employees in the community;
- generating positive media coverage;
- building goodwill among decision makers.

Sponsorship processes

Like all positioning support activities, sponsorship needs to be carefully planned and managed, as illustrated in Figure 42.2.

FIGURE 42.2   Sponsorship management cycle

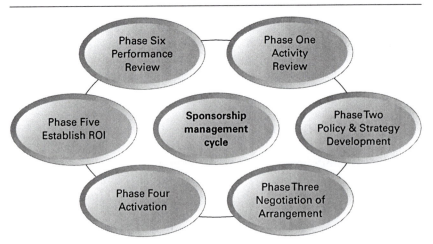

Phase 1: Existing activity review

The existing activity review should include all positioning support activities and how sponsorship can both complement and enhance them. It is important that any sponsorship programme is consistent with the creative aspects used in other communications and that timings of activities can be co-ordinated. If, for example, sponsorship is for a high-profile event, other communication activities need to support the build-up to the event, and then consolidate the position as the event fades from the public's mind.

Getting the right balance of activities is particularly important if sponsorship is to be used to support brand positioning where consistency of brand values is paramount. Sponsoring a poor performing Formula One racing team, for instance, may not enhance the brand value as much as desired. Similarly, to ensure return on investment, sponsoring a televised event must take into consideration the expected audience profiles and viewing figures to be worthwhile.

Phase 2: Policy and strategy development

A sponsorship strategy needs to be focused on the positioning objectives being pursued. The core decision is what or who should be sponsored, followed by plans for leveraging the association to the maximum cost-effective extent. In the early 2000s, Vodafone's sponsorship portfolio included Manchester United, the Australian Rugby Union Team and Ferrari. The intended association was excellence on a global scale and much effort was put into gaining as many spin-off benefits as possible.

Any sponsorship policy and strategy should include:

- measurable objectives (as far as possible);
- audience segmentation (including employees);
- brand essence or image being supported;
- fit with desired positioning;
- timescales and timings;
- geographical requirements;
- integration with other communications channels (spin-off opportunities);
- desired impact on behaviour of audiences;
- contingency plans if things change.

The key issue is to ensure a good business case for any sponsorship to avoid serving personal preferences rather than positioning objectives.

Phase 3: Negotiation

The objective of the negotiation phase is usually:

- an extension of a sponsorship programme;
- an extension subject to certain amendments;
- a new sponsorship agreement;
- termination of the old relationship.

Sponsorship negotiations vary depending on the respective bargaining strengths of the parties involved as well as the nature of the property involved. Whatever the case, however, it is important to ensure satisfactory legal arrangements, that the costs of sponsorship match the value of the intended returns, and that there is sufficient exclusivity.

Phase 4: Activation of the sponsorship programme

Negotiation of the right to associate with a sponsored 'property' is, however, only the first step in a sponsorship programme. Coca-Cola in the United States, for instance, spends upwards of four times the sponsorship rights fee in its activation of its FIFA football World Cup and Olympic Games properties. Activation activities based on Nike's sponsorship of US top basketball player Michael Jordan might include:

- advertising (Michael Jordan wears Nike);
- new media promotions (Nike/Michael Jordan websites);
- hospitality (come and join us at a Michael Jordan basketball match);
- licensing (special Michael Jordan Nike shoes);
- public relations (Michael Jordan visits Nike factory in Indonesia);
- promotions (free entry into a 'Dinner with Michael Jordan' competition with every Nike product purchase).

Phase 5: Return on Investment (ROI)

Establishing an overall ROI for a sponsorship programme can be tricky since it will be hard to link sales directly with sponsorship expenditure given the more powerful impact of other marketing activities. However, if measurable objectives have been set as part of the strategy and activation processes, it is possible to ensure the expected returns in other areas are achieved. These could include:

- expected media exposure and audience figures;
- increases in awareness, image, affinity etc;
- levels of association;
- attendance at sponsored events.

Phase 6: Review

Following measurements of the ROI of a programme, all experiences need to be evaluated and any lessons to be learnt established. These might include seeking answers to questions such as: 'did we sponsor too many events' and 'how did competitors respond to our sponsorships?' Sponsors may decide to withdraw sponsorship of, say, a football team if too many of its players get embroiled in violent conduct. Similarly, Tiger Woods lost many of his high-profile sponsors when details of his private life became public. Alternatively, a retailer might withdraw from sponsorship of equipment for schools if its competitors find a better way of offering the sponsorship. In the United Kingdom, supermarket giants Tesco and Sainsbury competed by offering vouchers with purchases that could be exchanged for computers and sports equipment respectively by schools. Who will lose momentum first remains to be seen.

Examples of sponsorship activities and deliverables include:

- supplements in a newspaper business section or colour supplement: sponsors secure prominent branding, editorial and advertising;
- a national awards dinner: sponsors select whom they wish to meet and sit next to at an invitation-only awards dinner;
- company visits: sponsors choose whom they wish to meet from among a list of companies that have performed well in various arenas;
- bespoke dinners: sponsors choose which dinners to host and select whom they wish to invite and sit next to.

Personal selling

Personal selling is normally seen as part of the communications mix. This is because the key role of the sales person is to present and promote the organization's offer and to engage in the two-way communications required to negotiate the terms of a sale. However, in order to perform these presentations and negotiations satisfactorily, sales people have to develop and maintain good relationships with their customers, particularly if repeat purchases are part of the desired outcome. Personal selling is, therefore, also an important aspect of the relationship market approach to business management. In fact, in organizations where relationship marketing is poorly understood, personal selling is seen as the equivalent of relationship marketing.

The majority of sales people operate in the field of industrial or trade marketing. However, personal selling is also a part of some areas of consumer marketing such as retailing, personal financial services or home improvements. Whatever the arena, the sales process is very similar and the tasks the sales person has to undertake are effectively the same. For organizational customers, the main difference is that there is an added degree of complexity. This results from the greater number of people involved in the decision-making process, the more formalized procedures involved and the distinct steps that an organization tends to follow in the purchase decision.

For business-to-business selling, it is also important to distinguish between a new buy, a straight re-buy and a modified re-buy. The higher the degree of 'newness', the more people tend to be involved and the more involved the selling task becomes. If, in addition, the product is complex, the greater the range of roles the sales person has to play. The way such roles are performed is often critical in determining the strength of the relationship between buyer and seller. Under these circumstances sales representatives may need to deal with engineers, technologists and senior management, as well as financial personnel and purchasing officers, which may imply that a team approach is required. Thus, either a sales person has to become a technical consultant, systems designer or integrator, cost accountant, administrative expert, or business strategist, or the relevant specialists have to become sales representatives and deal satisfactorily with the whole range of customers' concerns.

The earlier a sales person can become involved in the decision-making process, the better he or she will be able to influence the outcome. This is particularly important given that commitment to a supplier usually grows through the successive stages of the buying process. The commitment of existing customers can also be strengthened if straight re-buy situations can be converted into modified re-buys as this is likely to enhance the involvement of the supplier with the customer and, therefore, the strength of the relationship.

The sales process

Prior to any selling encounter, sales people need to understand as much as possible about their prospects. Often, a great deal of effort is involved in such research, but it can save much time in the longer run if it means that sales people see the right people at the right time and can provide relevant information. The sales process, however, starts with territory planning and obtaining interviews. This is particularly important to ensure that the maximum time is spent selling as opposed to travelling, administration, wasted calls, and so on. In addition, a systematic approach to territory planning is needed to ensure that all customers receive enough regular visits to maintain good relationships.

Although some calls will be made 'on spec', the majority will be by appointment. Appointments between customers and sales people are usually arranged on the telephone or via e-mail. Thorough preparation is needed before the call to enable the sales person to decide who to speak to, the objective for the call and the lever that is to be used to arouse the prospect's interest. It is not always easy to get through to prospects or, once connected, to persuade them to agree to an appointment. This is equally true for consumer sales calls. Increasing use of e-mail and text messaging has eased this process and introduced flexibility absent when remote contact was more difficult.

In personal selling, effective conduct and management of the sales interview is vital. The sales person must establish clear objectives for each call and have a plan of how they intend to achieve these objectives. A useful sequence to follow in any call is the 'ABC' sequence. The sales person should gain the prospect's Attention (A), sell Benefits (B), and move to a Close (C). The sales offer also has to be pre-planned and the necessary facts, information and supporting sales-kit of literature, samples, data and other aids needed to achieve the interview objectives must be assembled. An alternative angle is the SPIN approach whereby the sales person focuses on asking questions about the prospect's Situation (S), Problems (P) Implication (I), and Need-payoff (N). The idea is that getting the buyer to explain their requirements and to state the benefits they need has greater impact while sounding a lot less pushy. This is based on the old saying that 'people do not buy because the salesperson knows the products they are selling but because they felt the sales person understood their problems'.

Since customers buy products and services for what they will do for them, that is, the benefits of having those products or services, the sales person must focus on selling these benefits rather than the features. For the sales person, a simple formula to ensure this customer-orientated approach is adopted is always to use the phrase 'which means that' to link a feature to the benefit it brings. In this, sales people should seek to identify standard benefits (those benefits that arise directly from the features of what they offer), company benefits (benefits that are offered by the sales person's company) and differential benefits (those benefits that differentiate between the sales person's product or service and those of their competitors). A 'benefit analysis form' can be used to ensure a methodical analysis is conducted and proof should be given to substantiate every claim.

A buyer will almost invariably raise objections during a sales interview. An objection is a statement or question that puts an obstacle in the path leading towards closure of the sale. Buyers may raise fundamental objections when they cannot see a need for the product or service on offer. They may raise standard objections when they recognize their need but either wish to delay a decision, or need further convincing before concluding a deal.

When faced with a fundamental objection, the sales person has to sell the need for the product in question rather than the benefits entailed. There is a range of techniques for dealing with standard objections but if the buyer continues to raise objections without actually concluding the interview, there may be a hidden objection. It is often possible to discover what this is by asking an incomplete question, such as, 'and your other reason for not deciding is...?' Other objections, such as a price objection, can usually be overcome by talking in terms of value rather than cost.

The sale is closed when the buyer makes a firm commitment to place an order. The sales person should constantly look for opportunities to close the sale. The buyer will often show interest, make committing statements and ask questions; these are buying signals the sales person should follow up by asking a question that confirms they have correctly interpreted the buying signals.

A trial close can be used throughout the sales offer to test the buyer's reactions, uncover objections, determine buyer interest and speed up the sale. Trial closes also help the sales person to retain the initiative and to accumulate small commitments from the buyer. The sales person may also use direct and indirect questions to obtain buyer commitment. It is sometimes possible to offer alternatives that lead the buyer into stating a preference, which, once expressed, can pave the way to an immediate close. Other opportunities to close can be created by the summary technique, giving a quotation or by offering a concession.

The close, however, is not the end of the matter; it is just a step in a continuous process. Sales people must always remember that their objective is not only to close the sale, but also to open up a lasting relationship with the customer. In the final analysis, this is what makes a successful sales person.

Running a sales force, however, is an expensive form of communications and relationship building. The decision to use personal selling must, therefore, be carefully considered and will be based on the appropriateness of the advantages a sales force can provide as shown in Table 43.1. One response to the cost issue has been to use call centres as a substitute for travelling representatives. In some cases these default to order-taking facilities but well run centres staffed with skilled sales people can be a very cost-effective form of personal selling and provide much greater flexibility for the variable needs of employees.

Clearly, in different markets, different weightings will be given to the various forms of communication available. In industries with few customers such as capital goods or specialized process materials, an in-depth understanding of customers is required and personal contact is of paramount importance. In contrast, many fast-moving industrial or consumer goods are sold into fragmented markets for diverse uses. In these areas, other forms of communication are likely to be more cost-effective.

TABLE 43.1   The advantages of personal selling

- It is a two-way form of communication, giving the prospective purchaser the opportunity to ask questions of the sales person about the product or service.

- The sales message itself can be made more flexible and therefore can be more closely tailored to the needs of individual customers.

- The sales person can use in-depth product knowledge to relate their messages to the perceived needs of the buyers and to deal with objections as they arise.

- As a purchase is concluded, the sales person can move rapidly from persuasion to reinforcement and maintain appropriate relationships.

- Most important of all, the sales representatives can ask for an order and perhaps negotiate on price, delivery or special requirements.

Managing the sales team

As the importance of managing relationships with customers has increased and alternative communications channels have proliferated, organizations have had to pay particular attention to the role and productivity of one of their scarcest and most expensive resources: the sales force. The standard measures of sales force productivity have traditionally included call rates, revenue targets, volume targets and an increased client base. In more enlightened organizations, results-oriented sales managers have come to recognize that other objectives and productivity yardsticks are also required and that they are also dealing with a new breed of 'game-savvy' socially networked sales recruits that do not respond well to traditional sales management techniques. At the same time, customers now require sales representatives to provide instant responses and to be more readily accessible – and not just via the telephone. This has led to the recognition that organizations have to pay closer attention than ever to issues of motivation and training to complement this expanded set of requirements.

Sales force objectives

One of the major problems in achieving sales force productivity is that the way sales people spend their day leaves comparatively little time available for selling. Much of it is occupied in planning, travelling, sales administration and so on. In these circumstances, it is crucial that an organization should know as precisely as possible what objectives it wants its sales force to achieve. The sophistication of these objectives has led to the development of both quantitative and qualitative targets for sales activities.

The principal quantitative objectives employed are usually concerned with:

- how much to sell (the value of unit sales volume);
- what to sell (the mix of unit sales volume);
- where to sell (the markets and the individual customers that will take the company towards its marketing objectives);

- the desired profit contribution (where relevant and where the company is organized to compute this);
- selling costs (in compensation, expenses and supervision).

The first three types of objectives are derived directly from an organization's marketing objectives and constitute the principal components of the sales plan. However, there are many other kinds of quantitative objectives that can be set for the sales force; these are summarized in Table 44.1.

TABLE 44.1   Further quantitative objectives for a sales force

- Number of point-of-sale displays organized
- Number of e-mails sent to prospects
- Number of telephone calls to prospects
- Number of reports turned or not turned in
- Number of blog submissions made
- Number of trade meetings held
- Use of podcasts
- Number of service calls made
- Number of customer complaints
- Recruitment to the social media community
- Collections made
- Training meetings conducted
- Competitive activity reports submitted
- General market condition reports delivered

Qualitative objectives are more intangible in nature and can be a source of problems if sales managers try to assess the performance of the sales force along dimensions that include abstract terms such as 'loyalty', 'enthusiasm' and 'co-operation', since such terms are difficult to measure objectively. Where sales managers resort to highly subjective interpretations of performance, the result is too often resentment and frustration among those being assessed with accusations of favouritism, discrimination or intimidation.

However, it is perfectly possible for managers to set and measure qualitative objectives that directly relate to the performance of the sales force. It is possible, for example, to assess the skill with which a person applies his or her product knowledge for a customer, the skill with which the work is planned, or the skill with which a representative overcomes objections during a sales interview. While still qualitative in nature, these measures relate to standards of performance that are likely to be understood and accepted by the sales force.

Given such standards, it is not too difficult for a competent field sales manager to identify deficiencies; get agreement on them; coach in skills and techniques; build attitudes of professionalism; show how to self-train; determine which training requirements cannot be tackled in the field; and evaluate improvements in performance and the effect of any past training. Table 44.2 shows an example of setting objectives for an individual sales representative.

TABLE 44.2   Setting objectives for an individual sales representative

Task	Standard	How to set standard	How to measure performance	Performance shortfalls
• To achieve personal sales target	Sales target per period of time for individual groups and/or products	Analysis of: – territory potential – individual customer's potential Discussions and agreement between salesman and manager	Comparison of individual salesman's product sales against targets	Significant shortfall between target and achievement over a meaningful period
• To sell the required range and quantity to individual customers	The achievement of specified range and quantity of sales to a particular customer or group of customers within an agreed time period	Analysis of individual customer records of: – potential – present sales Discussion and agreement between manager and salesman	Scrutiny of: – individual customer records – observation of selling in the field	Failure to achieve agreed objectives Complacency with range of sales made to individual customers
• To plan journeys and call frequencies to achieve minimum practicable selling cost	To achieve appropriate call frequency on individual customers. Number of live customer calls during a given time period	Analysis of individual customer's potential. Analysis of order/call ratios. Discussion and agreement between manager and salesman	Scrutiny of: – individual customer records Analysis of order/call ratio Examination of call reports	High ratio of calls to individual customer relative to that customer's yield. Shortfall on agreed total number of calls made over an agreed time period

TABLE 44.2 *continued*

Task	Standard	How to set standard	How to measure performance	Performance shortfalls
• To acquire new customers	Number of prospect calls during time period. Selling new products to existing customers	Identify total number of potential and actual customers who could produce results. Identify opportunity areas for prospecting	Examination of – call reports – records of new accounts opened – ratio of existing to potential customers	Shortfall in number of prospect calls from agreed standard. Low ratio of existing to potential customers
• To make a sales approach of the required quality	To exercise the necessary skills and techniques required to achieve the identified objective of each element of the sales approach	Standards to be agreed in discussion between manager and salesman related to company standards laid down	Regular observations of field selling using a systematic analysis of performance in each stage of the sales approach	Failure to identify: – objective of each stage of sales approach – specific areas of skill, weakness – use of support material

Based on original work of Stephen P Morse when at Urwick Orr and Partners

Motivating the sales force

Sales force motivation has received a great deal of attention in recent times, largely as a result of the work undertaken by psychologists in other fields of management. It is, therefore, now widely accepted that it is not enough to give someone a title and a smart phone and expect them to achieve good sales results. Effective leadership is as much 'follower determined' as it is determined by management, and it is important to remember some of the main factors that contribute to effective management of the sales force.

If a sales manager's job is to improve the performance of his or her sales force, and if performance is a function of incentives minus 'disincentives', then the more he or she can increase incentives and reduce disincentives the better performance will be. Research has also shown that an important element of sales force motivation is a sense of doing a worthwhile job. In other words, the desire for praise and recognition, the avoidance of boredom and monotony, the enhancement of self-image, the freedom from fear and worry and the desire to belong to something believed to be worth-while, all contribute to enhanced performance.

Other methods and ideas that have been used to improve the productivity of sales forces over recent years have included:

- the development of imaginative and thorough training modules covering areas such as communication techniques, body language, human behaviour and motivation, observation skills, NLP approaches, transactional analysis and effective planning;
- the introduction of performance measurement, supported by evaluation procedures;
- the design of creative and productive sales aids;
- the establishment of systems for tapping and cross-fertilizing creative ideas generated by the firm's sales force;
- the development of effective incentive systems.

Remuneration

Remuneration will always be a very important determinant of motivation. This does not necessarily mean that to motivate a sales person you simply pay them more money than anywhere else. Clearly, there have to be sufficient financial motivations within a company to retain staff, but money is now accepted as a 'hygiene' factor, ie increasing levels of reward have diminishing impact on satisfaction. Very high levels of reward, such as has been the case in investment banking, usually indicates an absence of other motivational factors. When drawing up a remuneration plan, which would normally include a basic salary plus some element for special effort such as bonus or commission, the objectives summarized in the following list should also be considered:

- attract and keep effective people;
- remain competitive;
- reward sales people in accordance with their individual performance;
- provide a guaranteed income plus an orderly individual growth rate;
- generate individual sales initiative;
- encourage teamwork;
- encourage the performance of essential non-selling tasks;
- ensure that management can fairly administer and adjust compensation levels as a means of achieving sales objectives.

A central concept of sales force motivation is that the individual sales person will exert more effort if he or she is led to concentrate on:

- expectations of accomplishing the sales objectives;
- personal benefits derived from accomplishing those objectives.

The theory of sales force motivation is known as the path–goal approach because it is based on the particular path that the sales representative follows to a particular sales objective – and the particular goals associated with successfully travelling down that path. Representatives estimate the probability of success of travelling down various paths or sales approaches, and estimate the probability that their superiors will recognize their goal accomplishments and will reward them accordingly. Stated less formally, the motivational functions of the sales manager consist of increasing personal pay-offs to sales representatives for work–goal attainment, making the path to these pay-offs easier to travel by clarifying it, reducing road-blocks and pitfalls and increasing the opportunities for personal satisfaction en route. Knowing what your sales people consider to be a 'worthwhile endeavour' becomes highlighted as an important objective for any ambitious sales manager.

Key account management

The concept of key account management (KAM) has evolved as a natural development of greater customer focus and relationship marketing in business-to-business markets. The emphasis is on moving away from one-off, 'exploitative' transactions to longer-term synergistic relationships. This implies that a KAM relationship will enable buyer/seller companies to come together and create value in the market place above and beyond that which either could create individually. The evolutionary nature of KAM makes it possible to identify five distinct stages in the development of relationships between selling and buying companies. Identifying which stage the company is at is helpful in preparing for the challenges ahead and their implications for company organization and staffing.

Developmental stages of KAM relationships

As the nature of the relationship with the customer develops from being an 'anonymous buyer' to something approaching a 'business partner', the level of involvement with them becomes correspondingly more complex. This gives rise to some characteristic positions on the evolutionary path, which can be labelled Exploratory KAM, Basic KAM, Co-operative KAM, Interdependent KAM and Integrated KAM, as shown in Figure 45.1.

Each stage is distinguished by the nature of the problems faced by the selling company and how it organizes itself in response. As with personal relationships, those between businesses can founder for a number of reasons. The market position and priorities of the buying or selling company may also change over time in a way that negates the strategic necessity for a close working relationship. The evolutionary stages provide an overview of what can happen if all mishaps are avoided, rather than any form of predictive model.

FIGURE 45.1 Evolutionary nature of KAM relationships

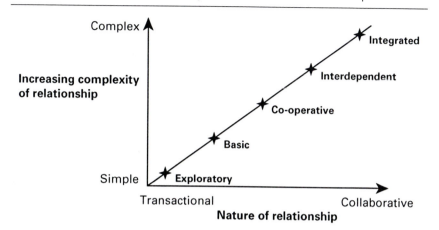

Adapted from a model developed in Millman, AF and Wilson, KJ (1995) 'From Key Account Selling to Key Account Management', *Journal of Marketing Practice: Applied marketing science*, **1** (1), pp 9–21

Exploratory KAM

This is a 'scanning and attraction' stage, where both seller and buyer are sending out signals and exchanging messages prior to the decision to get together. Both parties are interested in reducing costs. Commercial issues such as product quality and organizational capability are more important than establishing social bonds. Negotiation skills are paramount in the inevitable discussions that take place about price. It is unlikely that either party will disclose confidential information at this stage.

Here one of the greatest organizational problems is the ability of a key account manager to persuade the selling company to improve its production processes or to change its internal procedures in ways that will enable them to serve the target customer(s) better and more cost-effectively.

Basic KAM

Transactions have begun and the supplier's emphasis shifts to identifying opportunities for account penetration. In turn, the buying company will still be market testing other suppliers for price as it seeks value for money. It is essential, therefore, that the selling company concentrates on the core product/service, including all the intangibles, in an attempt to tailor-make a customer-specific package.

Although there may still be a lack of trust, there has been a subtle change organizationally. The key account manager and the main contact in the supplier organization are closer to each other and their organizations are beginning to be aligned behind them, as shown in Figure 45.2.

FIGURE 45.2   The basic KAM stage

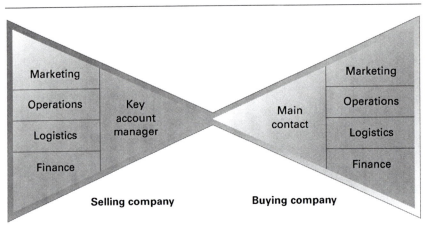

Co-operative KAM

By this stage trust will be developing and the selling company may have become a 'preferred' supplier. However, the buying company may still periodically test the market to check alternative sources of supply. With this increasing trust comes a greater willingness to share information about markets, short-term plans and schedules, internal operating systems and so on. Staff in the selling company are likely to be involved in discussions with their counterparts in the buying company, forging links at all levels from the shop floor to the boardroom. There is often a social context, sometimes in the form of organized events such as golf days. The structure of the relationship is illustrated in Figure 45.3.

It is this network of interactions that brings a new strength to the relationship. With it comes the realization that customer service operates at many levels and should be driven by a desire not to let down personal contacts. The relationship is still fragile, however, because of the difficulties in making the transition to higher levels of trust and mutual regard. It is not a highly organized relationship and there are many things that can go badly wrong, particularly if there is high staff turnover in either organization.

FIGURE 45.3 Co-operative KAM

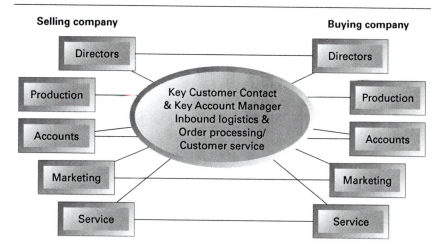

Interdependent KAM

When this stage is reached, the buying company sees the selling company as a strategic external resource. The two should be sharing sensitive information and engaging in joint problem solving. Each will allow the other to profit from their relationship and there is also a tacit understanding that expertise will be shared. At this stage, the selling and buying companies should be closely aligned and communicating at all levels, as shown in Figure 45.4.

FIGURE 45.4 The interdependent KAM stage

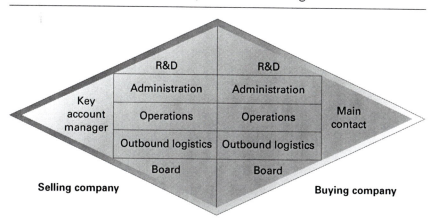

The various functions in each partner communicate directly. The role of the key account manager and the main buyer contact is to 'oversee' the various interfaces and ensure that nothing occurs to discredit the partnership, rather than being the mainstays of the relationship; the 'hero' model of a key account manager.

The partnership agreement will have long-term profit margins, although there will usually be several categories of performance expectations that are reviewed and renewed on a regular basis. It will be in the 'spirit of partnership' for the selling company to meet all of these consistently and to the highest possible standards.

Integrated KAM

If the seller/buyer relationship can extend beyond being just interdependent so that in effect the two companies operate as an integrated whole, but maintain their separate identities, a more synergistic situation can be created.

The interfaces between the two organizations at all levels will function as focus teams in a way that is largely independent of the key account manager, as illustrated in Figure 45.5. These teams, consisting of personnel from both companies, will generate creative ideas and overcome problems. Such problems may be functional, issue based, project based or perhaps serve a motivational purpose. Electronic data systems become integrated, information flows are streamlined, business plans are linked and the 'unthinkable' is explored.

About the only issue that remains sacrosanct for the selling company is likely to be its brand. Any requests from the buying company that could undermine this should be greeted with great suspicion.

FIGURE 45.5   The integrated KAM stage

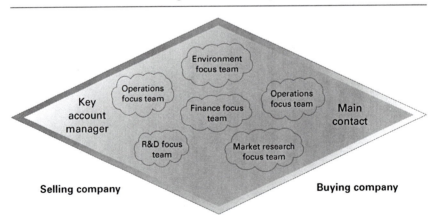

Challenges for the future

Although transforming the tactics of repeat business into a strategic thrust sounds deceptively simple, the implementation of KAM has proved to be more problematic. Many organizations have tried the partnership approach while failing to recognize the demands that true partnership brings. There are obvious benefits to be had, but it is important to acknowledge that managing the transition from traditional selling to general accounts to KAM will not be easy.

For most organizations, an interdependent relationship is likely to be the closest that can be achieved given the loss of autonomy an integrated relationship implies. There are very few examples of organizations that have sustained an integrated relationship for very long. For others, a co-operative relationship is the most that can be hope for. However, as shown in Table 45.1, there are a number of key questions that need to be addressed if the KAM approach is to provide a relevant model for organizations faced with the changing demands of continuously evolving markets.

TABLE 45.1   Key questions for the future of KAM

- How are organizations going to find or develop KAM executives with sufficient skills to build buyer/seller relationships?
- Is Integrated KAM the ultimate stage in the evolutionary development of KAM or will another form emerge?
- What is the best way to build key account teams?
- What are the particular problems for key account managers operating in complex supply chains or on a global basis?
- What are the organizational implications of global KAM?
- What kinds of decision support systems are required for effective KAM?
- How should the differences between key accounts and non-key accounts be managed?
- At what level may the KAM relationship be seen as a barrier to competition and fair trade?

Implementing key account management

In order to implement KAM effectively, organizations need a clear understanding of the areas in which KAM differs from traditional account management. In too many organizations, introducing KAM has simply involved giving general account managers new titles without changing anything else. As such, the potential benefits of KAM are never attained.

Difference between KAM and traditional selling to general accounts

Account management has long been recognized as an important sales function in business-to-business markets. However, general account management systems are notorious for being difficult to extend beyond a sales-based relationship. The tendency is for the performance of the account manager to be measured in terms of numbers of transactions and contract renewals. Negotiations are invariably focused on cost, product availability and quality issues. The aim of sellers is to keep their liabilities to a minimum while buyers are focused on value for money and are keen to keep options open. Under a general account management system, account turnover is accepted as a fact of life, new customers are constantly being sought and little differentiation is made between different customers except, maybe, in terms of size or location.

Recasting these efforts as a KAM system recognizes that it may be more cost-effective for a supplier to focus resources on retaining existing profitable accounts rather than constantly signing up new customers. Further, it recognizes that not all customers have the potential to be long-term partners and that developing such relationships requires the allocation of disproportionate resources. The emphasis becomes one of tailored service rather than sales plus supply co-ordination rather than delivery. Accounts are considered whole entities instead of buying points and key account managers become responsible for the quality of the relationship as well as the negotiation of sales.

As an example of the flexibility required, DHL operate a Global Account policy that enables them to offer a strategic partnership to customers, with a Global Account team located either in the country that the customer prefers to deal with or based at DHL's headquarters.

Strategic marketing benefits of KAM

The first benefit of successfully developing a KAM system is that less profitable accounts are identified and managed accordingly, thereby consuming fewer resources. Similarly, if key accounts are identified and kept for longer, less effort is required to attract new customers, except for those with the potential to become longer-term customers.

Broadening the relationship so that it goes beyond sales negotiations will increase the amount of two-way communications between the seller and buyer organizations. At a simple level, as communications increase, so do the chances of doing more business. If, at the same time, customer satisfaction levels can be raised, a virtuous circle can be created in which it becomes easier to sell to satisfied customers, as shown in Figure 46.1.

FIGURE 46.1   Customer satisfaction: virtuous circle

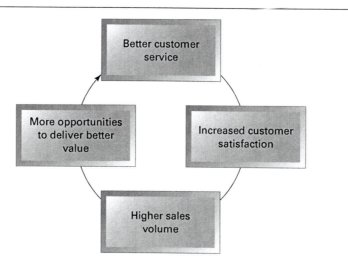

Organizations that use KAM systems to evolve accounts successfully into business partners also become more strategically secure. Their customers become less fickle and more willing to accommodate mistakes. Mutual problem solving will reduce the costs of 'doing business' and resources can be devoted to creating value for customers further along the supply chain.

In addition, buying companies will benefit by having their supplies safeguarded in terms of both quality and quantity, and are able to concentrate their resources on operations rather than procurement or supply management.

Skills required of a key account manager

Key account managers must be able to recognize how a relationship with a customer changes and how to respond positively to events in a way that enhances the relationship. This requires an ever-increasing repertoire of skills and knowledge as the scope of KAM widens and becomes more complex, particularly in global markets. Different skills are needed at each stage of the KAM relationship.

- In the early stages, as the main point of contact for a buying company, key account managers must represent the selling organization in a way that makes it appear competent. In this, they must appear likeable, approachable and trustworthy while at the same time demonstrating sound selling skills and good product knowledge. As such, there will be little to differentiate a key account manager from a competent sales person.

- As the relationship moves to interfaces at several levels within each organization, high-level business skills are required of key account managers; particularly since they have to act as a key facilitator between the different areas of their and the customer's business. In this, they will need an understanding of department or functional issues and how these might impact on the key account.

- Key account managers also require general management or leadership skills so that they are equipped to deal with any tensions that arise over differing organizational priorities. These can occur as a result of demands on staff who report to other functional managers as well as the key account manager, and the cross-functional nature of advanced KAM. The key skill will be influencing without authority and the ability to facilitate interactions.

- Where key account managers have team responsibilities, they must keep all members fully briefed about operational and strategic issues that have a bearing on the KAM relationship. This requires high level organizational and team leadership skills.

- Key account managers also require strategic business skills to deal with a key account's specific problems or needs, particularly as they become more involved in all aspects of managing an account. A strong strategic perspective will be an important attribute.

Organizational positioning

Organizationally, KAM must be supported at the highest level as a result of its potential strategic impact and the authority that the key account manager requires in order to call in resources from across the organization. This positioning should reflect the significance of the role in bringing about and maintaining large tranches of long-term business. In order to be effective, KAM cannot be perceived within the organization as a simple re-titling of the existing sales group.

The authority and status of the key account manager can easily be undermined if the buying organization is allowed to gain the ear of somebody higher in the business. Thus, when dealing with key accounts, more senior managers and directors should be seen to defer to the account manager. Such authority will also help to overcome adversity within the selling organization during the early stages of the KAM relationship as other managers seek to fight proposed changes to the internal procedures needed to support the development of the relationship.

Implementation issues

For the effective implementation of KAM, organizations need to address all of the above areas and to develop policies to accommodate them. In particular, it is important that specific measurements are put in place to measure its success. These might include: key account sales relative to general accounts; industry and own customer satisfaction systems, and executive feedback and development procedures.

Ignoring the differences between KAM and traditional selling to general accounts, the skills required, or the strategic organizational positioning of KAM, are likely to create difficulties in implementation. At the same time it is important that the entire organization appreciates the benefits that adopting KAM can bring to the long-term profitability of the business.

Channel strategy

A major concern for any organization is how they can best make their products available to the market place. The options available are many and the wrong choice can have significant consequences for an organization's success. In addition, once made, such choices tend to be long term in that a distribution system takes time to build and make effective and, once established, is not easily changed. From a customer's point of view, the channel through which they purchase provides the most direct relationship with the supplier. The development of a strategy for the channels is, therefore, important for the relationship an organization has with its customers.

Evaluating the use of intermediaries

The basic channel strategy decision is whether to sell directly to users or whether to use some form of intermediary. The choice may be straight-forward in that the costs incurred by selling direct may be just too high. Thus Volkswagen would have difficulty finding enough capital to fund a retail network for the sale of its cars in Germany, its home market, let alone the rest of Europe or the rest of the world. Traditionally, a specialist supplier such as a pharmaceutical company selling above-the-counter products to the public would have to sell a large number of competitor manufacturers' products in addition to its own before it could consider owning retail outlets that would be of interest to shoppers and have sufficient turnover to cover the overheads of retail premises. Recently, however, there has been an increase in the number of one-brand-only retail chains in High Streets and malls such as Lush soaps and cosmetics or Levi's clothing. In addition, the ability to provide online shopping has made the potential for going direct easier.

As the decision to use intermediaries is not clear-cut, the choice will depend on an evaluation of the their advantages and disadvantages. The main advantages include:

- Reduced distribution costs since an intermediary will be able to use the same transport and storage facilities for the output of a number of suppliers and spread the costs across a greater number of products.

- Better access to remote or fragmented markets, which would be too costly to service directly, or markets about which an intermediary has special knowledge and in which they can operate more efficiently.
- Reduced financial and physical problems associated with stock holding. If intermediaries pay for goods on receipt, rather than when sold, and operate warehouse facilities that match the particular requirements of local markets, original suppliers gain working capital benefits without having to invest in supply chain facilities.
- Improved service response can be achieved by intermediaries who are closer to customers geographically, or who possess better local knowledge of the needs of customers in their area.
- Enhanced value for customers may be provided by: one-stop shopping; systems integration; special packaging, or just breaking bulk and supplying in smaller quantities.

The disadvantages to a supplier of using intermediaries are smaller in number, but can have significant consequences. Since intermediaries tend to be independent organizations, there is an inevitable loss of control on the part of the supplier. Thus, there will be no guarantee that the products will be presented or positioned in the most appropriate way, or that intermediaries will actively sell your products rather than another's. The other problem that can result from the use of intermediaries is a loss of customer contact and the information such contacts provide. Apart from the inconvenience involved in passing information to a supplier, intermediaries will often be keen to hold on to information for the power it can add to their side of the relationship.

The functions performed by intermediaries are not usually optional; they are all required in order to create satisfied customers. Strategic decisions about channels are, therefore, concerned with who should perform these functions and where they should be located. The decisions will be based on efficiency in terms of who can best execute a function, plus the other marketing requirements of a supplier. Thus, apart from being more cost-effective, an intermediary should also complement the supplier's product range, pricing aspirations and service policies.

Channel and intermediary alternatives

There is a very wide range of channel intermediaries that will perform sales, distribution and service functions on behalf of a supplier. The exact number and appropriate forms will vary enormously between industries. However, the major types in existence are illustrated in Table 47.1.

In reality, a particular intermediary may be a combination of two or more of the types listed. For strategic purposes, form is irrelevant. More important are the costs they incur and the advantages they provide. In general, many organizations utilize a combination of intermediaries, and may even operate a direct sales activity as well, to match the different markets in which they desire a presence.

TABLE 47.1   Major forms of intermediaries

- Retailers in or out of town
- Wholesalers
- Distributors
- Dealers
- Agents
- Value added re-sellers
- Catalogue distributors
- Original equipment manufacturers
- Online retailers
- Direct mail retailers
- Franchised outlets
- Freight forwarders
- Merchandise clubs
- Party sales organizers
- Licensed manufacturers/service operators

In addition to varying the types of intermediary, an organization will also include the number of intermediaries as part of their strategy. The first strategic option is to seek **intensive distribution** by having your products available in as many outlets as possible. Thus, milk can be made available through: doorstep delivery; supermarkets; convenience retailers; vending machines; garages; caterers, and in some cases, directly from the farmer. The second option is **selective distribution**, which involves some, but not all, of the intermediaries who would be willing to supply a product. This can be a cheaper option and allows a producer to concentrate his or her efforts more effectively and thereby maintain greater control. Many financial services and products with a high brand value are marketed in this way. The third option is to offer **exclusive distribution** by limiting the number of intermediaries that handle a product. While this will reduce market coverage, it offers the supplier the possibility of greater control, better access to information, and can encourage intermediaries not to stock competing products or brands. New automobiles, plant and equipment, spare parts, major appliances and high brand apparel are often distributed in this way.

The choice of distribution coverage has long-term implications because each party will require commitment from the other, and the creation of any supply arrangement will involve considerable investment of both time and money from both parties. Costs will derive from:

- familiarization activities;
- product or service training;
- stock holding;
- creation of trading routines and processes;
- investment in special tools, equipment or facilities.

The basis of the decision will be the trade-offs involved between control, cost and market objectives.

A supplier must also decide where to focus marketing efforts: on a push strategy, whereby attention is concentrated on the intermediary to 'sell in' more products, or on a pull strategy, whereby the supplier emphasizes the creation of demand so that intermediaries are encouraged to deal in that product. The strategy might also involve the development of different channels over time. For example, a direct sales force can help an organization to prove that a market exists through obtaining early market penetration, but is then replaced by dealers to obtain intensive distribution as a market grows. This may be followed by a move to exclusive distribution to create brand value in a mature market. The creation of Levi's only specialist retail outlets is a good example of using distribution to emphasize the brand value of the product. Whatever the case, the decisions involved are not easy, but can significantly influence success in the market.

Channel management

Having devised a channel strategy, a supplier organization has to develop appropriate relationships with its intermediaries to enable it to take good advantage of the opportunities the intermediary can provide. The two major drawbacks to using intermediaries, rather than supplying direct, are the loss of control that intermediaries imply and the lack of access to direct feedback from user markets. Some argue that the margin taken by intermediaries is also a drawback. This should not be the case as the intermediary's margin pays for the services they provide. If the supplier could provide those services more cheaply, they have made a poor strategic choice in using intermediaries.

Channel or distribution managers must, therefore, seek to work with intermediaries so that the channel complements the suppliers' marketing objectives and minimizes the problems of control and access to market information. Organizations can achieve this through attention to channel motivation, treating intermediaries as business partners and managing channel conflict.

Motivating intermediaries

Intermediaries' prime focus of attention is their customers, since it is the customers who provide them with their income. Apart from the usual marketing issues involved in attracting and retaining such customers, the nature of the job performed by intermediaries also highlights issues of stock turnover and margins. Stock turnover is an important issue because of the working capital implications of holding inventories. Margins are important since production costs are outside an intermediary's control, which means that profitability is very dependent on the bought-in price and margin management. In addition, intermediaries will tend to concentrate their efforts on the products they can sell most easily.

Suppliers must work hard if they are to motivate intermediaries under these circumstances. The simple solution is to reduce prices to make products easier to sell, or make the margin available to the intermediary more inviting. Reducing an intermediary's stock costs and the risk of stock-outs by intermediaries, which may result from their reluctance to hold large inventories, should also be a focus. At the same time, suppliers must encourage intermediaries to promote their products rather than just wait for customers to turn up.

Possibly the most important aspect of motivating intermediaries is to remember that they are, themselves, a market and not just middlemen being paid to provide a service for the supplier. If the latter approach is adopted, the tendency will be for suppliers to seek the compliance of their channel members rather than any more substantial form of co-operation. This can lead to interactions based on transactions rather than a relationship built on mutual long-term needs. In transaction mode, motivation will tend to be 'deal-orientated' and focus on discounts, advertising allowances, merchandising arrangements and sales incentives. While these tools are not, in themselves, inappropriate, they need to be used as part of a wider marketing approach if they are to provide longer-term co-operation and stability.

As a market, intermediaries' problems need to be solved in a way that encourages them to become 'advocates' for their suppliers. This requires an understanding of how value can be supplied, rather than looking at the problem as one of efficiency or a simple transfer of cost. Important areas of value to middlemen that go beyond the approaches implied by a deal-orientation include:

- sales support materials;
- market research about intermediaries' markets;
- advanced information about product development;
- fast responses to technical queries;
- the creation of market pull;
- rapid fault tracing;
- product training;
- collaboration on product improvements.

Developing partnerships

An organization's relationships with its intermediaries is often better managed if it can be formed into a partnership. Under a partnership arrangement, intermediaries are more likely to see themselves as a meaningful part of their supplier's enterprise. The essence of this will be agreement between supplier and intermediary about the supplier's general market policies plus positive demonstrations of commitment. Agreement and commitment between supplier and middleman will reduce the need to exert control, since the intermediary should now, voluntarily, implement supplier policies and increase the flow of information from end-users to suppliers. Having the incentive to collect data they should be more willing to pass it back.

One way of promoting agreement within channel partnerships is through the creation of distributor panels, in the same way that equipment suppliers might set up user groups. Two-way communications between people at different levels of each organization will also be a means of cementing relationships. At a deeper level, this might include cross-board membership, personnel exchanges and participation in the marketing planning process. The potential for creating a social media to perform this function makes this a more enticing proposition.

Commitment to creating a feeling of partnership can be demonstrated in a number of ways. One significant action is the referral of customer enquiries to the relevant intermediary. Others can be:

- inclusion in public statements;
- mentions in company newsletters;
- invitations to trade entertainment events;
- acknowledgement of achievements;
- business consultancy advice;
- technical support for areas of weakness such as financial management or search engine optimization;
- not opening competing outlets in their territory.

A significant demonstration is to devote a specific part of the supplier's marketing management structures to channel marketing to show that the relationships are important.

This is not to say that channel partnerships cannot be changed. As a product matures through its life cycle in the market, different arrangements may be required to match different market developments. As a simple example, mass markets need to be addressed in a different way from niche markets, and products that are tending towards commodity status do not require the same level of dealer sophistication to be competitive. Similarly, as the competitive status of a product improves through, for instance, brand value development, different types of intermediary may be required to maintain product positioning. In the early 1990s in the United Kingdom, both Nissan and Mazda (Japanese car manufacturers) made significant changes to their franchised dealer network; the former to gain better control, the latter to upgrade the quality of their dealers in order to complement better the perceived quality and status of their newer models.

Channel conflict

Since channel members are normally independent organizations there is always the potential for conflict, either between channel members themselves or between an intermediary and their supplier. Resolution of such conflict is important so that intermediaries will remain responsive to efforts to motivate them and a partnership relationship can be maintained.

The majority of the conflict between intermediaries and suppliers usually occurs because suppliers have not paid proper attention to, or are inconsistent about, their channel management policies. As an example, equipment manufacturers will naturally want distributors to offer high levels of service, local advertising and competitive prices. They will also want their products promoted, presented and displayed, to the disadvantage of their competitors. If intermediaries were to adopt such policies unconditionally, they would incur significant costs, but not necessarily fulfil their own profit objectives or provide the right type of service for their customers. As indicated above, suppliers need to take channel members' ambitions and problems into account before demanding gold-star service for knock-down prices from them.

Inconsistent channel management can also arise when suppliers make their products available through a number of competing intermediaries. In the more extreme cases, suppliers find themselves competing directly with their intermediaries, which can leave channel members feeling a little betrayed. During the 'shake-outs' in the world personal computer markets in the late 1980s and early 1990s, many manufacturers and volume wholesalers started bypassing their intermediaries in an effort to survive. It must be added that this was only necessary as a result of poor channel relationships and short-sighted channel management in the first place. More recently, many insurance companies now sell direct as well as through traditional insurance brokers. A similar situation can also be seen with mobile phone handsets.

Conflict between channel members, rather than between intermediary and supplier, can occur for a number of reasons. One cause can be the appointment of too many intermediaries in one geographical area or for one communications media. In consequence, they end up competing with each other and finding it difficult to sustain sufficient sales volumes to make it worthwhile doing business. Another can result from the supplier seeming to favour one channel member against another.

Alternatively, individual channel members may start 'letting the side down' by engaging in over-vigorous competitive activities or reductions in quality. Here, suppliers must fulfil a role of **channel captain** and seek to maintain a state of distribution equilibrium.

One example where the intermediary acts as the channel captain is provided by Amazon who have pioneered a new business model in which it makes available products that compete with those it supplies itself. These are from approved competitors to whom it provides a link directly from its own site. Partner suppliers and distributors must conform to certain standards to remain linked with Amazon. eBay performs a similar role with suppliers who set up 'eBay Shops'. Although intuitively uncomfortable, it has proved successful so far and demonstrates that there are no 'recipes' for success and that there is always room for innovation.

Conflict is best resolved by anticipating its occurrence and avoided by trying to pre-empt the causes. Well-motivated intermediaries who see themselves as partners can significantly reduce the potential for such conflict. A well-developed strategy should seek to balance the needs of suppliers and intermediaries so that it adds value to products beyond the costs they generate and advance the strategies of both.

Customer service strategies

ustomer service is an increasingly important factor both for competitive advantage and customer retention. Indeed, the service element of many product offerings is sometimes the only aspect that distinguishes an organization's offer from its competitor's. In addition, once a supplier/customer relationship has been established, customer service provides a significant contribution to the augmented product offering that enhances the value of a purchase and cements relationships. To manage this adequately, some organizations treat customer service as a separate aspect of the marketing mix for which individual plans and strategies are created.

Customer service is most easily thought of as all those activities that support a customer's purchase from the time they decide to buy from a particular organization to the point at which they take full ownership and responsibility for the product. While this is obviously a simplification, the approach covers most of the major elements that need to be considered when devising a customer service strategy.

Elements of customer service

The key elements of customer service cover:

- The organization's response to placing the order, which provides the initial encounter. The ease by which an order is placed, taken and facilitated can provide a lasting impression and can win and sustain customers if managed more effectively than by other organizations. Apart from just being accessible, this can also involve advice, assistance in creating a specification and personal attention.

- The information provided by a supplier while an order is being processed and delivered will also influence a customer's experience of an organization. Such information could include: order confirmation; delivery notification and delivery variations; plus information that will facilitate installation or utilization. Regular contacts with a supplier will reduce the possibility of customers feeling isolated or forgotten and can increase a customer's feelings of being important to a supplier.

- Final delivery of the goods or service, which will also affect a purchaser's experience of a supplier. This does not just involve availability and delivery lead times, but also the way in which the product is delivered. Thus, the ability to deliver at specific times, the degree of delivery time variability, the completeness of an order and fill rates (the percentage of orders shipped complete), will all contribute to customer service levels.

- The support provided after sales have been completed, which can substantially enhance or reduce the value of a purchase. In fact, customer service is often taken to mean after-sales service, despite the other elements customer service covers. Post-sales support ranges from straightforward maintenance and repairs to training activities; helplines; assistance with, and notification of, upgrades; instruction manuals; returns policy; and fault tracing.

- The ease with which problems are solved, which can be the true test of an organization's commitment to customer service. This is particularly the case for many service organizations in, for instance, insurance, transport and hotels. Here the core product is, effectively, customer service, but where customers often only learn of an organization's true qualities when something goes wrong. This is also true for tangible products in terms of action on complaints, crisis repairs and an organization's ability to respond to emergency orders. Also included here will be the way in which an organization deals with problems such as design faults, contamination or other supply problems that can arise from time to time.

Developing a strategy

Forming a customer service strategy first involves the identification of the critical elements of service associated with an organization's activities. Some of these will be 'order-qualifying-type' activities in that they have to be provided for an organization to be on the shortlist of potential suppliers. For some computer or complex office equipment vendors, for instance, the ability to offer 'on-site' or 'next-day' service contracts falls into this category. Others can be characterized as 'order winning', in that they will act to differentiate one supplier from another.

Once identified, an enterprise can then compare its performance in these customer service elements with the expectations of customers and the performance of competitors. This will provide appropriate targets for customer service levels, for which policies and processes can be established. As an example, many organizations now operate a 'three-rings' policy, which tries to ensure that any telephone call is answered on, or by, the third ring to avoid the frustration a caller can experience from not knowing whether they have the right number; or from just feeling ignored. Other targets may involve on-time delivery levels, minimum notification times for late deliveries, emergency response times, and so on. Many internet suppliers now offer an order-tracking facility as part of the purchase experience. Similarly, mobile phones and GPS have enabled logistics and door-to-door delivery organizations to offer increasingly narrow delivery windows to avoid purchasers having to wait in all day for a delivery.

A good method for establishing customer service priorities is to perform trade-off analysis with customers. This asks respondents to prioritize different aspects of customer service against each other, such as delivery time variability against order lead times (see Table 49.1). In this example, it is assumed that all customers would find a short order lead time with no delivery time variability the most preferable combination (scored 1), and the converse the least acceptable (scored 9). Customers are then asked to complete the remaining boxes with the numbers 2 to 8 to represent their order of preference. These rankings will show exactly where customer preferences lie. If this is performed for the half-dozen or so elements that are critical for attracting new customers or retaining existing ones, it is possible to develop quite sophisticated customer service programmes. It is also possible to use such an analysis for segmentation purposes so that differing requirements can be serviced at the appropriate levels, should distinct patterns of need appear.

The final decision in creating a customer service strategy revolves around the implementation of the service programme. The basic options are contracting out, or doing it yourself.

Here, the decisions will depend on the resources available to an organization, plus the trade-offs between costs, quality and control. As an example, while it may be cheaper to subcontract repairs, it may be hard to monitor quality. Similarly, while good asset management might dictate using third

TABLE 49.1 Example of customer service trade-off matrix

		Delivery time variability		
		On time	+/– One day	+/– Two days
Order lead times	One week	1		
	Two weeks			
	Three weeks			9

parties for infrequently used and expensive service operations, a situation of rapid change might make it more desirable to keep the activity in-house to retain control over market or new product developments.

One answer to the problems of managing customer service has been to reduce the need for service by allowing customers to perform certain activities themselves. Thus, the developments in electronic data interchange (EDI) have enabled customers to place orders via terminals on their own premises, thereby reducing the need to order during opening hours. Similarly, central diagnosis facilities via EDI can locate equipment faults and perform tests that can save much time and expense for both parties. In addition, 'plug-in maintenance', whereby a whole module or aspect of a product is replaced, sometimes by the customers themselves, rather than sending out a specialist to locate a faulty part, has reduced the need for service calls. The ability to provide video demonstrations on the internet of how to perform a repair that previously required a specialized technician has improved this as an option.

Overall, then, customer service is a powerful contributor to the competitive position of an organization and its ability to maintain good customer relationships. As product reliability improves, the need for after-sales service decreases. However, a customer service package covers more than just after-sales service and should facilitate much of a customer's experience of dealing with a supplier.

Multi-channel integration

The advent of the internet plus the enormous growth in digitized products and service has meant that there has been significant innovation in routes to market, ie the channels used to both communicate with customers and to deliver products. The significance of this is that the channels used directly impact on an organization's relationships with its customers. Companies such as Direct Line in the United Kingdom and State Farm Insurance in the United States, plus easyJet, Southwest Airlines, eBay and Amazon are already competing by exploiting a range of IT-enabled remote channels to add value and/or reduce costs. For other businesses, the challenge is deciding how to respond to the opportunities and threats these pose and deciding what range of channels should be encompassed.

Packages for sales force automation, direct mail, telemarketing, customer service, e-commerce and marketing analysis have all been available for some time, both individually and in combination, as integrated customer relationship management systems. But these packages, while providing an essential infrastructure, need to be supplemented by managerial processes to address such questions as: 'which channels to use' and 'how should they work together to deliver customer value?'

Research from Cranfield School of Management suggests that companies will select from the following broad channel options:

- A single channel strategy uses one channel for the bulk of customer interactions. Direct Line and First Direct, for example, both started as telephone operations. In the internet world, being an internet only business, such as Amazon and eBay, is referred to as a 'pure play' business model.

- A migration strategy starts with one single channel and then migrates customers to another channel on the grounds of increased value or reduced cost. Thus, easyJet initially sold tickets by telephone but now provides financial incentives to its price-sensitive customers to buy online – most of whom now do so. State Farm started using agents and brokers, but now has a multitude of channel options for its customers.

- A discrete multi-channel strategy uses different channels to perform different tasks over a customer's life cycle. As an example, Thomas Cook's corporate foreign exchange business uses the internet to generate leads, a direct sales force to sign up new clients and a call centre or the internet to take orders. Other organizations will recruit new customers by direct mail, e-mail or call centre and then use the internet to manage transactions and then the telephone to check on customer satisfaction and to ensure repeat purchases.

- An integrated multi-channel strategy involves offering different channels to the customer without attempting to influence which one the customer uses. First Direct, for instance, now offers both telephone and internet channels as equal alternatives, although the internet has much lower unit costs and has also proved better for cross-selling. However, since First Direct competes on the basis of customer service, it accepts the higher costs generated by telephone customers without penalty or the offer of reward to internet users.

- A channel segmentation strategy offers different channels to different customer groups to meet their varying needs. Each of these routes to market may use the same or different brand names. The insurer Zurich's multiple brands (Allied Dunbar, Zurich, Eagle Star and Threadneedle) use different routes to market (a direct sales force, independent financial advisers and company pension schemes etc) in order to serve customer groups with differing needs and attitudes.

- A customer value strategy uses channels selectively according to the financial value of the customers. Many IT firms use account managers for high-value customers but steer smaller customers to lower-cost channels such as the internet, call centres or value-added resellers. Some insurance companies will similarly use brokers for larger clients and the internet for smaller accounts.

Customer preferences

When deciding on the extent to which an integrated channel strategy is required, the starting point must be customers themselves. If organizations do not offer them the channels they prefer, a competitor will. However, the business risk of using new channels requires organizations to attempt to predict customer take-up. Figure 50.1 illustrates a simple technique for doing this based on the 'customer value curve'.

The first step is to establish those factors that determine a customer's choice of supplier. These are shown on the horizontal axis of Figure 50.1, along with weightings out of 100 representing their relative importance in the buying decision. These factors will vary by customer segment. In the segment illustrated, customers are most interested in the cost they incur –

FIGURE 50.1   Choosing channels: the value curve

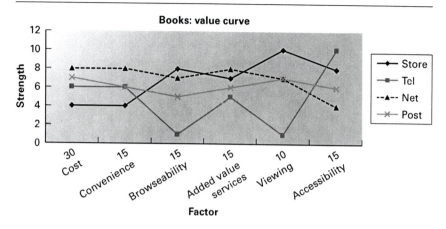

the book price plus any other charges such as delivery – but are also concerned with a number of other factors such as convenience of purchase and the ability to browse for the book they want. The channel choices might include a traditional bookshop; telephone ordering from a magazine advert; an internet store such as Amazon, or purchase through the post from a book catalogue.

The ability of each current or future channel to deliver against each factor is then either researched or subjectively assessed and allocated a score out of 10. In this example, it can be seen that taking all the factors together, the internet and physical stores have the best matches.

One factor in assessing a channel's economics is the transaction costs involved. The TPN Register (an interactive catalogue-management service now owned by General Electric) enables a purchaser to develop and customize a private catalogue that reflects their preferred suppliers and negotiated terms of business. This allows customers and suppliers to gain transaction cost savings. However, customer acquisition and retention costs should not be forgotten. The 'dotcom' arm of one retail chain recently discovered that customer acquisition through banner advertising was costing £700 per customer, when the average sale was only £50 – good news for this bricks-and-clicks retailer in its competition with pure-play 'dotcoms', as it could leverage its physical stores for customer acquisition at a cost of just £13 per customer.

How channels work together

In most markets, purchasers use a number of channels in combination to meet their needs at different stages of their relationship with a supplier.

This can be demonstrated using channel-chain analysis as illustrated in Figure 50.2.

FIGURE 50.2   Channel-chain analysis: the corporate PC market

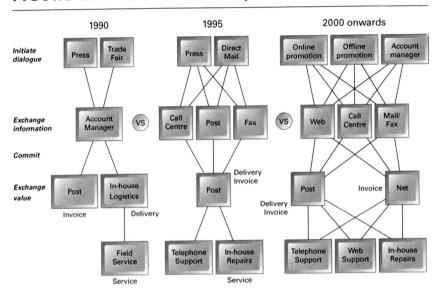

A useful tool in looking at how channels need to work together is channel-chain analysis. This involves identifying which channels are used at which stages of the purchase and value delivery process. In this example from the business-to-business PC market, three of the common channel-chains being used by various competitors are illustrated. The stages of the process are listed on the left of the diagram, and the channels used at each stage are listed against that stage. The channel used for one stage will often affect which channel is likely to be used at the next stage, as shown by the lines joining each box.

The channel-chain on the left shows the traditional account management approach, as used by most competitors at the start of the 1990s, when the sales process was largely handled face to face by account managers. In those days, the purchase of any PC usually went through a direct sales person or a value added reseller. This approach continues to be used for the sale of larger computer installations or systems development contracts.

With the introduction of 'selling from the page' in the mid-1990s, as illustrated in the middle of Figure 50.2, press advertising became the dominant marketing tool for the early stages of a purchase, with further information being provided by product brochures and call centre staff. The actual order could be placed by a number of means – often a traditional fax or mailed order placed by the accounts department.

More recently, many competitors have added the internet to the channel mix, as illustrated on the right. However, most of these are not pure-play internet providers. Account managers might serve major accounts, building relationships and negotiating service contracts and discount levels while using their websites to allow customers to configure their products and establish base level prices. The order itself is as likely to be placed over the web and confirmed by e-mail.

Having drawn the channel-chains in current use, the next step is to consider possible future channel-chains. For some markets, e-tailers are replacing store-based business and interactive TV is expanding in the range of products it sells. This requires experimentation with channel-chain diagrams to think through, not just how sales can be made, but also how all aspect of a customer's needs will be satisfied. For example, will a mobile phone purchaser buying over the web be able to return a faulty phone to a nearby store? Will an e-hub be able to handle not just price negotiations, but also information flows on stock levels, complaints, returns and product development – and if not, what additional channels will be needed?

The acid test of whether a channel-chain will flourish is whether it represents a better value proposition to some group of customers. Channel-chain analysis can be a useful way of evaluating the alternatives.

Integrated marketing communication and distribution channels

As distribution channels proliferate with the advent of new media and improved physical distribution infrastructure, the distinction between communications channels and sales and distribution channels is steadily reducing. At the same time, this increase in choice has encouraged further fragmentation within markets with individual customers preferring different sales and communications channels. Integrating these channels within a coherent strategy is not an easy task. The first task is to choose which medium to use for which customer interactions. The choices are illustrated in Figure 51.1.

FIGURE 51.1   Communications plan

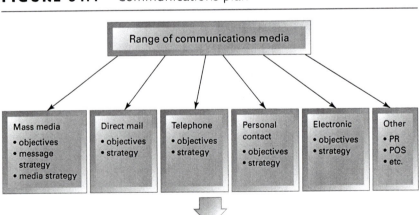

Integrated marketing communications plan

The choice of medium is generally a complex one involving different media for different communications and product delivery with the same customer. For example, a Hewlett Packard (HP) customer may find out about the company from colleagues or from press advertising; investigate which product to buy, what the price is and what configuration is required using the HP website, a PC retailer and web-based discussion groups; print out order details and pass them to the purchasing department to place the order via phone, e-mail or direct via their website; check on the delivery time via telephone or interactive web dialogue; take delivery via a parcels service or from a retailer; and obtain customer service using technical help telephone lines or e-mailed communications. Customers are no longer content to have the medium dictated by the supplier.

From this illustration, it can be seen that the choice of communications medium has to be closely connected to the distribution strategy. Distribution channels often have a mix of purposes:

1 conveying a physical product to the customer;

2 adding value through packaging, extras, product information etc;

3 communicating and exchanging information with the customer.

A garage selling motor cars, for example, provides product preparation (cleaning, testing accessories), comparative information on the model, an opportunity for a test drive, a location where price negotiations can occur, and a location for the physical delivery of the car to the customer, as well as post-purchase service and problem-solving. A clothes shop provides a location where information about a garment can be exchanged by trying it on, feeling it, examining labels and talking to a shop assistant. Such detailed information exchange would be hard to replicate using cyber-marketing approaches.

Basing promotional strategies on information exchange in this way encourages an organization to forge close linkage with the physical issues of distribution. As illustrated in Figure 51.2 the physical development of a tangible product and many service products provides numerous opportunities for communications with the market and individual customers/consumers. This is a far more sophisticated model of marketing communications and forces a direct link with operations distribution channels.

In this model, sales personnel will be included in communications plans as the key messages at the core of a communications plan will need to be supported by field and call centre sales staff. Key sales people and managers will therefore need to be included in both formal presentations and informal briefings and decision making. Performance targets in terms of message continuity, sales seminars and the reporting of customer information exchanges could all have measurable objectives associated with them.

Thinking of communications as an interactive process, rather than a one-way stream of promotional activity, adds new dimensions to sales planning. A classical sales and communications programme might include a direct

FIGURE 51.2 Value Chain and associated communications activities

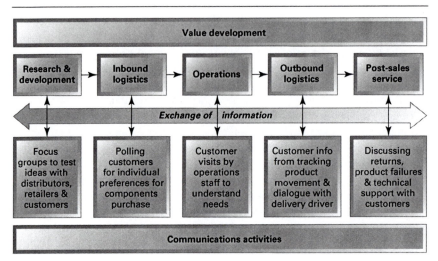

mail campaign, banner adverts on various websites, participation in a number of web forums or webinars, some in-store promotions, and so on. The overall approach can be described as a 'push' strategy whereby customers are identified and/or found, and then invited and/or persuaded to make a purchase. Under an interaction approach, communications are seen more as a dialogue in which information is exchanged and the propensity to purchase becomes the subject of negotiation. As product customization becomes increasingly feasible in a larger number of industries, and markets become more fragmented, the potential for sales based on such interactive dialogue becomes much greater.

The ability to capitalize on these developments and the potential for integrating communications and distribution channels does, however, depend on senior managers understanding the opportunity and adjusting the organization's processes accordingly. As an example, an international business-to-business financial services organization was one of the first in its sector to develop a website. Their early experience immediately identified that the site enabled them to reach new customers considerably more cost-effectively than their traditional sales force. When the website was first launched, potential customers were finding the company on the web, deciding the products were appropriate on the basis of the website, and sending an e-mail to ask to buy. So far, so good.

However, stuck in a traditional mindset about the sales process, the company allocated the e-mail or 'lead' to a salesperson, who would phone up and make an appointment, perhaps three weeks hence. This gave the customer plenty of opportunity to investigate other suppliers and even to purchase from a competitor who could respond faster. Those that didn't were subjected to a sales pitch complete with glossy materials, which was totally unnecessary, the customer having already decided to buy. Those that were not put off would proceed to be registered as able to buy over the web, but the company had lost the opportunity to improve its margins by using the sales force more judiciously.

In time, the company realized its mistake, and changed its sales model and reward systems to something close to the interactive model. Unlike those prospects that the company proactively identified and contacted, which might indeed need 'selling' to, many new web customers were initiating the dialogue themselves and simply required the company to respond effectively and rapidly. The sales force was increasingly freed up to concentrate on major clients and on relationship building.

The changing perspective of sales processes and broader communication opportunities clearly raises questions for the design of marketing communications, such as: Who initiates the dialogue, and how do we measure the effectiveness of our attempts to do so across multiple channels? How do we monitor the effectiveness not just of what we say to customers but what they say back? And how about the role of marketing communications as part of the value that is being delivered and paid for, not just as part of the sales cost?

PART SEVEN
Planning and control

Forecasting sales

Forecasting sales is a core organizational driver on the back of which resource and production activities depend. Unplanned changes to capacity are always expensive and usually lag behind the need that led to the requirement for change. During times of relative economic stability or consistent growth rates, sales forecasts could be made with some degree of certainty and the variation between forecast and actual sales tends not to be large. As the 21st century unfolds, however, the size and complexity of the marketing task in all areas of economic activity has increased substantially. At the time of writing, the collapse of the financial 'bubble' created by mortgage lending unsupported by the values of the properties being lent against has instigated global economic instability. Taken together with the consequences of extreme weather, many markets are now subject to a regular cycle of unpredictable crises so that the norm is now uncertainty rather than the extrapolation of trend.

Where there are trends, they are in terms of shorter product life cycles; changed distribution channels; growing internationalization; almost instant spread of information and huge increases in the volumes of information available. Although trends, they have not made forecasting any easier. In consequence, forecasting cannot be performed with anything like the accuracy that was possible when markets were more stable. Nevertheless, it is a necessary task and one that has to be done well given the impact that a sales forecast has on capacity management. Crucial to forecasting that will have positive benefits is a good understanding of the differences between macro and micro forecasting and the ability to utilize both qualitative and quantitative methods.

The selection of an appropriate forecasting approach or set of techniques is dependent on four main factors:

- the degree of accuracy required, which will depend on the risk associated with the decisions that will be based on the forecast;
- the availability of good data and information, which will determine the techniques that can be utilized for making forecasts;
- the time horizon required, which will be determined by the time it takes to alter capacity within the organization;

- the length of a product's life cycle and its position on it, which will influence both the time horizons and types of data sought.

Macro and micro forecasting

Macro forecasting is essentially concerned with forecasting markets in total. In adopting a macro approach, the emphasis is on observing the broad picture and, from that, deducing the implications for the products and markets in which an organization is interested. Some form of macro forecasting has to precede the setting of marketing objectives and strategies. Other forecasts should come after the enterprise has decided which specific market opportunities it wants to take advantage of and how this can best be done.

Micro forecasting is more concerned with detailed unit forecasts and should normally come after the organization has set its major objectives and strategies. These obviously deal with shorter time horizons such as an organization's sales predictions for the next period. For this type of forecast, extrapolative techniques may be appropriate, although the frequency of disruption and the length of a time period will determine how appropriate. Because extrapolation is based on the assumption that what has happened in the past will be a guide to what will happen in the future, it is a technique that must be used cautiously. A more appropriate micro approach is to build up, from an individual customer level, an estimate of what the total sales of a product could be for the period in question.

Forecasting techniques

While there are many techniques that can be used for forecasting, they usually fall into one of two categories: quantitative techniques and qualitative methods. Quantitative approaches, as the name implies, refer to a forecast made on a numerical basis of some kind and mostly involve some form of statistical analysis. Qualitative estimates are more intuitive in nature and rely on the skills of individuals in interpreting the world around them as they see it, based on their experience, the quality of their imagination and their knowledge of the area under discussion. In the end, the outcome of a qualitative forecast should, of course, also be quantitative in nature. It is the methods of arriving at the projection that differ.

It is also the case that, particularly at a macro level, it would be unusual if either of these methods were used entirely on their own, mainly because of the inherent dangers in each. Thus a combination of approaches is usually far more appropriate. As an example, it is comparatively easy to develop an equation that will extrapolate statistically the world population up to, say, the year 2020. The problem here is that the method would not have taken account of likely changes in past trends. Better would be an approach that listed a whole series of possible events that could affect world population, and then assigned probabilities to the likelihood of those events happening. From this, a more sophisticated and more realistic forecast could be produced.

A similar approach is adopted by many business forecasters who use leading indicators, ie indices of related or even non-related activities as aids to estimating changes in market conditions at a macro level. Examples include:

- any of the internationally recognized Ordinary Share Indexes, which are reckoned to provide a lead of about six months;
- new housing starts, which can give a lead of about 10 months;
- the net acquisition of financial assets by companies, which can be used as a lead for about 12 months.

Such indicators will only provide approximate pictures of general business conditions and cannot be guaranteed to offer consistent correlations. On the other hand, forecasters' experience and understanding of business may lead them to see a close fit between seemingly unrelated activity and the sales performance of a particular product.

In recent years, there has also been a considerable growth in the use of marketing models to provide a macro-type basis for sales estimation. Generally, these models incorporate a number of statistically derived relationships drawn from empirical observations, the purpose of which is to explain the observed market behaviour in terms of marketing trends. However, not everybody is enthusiastic about such models, particularly if they are used for large-scale situations, because of the problems of quantifying what are often qualitative and intangible relationships. In addition, such relationships will often change considerably over time, thereby making the model obsolete. Another factor militating against the use of models is the considerable expense involved in collecting the necessary data.

An example of a qualitative macro estimation technique is the Delphi forecast (named after the Greek oracle who foretold the future). Here, a group of experts discuss a problem, such as, 'how will retailing be structured by the year 2025?' and give their consensus of the answer to this problem. An alternative qualitative technique, 'scenario development', involves alternative futures being established based on different outcomes in key areas of uncertainty. The internet has also enabled advances in crowd forecasting, which is based on the maxim that the crowd (the mob, the masses) collectively know better than the individual expert. At present this is gaining popularity in financial markets but is equally applicable to a wide variety of market circumstances.

As noted, good micro approaches are based on building up, from an individual customer level, an estimate of what total sales of the product could be in a given period. Quantitative micro methods often involve surveys of actual and/or potential customers or seek to extract information from internal sources. The ability to seek views from online purchasers by persuading them to take a quick survey following completion of the purchase has significantly aided this process. Although the procedures involved can be quite sophisticated, these studies still rely on indications from respondents as to their likely purchasing behaviour. Qualitative micro estimates will be derived from a variety of assessments such as the judgement of members of the sales force concerning future sales, the level of retailer optimism or detailed observation of an individual's purchase behaviour.

Forecasting and uncertainty

Because forecasting deal with uncertainties, market forecasters need to establish the nature of the 'either/or' associated with the area under study. Thus, the output of a forecast should be expressed in terms of a range of possible outcomes. Beyond this, it should also be recognized that the process by which any market prediction is achieved is essentially probabilistic. Forecasts thus can, and should, be made to incorporate the probabilities that are implicit in a marketing environment.

As an example, sales forecasters will want to establish the proportion of a total market that will represent their 'addressable' market and the share they will be able to gain. This will be based on an assessment of the barriers to trade plus the effect of a specific marketing programme in competition with alternative means of satisfying the same need. The danger here is that such estimates become self-fulfilling prophecies in that both the estimate and the marketing mix programmes are dependent on each other. In this sense, a given level of market achievement is predicted by what an organization believes to be potentially achievable. More useful, here, would be alternative scenarios based on different probabilities so that optimum levels of investment can be assessed and risk factors built into the various activities of the organization.

The task of marketing managers, then, when adopting a forecasting role, is to take whatever relevant data are available to help predict the future. They must apply to them whatever quantitative techniques are appropriate, but then use qualitative methods, such as expert opinions, market research, analogy, and so on, to predict what will be the likely discontinuities in the same time series. It is only through sensible use of the available tools that management will begin to understand what has to be done to match its own capabilities with carefully selected market needs. Without such an understanding, any form of forecasting is likely to be a sterile exercise.

Marketing planning

All organizations operate in a complex environment, in which hundreds of external and internal factors interact to affect their ability to achieve their objectives. Managers need some understanding, or view, about how all these variables interact and they must try to be rational about their decisions, no matter how important intuition, feel and experience are as contributory factors in this process of rationality. Most managers accept that some kind of formalized procedure for planning the organization's marketing helps to sharpen this rationality so as to reduce the complexity of business operations and add a dimension of realism to the organization's hopes for the future.

The essence of marketing planning

The contribution of marketing planning to organizational success, whatever its area of activity, lies in its commitment to detailed analysis of future opportunities to meet customer needs, and a wholly professional approach to selling to well-defined market segments, products or services that deliver the sought-after benefits. Such commitment and activities, however, must not be mistaken for budget forecasts, which have always been a commercial necessity. The process of marketing planning is a more sophisticated approach concerned with identifying what, and to whom, sales are going to be made in the longer term to enable revenue budgets and sales forecasts to have any chance of being achieved.

In essence, marketing planning is a managerial process, the output of which is a marketing plan. As such, it is a logical sequence and a series of activities leading to the setting of marketing objectives and the formulation of plans for achieving them. Conceptually, the process is very simple and is achieved by means of a planning system. The system is little more than a structured way of identifying a range of options for the organization, of making them explicit in writing, of formulating marketing objectives that are consistent with the company's overall objectives and of scheduling and costing the specific activities most likely to bring about the achievement of the objectives. It is the systemization of this process that lies at the heart of the theory of marketing planning.

Types of marketing plan

There are two principal kinds of marketing plan:

- the strategic marketing plan;
- the tactical marketing plan.

The strategic marketing plan is a plan for three or more years. It is the written document that outlines how managers perceive their organization's position in their markets relative to their competitors (with competitive advantage accurately defined), what objectives they want to achieve, how they intend to achieve them (strategies), what resources are required, and with what results (budget). Three years is the most frequent planning period for strategic marketing plans. Five years is the longest period and this is becoming less common as a result of the speed of technological and environmental change. The exceptions here are the very long-range plans formulated by a number of Japanese companies, which can have planning horizons of between 50 and 200 years!

The tactical marketing plan is the detailed scheduling and costing of the specific actions necessary for the achievement of the first year of a strategic marketing plan. The tactical plan is thus usually for one year.

Research into the marketing planning practices of organizations shows that successful ones complete the strategic plan before the tactical plan. Unsuccessful organizations frequently do not bother with a strategic marketing plan at all, relying largely on sales forecasts and the associated budgets. The problem with this approach is that many managers sell the products and services they find easiest to sell to those customers who offer the least line of resistance. By developing short-term, tactical marketing plans first and then extrapolating them, managers merely succeed in extrapolating their own shortcomings. Preoccupation with preparing a detailed marketing plan first is typical of those companies that confuse sales forecasting and budgeting with strategic marketing planning.

The contents of a strategic marketing plan

The contents of a strategic marketing plan are:

- Mission statement: sets out the raison d'être of the organization and covers its role, business definition, distinctive competence, and future indications.

- Financial summary: summarizes the financial implications over the full planning period.
- Market overview: provides a brief picture of the market and includes market structure, market trends, key market segments, and (sometimes) gap analysis.
- SWOT analyses: the strengths and weaknesses of the organization compared with competitors against key customer success factors plus the organization's opportunities and threats, which is normally completed for each key product or segment.
- Issues to be addressed: these are derived from the SWOT analyses and are usually specific to each product or segment.
- Portfolio summary: a pictorial summary of the SWOT analyses that makes it easy to see, at a glance, the relative importance of each area of activity. It is often a two-dimensional matrix in which the horizontal axis measures the organization's comparative strengths and the vertical axis measures its relative attractiveness.
- Assumptions: assumptions that are critical to the planned marketing objectives and strategies.
- Marketing objectives: quantitative statements in terms of profit, volume, value and market share, of what the organization wishes to achieve. They are usually stated by product, by segment, and overall.
- Marketing strategies: activities that will enable the objectives to be achieved and often involve the four Ps of marketing: product; price; place; and promotion.
- Resource requirements and budget: the full planning period budget, showing in detail, for each year, the revenues and associated costs.

The contents of a tactical marketing plan

The contents of a tactical marketing plan are very similar, except that it often omits the mission statement, the market overview and SWOT analyses, and goes into much more detailed quantification by product and segment of marketing objectives and associated strategies. An additional feature is a much more detailed scheduling and costing of the tactics necessary to the achievement of the first year of the plan.

The marketing planning timetable

While Figure 53.1 depicts the relationship between the marketing planning process and the output of that process, the strategic and tactical marketing

FIGURE 53.1 Strategic and tactical marketing plans

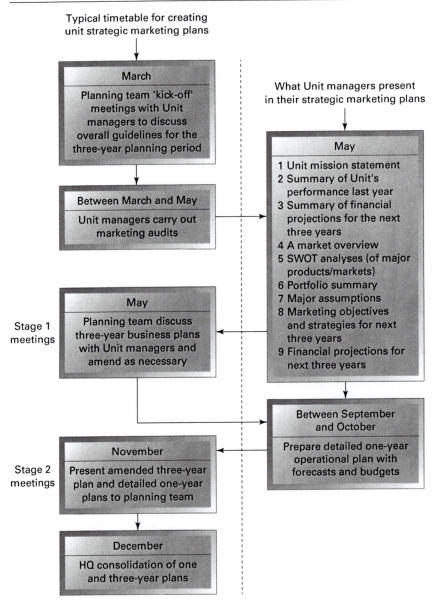

Typical timetable for creating unit strategic marketing plans

March
Planning team 'kick-off' meetings with Unit managers to discuss overall guidelines for the three-year planning period

Between March and May
Unit managers carry out marketing audits

Stage 1 meetings

May
Planning team discuss three-year business plans with Unit managers and amend as necessary

What Unit managers present in their strategic marketing plans

May
1 Unit mission statement
2 Summary of Unit's performance last year
3 Summary of financial projections for the next three years
4 A market overview
5 SWOT analyses (of major products/markets)
6 Portfolio summary
7 Major assumptions
8 Marketing objectives and strategies for next three years
9 Financial projections for next three years

Between September and October
Prepare detailed one-year operational plan with forecasts and budgets

Stage 2 meetings

November
Present amended three-year plan and detailed one-year plans to planning team

December
HQ consolidation of one and three-year plans

Note: The marketing planning progress must not be confused with what appears in the plan itself, which is described on the right.

plans, Figure 53.2 shows the same process in a circular form. This indicates more realistically the ongoing nature of the marketing planning process and the link between strategic and tactical marketing plans.

FIGURE 53.2   Strategic and operational planning cycle

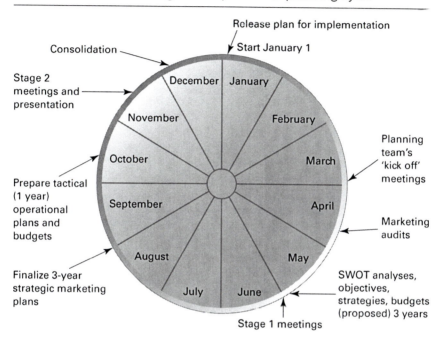

Marketing vs business plans

Good marketing plans and business plans have many overlaps since they both try to provide an overview of important managerial processes. However, marketing plans do not cover other areas of a business such as operational activities, financial management and HR developments, which are all areas that will be referenced in a full business plan. A marketing plan should, however, provide clear market-based performance requirements that will act as a starting point for, say, engineering plans, cash flow forecasts, logistics planning, and so on, so that they are co-ordinated with the relevant aspects of the marketing mix. The challenge for senior managers is finding a way of bringing all these together in one larger and comprehensive corporate or business plan.

Barriers to implementing marketing planning systems

Successfully implemented marketing planning systems will have profound benefits for a business. However, recent research has confirmed that 80 per cent of organizations do not have an integrated, co-ordinated and internally consistent plan for their marketing activities. The most frequently encountered barriers to successful marketing planning are shown in Table 54.1 and elaborated below.

TABLE 54.1   Barriers to the integration of strategic marketing planning

1   Weak support from the chief executive and top management.

2   Lack of a plan for planning.

3   Lack of line management support.

4   Confusion over planning terms.

5   Numbers in lieu of written objectives and strategies.

6   Too much detail, too far ahead.

7   Once-a-year ritual.

8   Separation of operational planning from strategic planning.

9   Failure to integrate marketing planning into a total corporate planning system.

10   Delegation of planning to a planner.

Weak support from chief executive and top management

Since the chief executive and top management are the key influencers in a company, without their active support and participation any formalized marketing planning system is unlikely to work. Any sign of indifference or greater interest in another area of activity will very quickly destroy the credibility that emerging plans might have had. This is the most frequently encountered barrier to effective marketing planning.

Lack of a plan for planning

The next most common cause of failure is the belief that, once a system is designed, it can be implemented immediately. One company became very worried when it achieved virtually no improvement in the quality of the plans coming into headquarters a year after the introduction of a very sophisticated system. Evidence indicates that in fact a period of around three years is required in an organization of any size before a complete marketing planning system can be implemented. Failure or partial failure is often the result of ignoring the:

- requirement to communicate the reasons a marketing planning system is necessary;
- need to recruit top management support and participation;
- necessity to test the system out on a limited basis to demonstrate its effectiveness and value;
- importance of training programmes, or workshops, to train the management in its use;
- lack of date and information in some parts of the world;
- shortage of resources in some parts of the world.

Lack of line management support

Hostility on the part of line managers to the introduction of new marketing planning systems is a further barrier. This is usually because the person responsible for introducing the planning system has not developed a plan for implementing the system or engaging other functional managers. New systems inevitably require considerable explanation of the procedures involved and are usually accompanied by *pro formas*, flow charts and the like. Often these devices are most conveniently presented in the form of a manual.

When such a document arrives on the desk of a busy line manager, unheralded by previous explanation or discussion, the immediate reaction is concern that they it will take up too much of their time, that they won't be able to understand and comply with it, followed by anger, and finally rejection. They begin to picture headquarters as a remote 'ivory tower' totally divorced from the reality.

Allied to this is the fact that many line managers are ignorant of basic marketing principles, have never been used to breaking up their markets into strategically relevant segments, nor to collecting meaningful information about them. This lack of skill is compounded by the fact that there are many countries in the world that cannot match the wealth of useful information and data available in the United States and Europe. The problem of a lack of reliable data and information can only be solved through the investment of time and money. Where available resources are scarce, it is unlikely that the information demands of headquarters can be met.

Confusion over planning terms

The people given responsibilities for implementing a marketing planning system frequently use planning terminology that is perceived by operational managers as meaningless jargon. Those companies with successful planning systems try to use terminology that will be familiar to operational managers and where terms such as 'objectives' and 'strategies' are clearly defined, with examples given of their practical use.

Numbers in lieu of written objectives and strategies

Most managers in operating units are accustomed to completing sales forecasts together with the associated financial implications. They are not accustomed to considering underlying causal factors for past performance or expected results, nor to highlighting opportunities, emphasizing key issues, and so on. Their tendency is to extrapolate numbers and to project the current business unchanged into the next fiscal year. When a marketing planning system suddenly requires that they make explicit their understanding of the drivers for their business, they often struggle.

Too much detail, too far ahead

Connected with this is the problem of over planning, usually caused by elaborate systems that demand information and data that headquarters do not need and can never use. Systems that require vast quantities of data are generally demotivating for all concerned and give rise to the impression that HQ is a 'black hole' from which nothing ever emerges.

Once-a-year ritual

A very common problem with marketing planning systems is the ritualistic nature of the activity. In such cases, operating managers treat the writing of the marketing plan as an unpleasant duty. The *pro formas* are completed, but not always diligently, and the resulting plans are quickly filed away never to be referred to again. They are seen as something that is required by headquarters rather than as an essential tool of management. In other words, the production of the marketing plan is seen as a sort of game of management bluff.

Separation of operational planning from strategic planning

Most companies make long-term projections. Unfortunately, in the majority of cases these are totally separate from short-term planning activity. This separation tends to discourage operational managers from thinking strategically. In reality, detailed operational plans should be the first year of the long-term plan, and operational managers should be encouraged to complete their long-term projections and then continue in the same timeframe to develop their short-term projections. This will encourage managers to think about what decisions have to be made in the current planning year to achieve the long-term projections.

Failure to integrate marketing planning into a total corporate planning system

It is difficult to initiate an effective marketing planning system in the absence of a parallel corporate planning system. This is yet another facet of the separation of operational from strategic planning. Unless similar processes and timescales to those being used in the marketing planning system are also being used by other major functions such as distribution, production, finance and personnel, the sort of trade-offs and compromises that have to be made in any company between what is wanted and what is practicable and affordable, will not take place in a rational way.

Another facet of this is the lack of participation of key functions of the company, such as engineering or production. Where these are key determinants of success, as in capital goods companies, a separate marketing planning system is virtually ineffective. Where marketing is a major activity, as in companies with fast-moving goods, it is sometimes possible to implement a separate marketing planning system.

Delegation of planning to a planner

Planners should really act as co-ordinators of planning, not as creators of goals and strategies for other parts of the business. However, if operational management are unwilling to co-operate, a planner becomes powerless. If the board then demand presentations of a master plan, the planning manager often ends up formulating objectives and strategies unconnected with operational realities rather than admitting their ineffectualness. Thus, it is more the lack of line management skills and commitment plus inadequate organizational structures that frustrates the company's marketing planning efforts, rather than inadequacies on the part of the planner

The problems are compounded by the fact that when larger organizations appoint a person with the specific title of marketing planning manager, it is often a response to the difficulty of controlling businesses. This is particularly true for those that have grown rapidly in size and diversity, which can lead to a wide array of new problems to deal with.

The key tasks of a central marketing planning manager are essentially those of system design and co-ordination of inputs plus amalgamation of business unit plans into an overall marketing plan. Underpinning this is an ability to bring about behavioural change outside their areas of control so that line managers co-operate with the planning system. Such a requirement is far-reaching in its implications and affects training, resource allocation and organizational structures. As a catalyst for change, the planner, not surprisingly, comes up against significant political barriers, the result of which is that they often become frustrated and eventually ineffective.

Conclusion

Overall, to be successful it is important to distinguish between the process of marketing planning and the output. Indeed, much of the benefit of a planning system will derive from the process of analysis and debate among relevant managers and directors rather than from the written document itself. Being aware of the barriers to implementing a successful planning system will go some way to helping organizations overcome them and obtain these benefits.

International product planning

Although there are many factors that inhibit successful international marketing, inadequate product planning is one of the more significant contributions to poor performance. This is because the product is at the heart of the marketing mix that constitutes a supplier's offer and is the first factor to which customers respond. As the leading edge of the marketing mix, the product must be as 'right' as possible to avoid becoming another export casualty that fails once they move outside their home territory. The two key questions that need to be answered to enhance the chances of success are:

- Which of its product lines should an organization sell in overseas markets?
- Does it need to adapt them for those markets?

Product line choice

In all but the most exceptional cases, overseas markets will already have similar or competing products to those a domestic supplier wishes to export. This implies that the overseas market will already support a distribution infrastructure with existing trading practices, including exclusivity agreements and networked relationships. In addition, it will imply that there are established consumer habits and preferences, competitor promotional activities and accepted pricing structures. Choosing a product line for such a market will require the identification of an opportunity derived from a good understanding of these market features. This should include:

- an analysis of potential competitor product performance;
- market usage patterns and important application requirements;
- the dynamics of the market in terms of supply chain structures, the major determinants of price, communication channels and the major positioning variables;
- customer expectations of a product.

The analysis should also seek to highlight any trends in the market that will reduce the attractiveness of products currently available and to identify any products from existing suppliers that leave a gap between customer expectations and product performance. Where an organization can identify a product line that has a cost or performance advantage that fits one of the gaps identified, it has an opportunity that it may be possible to exploit. If it has neither of these, there will be no incentive for customers to switch brands. The one exception to this will be rapid growth markets where there is an excess of demand over supply. Good examples of this were provided by Eastern Europe following the collapse of the Soviet Union where large numbers of consumers were desperate for high-profile Western consumer goods such as mobile phones. Those retailers who could obtain supplies had long queues and were unable to satisfy demand and any supplier with products, whatever the quality, could make sales.

Whatever the case, before entering the market the business must engage in product trials to ensure that the line has no fundamental weaknesses that will prohibit sales or that will be too costly to adapt. This, in turn, will be a function of market potential, market accessibility and the possible margins available.

Product adaptation

Unfortunately, it is rarely the case that a domestic product can be introduced into an overseas market without any form of adaptation. Research has shown that some of the biggest problems in product internationalization have occurred when organizations have followed the rather naive belief that products are transferable from home to foreign markets without change of some kind. Thus, product application is hardly ever universal and even globally branded products such as Coca-Cola and McDonald's use different formulations for different parts of the world to accommodate taste variations between countries.

Apart from taste and cultural influences such as colour requirements, adaptations may be required by distribution complexities not encountered in home markets. Thus packaging and unitization practices may differ by country and aspects such as product tracking mechanisms will often require modification once consignments enter a foreign land. Additionally, there are often legal or semi-legal requirements that must be satisfied. Thus, if a similar product or service already exists in a target country, there is likely to be a standard for it to which products will need to conform. Organizations must, therefore, have regard for:

- legal requirements (such as environment/pollution legislation);
- mandatory standards (such as electrical safety standards);

- industry standards (such as light alloy wheels in Germany);
- voluntary standards (such as paper size).

A further complication here is that, whereas standards are always well defined, they tend to be:

- different by country;
- many in number as a result of covering measurement, quality, material, properties, performance and safety, etc;
- different in legal backing/adherence and rationale.

As well as standards, products may also require adaptation as a consequence of the way in which they are used. Thus, other product characteristics that need to be most carefully researched in all foreign countries include:

- physical properties, such as size, weight, materials, tolerances and instrumentation;
- performance characteristics, such as mechanical, electrical and raw materials;
- others, such as applications, symbols, codes, language, commissioning and service requirements.

As examples, in respect of physical characteristics, paper size is different in photocopiers in different markets and different flour quality affects the design of baking machinery. Similarly, with reference to performance, there are different generator-size requirements in different countries and in the case of application, tyre requirements differ significantly in hot countries, although the product is essentially the same. In addition, instruction and installation manuals will need to be rewritten and maintenance requirements may need to be altered to take account of service facilities in other countries.

Service products are no exception to these difficulties either. Different legislative regimes may make an insurance product inadequate for other countries or a different attitude towards litigation may require policies to be sold at a higher price to ensure an adequate loss ratio.

While it is tempting to stop at product/market analysis, it is also prudent to consider product adaptation at a much broader or company level. Thus, it might be important for an organization to consider whether it has: the design/technical capability; the raw material processing capability; the labour know-how; the equipment/technical know-how; the correct production processes, such as special assembly versus batch assembly; and so on. If inadequately thought through, there may be significant consequences for the organization. As an example, power cables manufactured in Europe had to be produced on different machines using additional tooling in order to create a product that conformed to the market requirements of another part of the world. In turn, this led to pressure on existing workflows resulting in a production plan change and consequent capacity constraints, slower throughputs, lower earnings for employees and, worst of all, increased production costs.

Overall, issues such as these imply that the financial risks involved in entering overseas markets need to be most carefully evaluated. In particular, an organization needs to be very interested in the costs of adaptation, the resulting margins, the investment requirement and the likely return on investment (ROI), leading to a preliminary assessment of the volume required in any specific foreign market. In particular, the successful international company should be looking continuously for synergy and cost savings from any essential product adaptation. These are possible from:

- economies of scale in production;
- economies in product research and development;
- economies in marketing as a result of consumer mobility;
- the impact of technology.

To plan satisfactorily for these circumstances, product managers thus have to be rigorous in their approach as summarized in Table 55.1.

TABLE 55.1 Areas requiring attention in international product planning

The product's functionality	Standardization Adaptation
Packaging and labelling	Protection/security Promotional/channel aspects Cultural factors Package size Language
Brands and trade markets	Global or national Legal Cultural Other marketing considerations
Warranty and service	Transferability of domestic terms and conditions Safety Varying quality control standards internationally Varying use conditions Service networks

Organizational structure and marketing

One of the problems organizations have with marketing is deciding where and how it should fit within their existing and developing structures. The first problem concerns whether or not to have a specific marketing department at all and then, if so, deciding what scope, or range of activities, it should oversee. Once a department's overall responsibilities have been determined, the next step is to decide how it should be structured and who should do what job. If it is felt that a discrete marketing department is not appropriate, establishing and maintaining strong marketing leadership throughout the organization becomes more than usually important.

The significance of these problems is that organizations can only provide the environment within which people carry out their work; they cannot determine how the work is performed. However, structures and the control systems associated with them provide evidence of how senior managers value a particular activity and the role it plays in the organization. Structure can also place hurdles in the way of people trying to get on with achieving their responsibilities by making communication, co-ordination and decision-making more difficult. Where possible, organizational structure should match the long-term objectives of the business.

Since most organizations start small, the typical evolutionary pattern for marketing is from a 'one-man-band' situation, where one person will perform all tasks and where sales essentially involve order-taking with small amounts of prospecting or advertising, to the multi-functioning super-department incorporating a whole range of specialist activities as illustrated in Figure 56.1. Thus, as an organization grows and becomes more sophisticated in its approach to marketing, the number of options for structuring its range of marketing activities increases.

FIGURE 56.1   Organizational structure and marketing

Typical evolutionary pattern of marketing

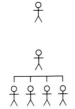

One-man band
Basically an order-taker, probably involved in technical side as well.

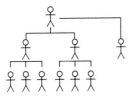

Sales team marketing
Sales people sent out to 'drum up orders'. Self-generated sales support materials.

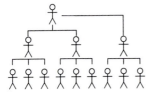

Sales force plus marketing sales support
Marketing provides materials and information which support sales activities.

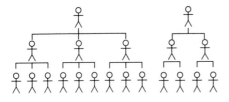

Sales force plus ancillary marketing
Marketing expands activities and employs specialists to manage a range of functions – still essentially sales support.

Separate sales and marketing departments
Marketing takes on product or brand management responsibilities and starts to coordinate/influence sales strategies.

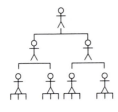

Unified sales and marketing departments
A sales and marketing director/VP appointed to coordinate all activities.

Central and decentralized activities

For multi-national or multi-region organizations, a choice has to be made between centralizing and decentralizing their marketing activities. Centralized operations make co-ordination much easier and are better at avoiding duplication. Decentralization allows for more flexibility and better exploitation of local opportunities. In this respect, there are no 'right' or 'wrong' options. The choice will depend on the organization's product diversity, the need for local variations and the management's ability to achieve a good balance between co-ordination and control. The latter is necessary to avoid fragmentation and to prevent managers feeling that they have no effective freedom of choice. Sadly, in many larger organizations, it is not uncommon for local (ie decentralized) marketing personnel to find themselves with no influence over product decisions, price or delivery and who then become frustrated at having to manage a marketing mix over which they have little control.

An ideal arrangement, of course, is to organize around a combination of both in order to gain the benefits of each. This involves putting marketing as close to the customer as possible, while also having some kind of centralized marketing function. In this way, the potential for costly and unnecessary duplication is minimized and the possibility of achieving economies of scale and effective knowledge transfer is optimized.

Departmental structures

For organizations with marketing departments, the second area of choice is the methodology for structuring the department's activities. The main decision is whether to organize around functions; products; markets; key accounts; geographical area, or some combination of two or more of these options. Traditionally structured marketing departments organize around functions such as: new product management; market research; customer service; advertising; market analysis; public relations; sales promotions/special campaigns, and so on.

A common alternative arrangement is to organize around a series of product managers who would be responsible for the whole range of activities associated with their products or brands. This usually includes co-ordinating with the sales force and third party re-sellers, as well as elsewhere within the organization. Structuring around markets usually involves the creation of market managers operating geographically, by sector, or by segment. Variations on this theme have been referred to as vertical marketing, trade marketing and industry marketing.

In cases where there are very few customers, some organizations organize around key accounts using key account managers, while others appoint marketing specialists with responsibility for all activities within a definable area. In many organizations, a combination of approaches is often in evidence.

As examples, some businesses organize around brand managers, but separate the functions of public relations, customer service, trade relations and planning, while others use both product and market managers in a matrix-type relationship as illustrated in Figure 56.2.

FIGURE 56.2 Matrix marketing department

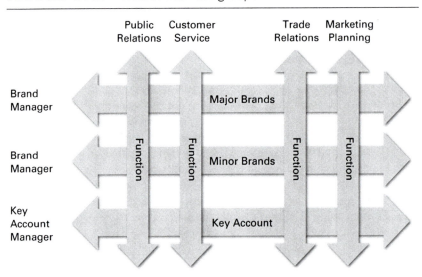

There are, however, a number of dangers inherent in any approach to the organization of marketing. For instance, if an organization structures around markets and market managers to emphasize the importance of a market orientation, they risk smaller brands being neglected, a dilution or loss of functional skills or product knowledge, and product customization increasing with a loss of the potential for economies of scale. Similarly, focusing on any area to the exclusion of others risks tasks in the other areas not being performed in as professional or as effective a way as possible. Additionally, if responsibility and control become imbalanced so that people are held accountable for areas over which they have no control, disillusionment and negative politics can result.

In fact, one of the key problems in operationalizing marketing in organizations is achieving the correct balance between responsibility and accountability in the management of the marketing mix. Marketing managers are obviously concerned to manipulate the mix to create an offer irresistible to targeted customers. Many of the elements of the marketing mix, however, are quite rightly under the control of non-marketing managers, since they require specialist or technical skills to be managed well. Marketing managers are therefore in the position of being responsible for the profitable sales of the organization's products, but without the authority to control the elements that will promote such sales. In many organizations, the conflict and poor relations that exist between sales and marketing, or operations and marketing, typifies this problem.

Process redesign

One attempt to overcome some of these difficulties has been to reorganize an organization's activities around its core processes that either obtain value from suppliers or deliver value to customers. Instead of structuring a business around its functional activities such as operations, finance and human resources, etc, some organizations have adopted processes such as new product development, order fulfilment and cost reduction as the basis for managing operating units. Each process is managed by a team, which has responsibility for delivering efficiency in that area and for meeting the objectives appropriate for competitive advantage. The teams may still be product or customer focused, depending on the nature of the business. The key difference between conventional structures and a core process, team-based approach, is that the team becomes multifunctional with responsibility for, say, inbound logistics, production, sales and supply, rather than each activity stage being a distinct and separate operation.

Under these circumstances, marketing functions would be provided by each of the teams, with ultimate marketing responsibility resting with the top team for each process. The organization would also include a specialist marketing unit, which would provide information, advice or assistance on specialist topics such as conducting market research or designing a customer service strategy. Marketing would thus be brought closer to the areas it needs to influence, since a good part of all the elements of the marketing mix would be the responsibility of the cross-functional process team. Under this approach, marketing expertise would be injected into the team either through consultancy, training or 'contracting out'.

Other developments

In addition to the 'business process redesign' described above, there are a number of other developments that can affect the position or structure of marketing within organizations.

The first of these is the decline of traditional brand management as retailers become more powerful and, in some cases, substitute brands. Rather than a brand's franchise in the market influencing the choice of supplier, retailers are now much more interested in costs, strategy alignment and response to regional differences as a basis for choosing suppliers.

The second development is the advancements being made in micro-marketing, which are encouraging marketing managers to look at differences between consumers in more elaborate ways and to use sales promotion activities and database marketing for more accurate targeting. At the time of writing, Amazon is probably the leading exponent of micro-marketing with its regular personalized e-mail communications based on previous purchases and browsing.

The third is the reduction in the effectiveness of mass advertising as media channels proliferate and as it becomes harder to reach mass markets. These trends will support moves away from national and international brand management as a basis for organizing marketing, towards market-focused management structures, either as part of a process team, as a framework based on relationships or just simply around ideas. During Christmas 2006, P&G sponsored luxury restrooms in New York's Times Square to promote Charmin toilet paper, the idea being to reach younger customers via the associated new media coverage (YouTube, Facebook, Twitter etc).

Fourth, the current popularity of category management as a basis for organizing consumer goods marketing is also affecting how suppliers organize their marketing activities. To match their retail customers, suppliers are organizing brand portfolios and appointing category managers, or 'champions', whose focus is on maximizing profit from a category for the retailer rather than developing brand franchises.

In the end, however, it must be remembered that structure is of only secondary importance in establishing marketing as an effective force within an organization. Of greater significance is the attitude of the managers working within the structures and the ways in which they are able to influence other managers towards a market-orientated approach to their own responsibilities. If a market orientation is well embedded and stretches across its range of activities, it is almost possible to argue that structure is irrelevant to marketing effectiveness.

Budgeting for marketing

One of the most vexing questions for any marketing manager, or indeed, any marketing organization, is 'How much, and where, should we spend on marketing?' The question is difficult because it requires an understanding of what should be included in a marketing budget, the way in which costs are generated and the relationship between marketing expenditure and the results sought. Each of these areas is problematic and often requires sophisticated financial information and analytical tools for the development of effective programmes and budgets.

Budgeting practices

For many organizations, such information and tools are not readily available. In their absence, the most appealing approach is to use last year's figures as the base and to project forward. This, of course, takes into account inflation plus prevailing market conditions, and adds on an amount that senior controllers will deduct at the budget review and reduces budgeting to a game of cat-and-mouse.

Zero-based budgeting

More preferable is an **iterative zero-based** approach that starts with marketing objectives and the programmes designed to achieve these objectives. Once activities have been identified, the incremental cost of these can be calculated and a budget can be established. If these are deemed to be too expensive, alternative activities or structures that will deliver the outcomes sought need to be investigated. If these alternatives still prove to be unacceptable, then the objectives need to be recast or the strategy reviewed. In this way, every item of expenditure can be traced back to specific objectives, and indeed, the overall corporate objectives of the organization. Unfortunately, many senior managers instruct their staff to reduce budgets but then expect them to deliver the same results; hence the cat-and-mouse budgeting noted above.

Variable cost budgeting

A less wide-ranging approach is to base the budget on **variable costs**, particularly for short-term budgeting, since certain costs, such as human resources and physical facilities, can only be significantly altered in the longer term. Periodically, however, this would require a zero-based approach to be used to review all products, markets and related activities. This would enable organizations to abandon obsolete and unnecessary features and to make appropriate structural alterations. Many of the moves away from brand management towards category, or business process management, are a result of such reviews.

Life cycle budgeting

Budgeting for marketing can also be based on **life cycle costing**. This involves assessments of the total costs involved in managing products over their life in the market. Such an approach requires marketing managers to plan ahead in terms of product upgrades, changing promotional activities, service and distribution support, and the way price is likely to alter over the life of a product. Long-term assessments of return on investment, payback and cash management can therefore be made, which will help both short-term budgeting control and organizational financial planning.

Operating and opportunity budgeting

A further approach utilizes the notions of **operating budget** versus **opportunity or exceptions budgets**. Operating budgets cover those activities that are a continuation of existing programmes. The key issues here are in terms of efficiency and the maintenance of expected performance levels. This highlights the fact that marketing managers should be seeking constant cost reduction plus better ways of managing the marketing mix and obtaining marketing information, while at the same time countering adverse developments. An opportunities budget should be developed for unexpected circumstances that can yield financial and marketing benefits for the organization. One of the critical roles of marketing managers is to spot such opportunities and to feed them into the general management of their enterprise. As an example, shortly after Hurricane Katrina hit the Gulf Coast, P&G sent a beverage trailer converted into a laundromat to New Orleans to wash survivors' clothes. The purpose was to support the positioning of Tide as a detergent that 'works wonders on the fabrics that touch your life'.

Marketing costs for budgeting

Since marketing management requires the development of an offer, which consists of the various elements of the marketing mix, a marketing budget should, in theory, include all costs associated with operationalizing this mix. In practice, marketing managers do not have control over all these elements. In addition, the activities over which they do have control will vary from one organization to another.

For an organization that buys in products to be sold via a direct sales force, a catalogue and a direct mail activity, the marketing budget may be comprehensive and include selling costs, order processing, stock-holding, merchandising, packaging, and credit. For a manufacturing concern with complex logistics, which sells via distributors or retailers and utilizes significant financial activities such as credit card or Electronic Data Interchange (EDI) facilities, marketing may be more focused on the generation of demand and market forecasting.

For budgeting purposes, the important factor here is to distinguish between **controllable** and **uncontrollable** costs. This is a particularly difficult problem when sales and marketing are organized as two separate activities. While marketing managers may be held accountable for sales and profits, they may have no responsibility for selling, merchandising and discounts. Thus, the contents of marketing budgets need to be set in the context of specific organizational structures, the way in which senior management see the priorities of their business and the role of marketing within it.

Costing marketing activities

Even where marketing responsibilities are clearly identifiable, budgeting problems can still arise as a result of difficulties in allocating costs between different marketing activities. As an example, the ultimate profit centre for a business is each individual customer. For industrial companies with only a handful of customers, costs and profits may be easy to identify on a customer basis. Where larger numbers of customers exist, the allocation of expenditures such as advertising, sales and customer service between customers becomes confused. This is especially so when some customers can be easy to sell to while others may require much greater efforts. Similarly, some customers may place great demands on their suppliers, while others may be more self-sufficient. In addition, some customers may take a very profitable mix of products while others may only purchase those with low margins.

As a response and to reduce confusion, some organizations have developed accounting systems that enable customer account profitability to be established. Thus, establishing the profitability of a customer may be a very confusing process. In others, it is differences in the costs generated by different products that are more significant. One product may be quick and easy to move around while others may be more awkward, require greater protective packaging or require more explanation for customers. Here systems that can identify direct product profitability are used.

The problem for marketing managers lies in determining the most profitable courses of action and in targeting the organization's activities in the best way possible. This requires good information about both customer profitability and product profitability, and as indicated, it may be hard to attribute costs in a way that will yield the appropriate information. In addition, the expected results of different types of campaign such as sales promotions, additional sales people, product upgrades and price adjustments may also be difficult to judge.

Some assistance can be gained from historical data, which can be used to assess trends or to establish relationships between expenditure and results. Unfortunately, simple input/output relationships rarely exist in marketing, except at a very low level, since purchases are the result of a complex series of events that are unlikely to repeat themselves from one time period to another. In the end, marketing managers must utilize both the information that does exist and their professional judgement based on experience plus sound marketing principles, to set their budgets.

Overall, then, budgeting for marketing is an imprecise science and will depend on an organization's structure, its approach to marketing and the sophistication of its information systems for its quality. The process can be enhanced by focusing on the areas that are important to a business and ensuring that expenditure is related to specific marketing objectives. Distinguishing between order-filling activities and order-getting activities can help identify marketing responsibilities and a basis for analysing the effectiveness of marketing activities. Ultimately, however, a marketing budget should be a managerial tool, not just a financial device. The interweaving of a market orientation into all areas of operations so that appropriate judgements can be made, will be most beneficial in directing and controlling marketing expenditure.

Legal issues in marketing

Marketers and general managers alike will probably know and understand the differences between, say, an Ansoff and a Boston Matrix. It is less likely that they will know the difference between contract and tort or, for that matter, the difference between civil and criminal law. More dangerously, they may be completely unaware that a claim in a news release could be subject to review by the Committee of Advertising Practice or that a promotional offer cannot be reneged upon if it proves too costly.

Unfortunately, ignorance of the law as it applies to modern marketing and marketing communication is no longer acceptable in today's highly litigious environment, which saw two giants of the mobile world slug it out over the rights to use the colour orange in 2006. A more recent example is provided by Apple's 2012 vigorous pursuit of Samsung for claimed patent infringements by various smartphones, media players and tablets that they had released in the preceding 12 months.

Rules and regulations have a purpose in business and marketing best practice should comply automatically with the laws of the country in which an organization operates. Thus, a business based in London should conform to British and EU laws; although given the very frequent changes, it can't always be assumed that this is always the case. Be that is it may, most law and regulation is based on common sense, so any person who finds themselves engaged in activities likely to discredit, rather than enhance, strengthen or protect, your organization's reputation, is highly likely to be doing something that is unlawful as well.

Navigating any legal quagmire, however, will require more than just cursory knowledge of basic legal issues. As a response, most countries have a series of (now online) resources that can assist interested parties to distinguish the legal from the illegal. For the United Kingdom, examples of sources of legal information include:

- Advertising Standards Authority (**www.asa.org.uk**)
- Brand Republic (**www.brandrepublic.com**)
- British Copyright Council (**www.britishcopyright.org**)
- Committee of Advertising Practice (**www.cap.org.uk**)
- European Commission Office (**http://ec.europa.eu/index_en.htm**)

- Ethics Resource Centre (**www.ethics.org**)
- Equality and Human Rights Commission (**www.equalityhumanrights.com**)
- Ministry of Justice (**www.justice.gov.uk**)
- Information Commissioner's Office (**www.ico.gov.uk**)
- Mailing Preference Service (**www.mpsonline.org.uk**)
- Office of Communications (**www.ofcom.org.uk**)
- Office of Fair Trading (**www.oft.gov.uk**)
- Pinsent Masons (**www.out-law.com**)

In the United States, there is a similar range of sites to help map the legal landscape, such as:

- Government (**www.usa.gov/topics/consumer.shtml**)
- US Patent and Trademark Office (**www.uspto.gov/inventors/patents.jsp**)
- Marketing Today (**http://marketingtoday.com/marketinglaws/usmarketinglaws.htm**)
- Federal Trade Commission (**www.ftc.gov**)

In general, there are three distinct ways in which laws and regulations impact the marketing practitioner, as illustrated in Figure 58.1.

FIGURE 58.1   Three faces of the law

Derived from A. Kolah, *Essential Law for Marketers* (2013)

Legal barriers to market entry

Barriers to market entry such as, for example, the qualifications legally required to practice as a doctor or barrister, are useful. Their existence means that supply of such services is tightly controlled and as a result, they can command a premium price in the market. Conversely, certain products, such as baby clothing, must comply with fire retardant regulations, which means that baby clothes that don't comply can't be lawfully sold in the market. A legal barrier to market entry therefore makes it difficult for competitors to enter the market and can indirectly help to protect the market share of existing companies already lawfully trading.

The key legal tools used in marketing to enforce the barrier to market entry are:

- Trademarks – legal protection stops other competitors from using the same or similar marks with protection extending to words (including personal names), designs, letters, numerals and even the shape of goods or their packaging, as is the case for a Coke bottle.
- Passing off – this stops others from producing imitation or fake merchandise, or pretending that their business is in some way linked to your own.
- Copyright – a useful legal measure to prevent competitors using someone's material or ideas without permission. This applies to literature, music, and dramatic and artistic works.
- Personality rights – important for celebrities whose image may be used in an advertising or marketing campaign as it stops others from using that person's image or endorsement without seeking permission first.

Legal requirements for marketing activities

This is really about staying on the straight and narrow. Some lawyers tend to like this area of the law because it helps them charge clients large fees by scaring the daylight out of them with the consequences of failing to comply with certain laws and regulations. In some cases, non-compliance can even lead to jail. Laws that place legal requirements on suppliers cover a very wide range of marketing and communications activities, including:

- Advertising, sales promotions and direct marketing – the Committee of Advertising Practice (CAP) in the United Kingdom and the Federal Trade Commission in the United States provide a body of regulations that organizations must comply with. These include the requirement that all marketing communications should be legal, decent, honest and truthful.

- E-mail and SMS campaigns – under most countries' laws, spamming is an offence and, subject to a few exceptions, businesses must always get the permission of the recipient to send a marketing e-mail or mobile text message that contains an offer or special promotion.
- Using databases for marketing – the UK Data Protection Act 1998 has had the biggest impact on marketing in the last 100 years. It gives individuals a legal right to know how a third party has obtained, recorded and held personal data. The 1998 Act also sets out detailed controls on the transmission, retrieval and protection of such data and makes the staff involved personally liable for any breach of these laws. In the United States, a combination of legislation, regulation and self-regulation is preferred.

Law as a weapon for competitive advantage

The above presents the law as something that is about limiting or controlling the way organizations conduct their marketing activities. However, there are several areas of marketing practice where knowing how to apply the law will make a difference to the nature and content of a business's marketing and communication efforts. As an example, some laws, such as the EU Directive on Comparative Advertising, have legitimized activities previously illegal in some countries. The Directive allows comparative advertising as being in the interests of competition and public information. However, the law also protects competitors from being attacked with untrue comparisons, but not where comparisons are valid. A similar situation exists in the United States where the Federal Trade Commission has recently tried to liberalize what can and cannot be said in comparative advertising.

One example that tested the limits of comparative advertising is provided by the case of British Airways vs. Ryanair concerning an advert that compared prices under the heading 'Expensive BAstards'. British Airways were unsuccessful as the core claim within the advert was substantially true. In a different vein, pharmaceutical companies can gain significant competitive advantage from careful manipulation of patent registrations to extend the life of a drug beyond the initial protection period.

Overall, and as is often the case, the law can be both a help and a hindrance for marketing and marketing communications. However, the existence of regulation and law does not necessarily make things easy for marketing practice. A good example is provided by patents where the dilemma is whether or not to register a technology advancement that provides competitive advantage. On the one hand, a patent signifies that the advancement should not be copied and infringement can lead to claims for compensation. On the other, publication will enable competitors to copy the advancement. For smaller enterprises, the legal costs of registering a patent nationally and internationally, and then pursuing a patent infringement, may well be prohibitively impossible.

Marketing due diligence

The purpose of a 'marketing due diligence' exercise is to assess the likelihood that an organization's marketing strategies will create or destroy shareholder value. This is done by evaluating a marketing strategy in terms of the risks associated with it plus the rate of return required from it. The difference is that normally, the financial focus within marketing strategies and plans is whether the predicted outcomes are sufficient rather than identifying the risks associated with achieving the outcomes. Financial outcomes are usually presented as single point certainties rather than being expressed as a range of possible outcomes based on the volatility of future business environments, ie the risks involved.

Marketing due diligence is important for four groups of organizational stakeholders:

1 investors and their proxies: as a way of seeing through the smoke and mirrors of 'investor relations';
2 for boards and equivalents: as a way to prove your value creation potential to financiers;
3 for strategy makers: as a way to prove your value to the board;
4 for strategy implementers: as a way to prove your value to your boss!

The process

The marketing due diligence process starts with identifying the specific risks associated with each element of a marketing strategy, so that individual probability assessments of success/failure and the consequent impact on financial outcomes can be assessed. This enables predicted financial outcomes to be directly adjusted, where necessary, in the light of identified risks. The level of any adjustment that is required clearly depends on how the forecasts were originally prepared. Plans that include extremely optimistic stretch targets ('best case' plans) will normally need more adjustment than more conservative plans that already allow for expected risks and consequent variation in financial returns ('most likely' plans).

As a simple example, if the predicted sales revenue for a particular product is £1 million, but after analysis it is felt that there is only an 80 per cent probability of achieving that revenue, the risk adjusted revenue should be £0.8 million.

In order to produce a shareholder value 'figure' from the marketing due diligence diagnostic process, probability adjusted sets of expected future cash flows should be compared to the financial return required by the business. This is done by assessing the 'true' capital required to implement the proposed marketing strategy. True capital includes the critically important, and often highly valuable, intangible marketing assets as well as the more obvious tangible assets of the business. These can include: product development resource; marketing processes; customer databases; relationships; brands, and so on.

As the specific risks of the proposed marketing strategy have already been taken into account in the diagnostic review, the return required on this capital employed can be calculated by reference to the company's normal cost of capital. In other words, there is no need arbitrarily to increase the required rate of return to try to take account of the complex myriad of risk factors.

There can, however, be one additional adjustment to the predicted financial return if the proposed marketing strategy places any existing assets at risk, and draws on the theoretical concept of 'capital at risk'. In this, the return required must be sufficient to cover any loss in capital value of an asset as a result of its incorporation into a marketing programme. As an example, an 'umbrella' or 'mother' brand' could be used to help the launch of a new product. If the new product fails or becomes toxic, its association with the higher-level brand could negatively affect its value. Coca-Cola suffered this when they launched Dasani in the UK and had to withdraw it after negative publicity and a contamination problem. Use of an existing asset in this way is done to reduce the required marketing expenditure, but the expected financial returns do not normally include the danger to the value of the existing asset if the strategy is not completely successful. Such an adjustment should be made as part of the full marketing due diligence review.

Even if the existing marketing planning information is not sufficient to enable a numerical value to be calculated, a big advantage of the marketing due diligence diagnostic process is that it will still highlight the key risk areas of any proposed strategy and show up the specific deficiencies in the current marketing plan. In many cases these deficiencies can be remedied by applying the therapeutic process within marketing due diligence, which reviews and improves the marketing planning process.

Thus, the critical resource allocation decisions at board level should be based on much better and more validly comparative information. Knowing this should provide great reassurance to external analysts and shareholders, as they can be more confident that in the future, marketing strategies will be shareholder value-enhancing.

Implementation

The implementation of a due diligence process will require the assistance of mathematically or statistically literate people. Such skills are common in areas such as investment banking and financial or economic modelling, but are rarely found in marketing staff. This emphasizes the need for marketing personnel to work outside their departmental boundaries in alliance with staff in other areas of the organization.

There are a number of different sources of risk that need to be taken into consideration in the due diligence process as outlined below.

Market risk

Market risk is the risk that the predicted market size will not be as large as hoped for by the plan. It is distinct from, but aggregates with (market) share risk and profit risk. Market projections can turn out to be wrong for a number of reasons: the targeted market is very new; the product category is very new; the product enters a new stage in its life cycle; or the uncertainty arising from this 'newness' is not compensated for by effective research and analysis.

Share risk

Share risk is the risk that the strategy will not create the degree of customer preference or competitive advantage that is needed to create the planned market share and hence fall short of creating shareholder value. It appears when what is offered to customers is not, in their eyes, valuable enough to them. This happens for a number of reasons: the wrong customers are targeted; they are offered the wrong things; or the strategy involves going head-on with a bigger, stronger competitor.

Profit risk

The required contribution to shareholder value can still founder as a result of profit risk, even if the strategy achieves the predicted market share and sales revenue. Profit risk considers the probability of creating the anticipated financial return from the predicted market share of the planned market value. Risks are greatest in relatively mature markets where established competitors are often fighting to obtain a larger share of a static, or even declining, total profit pool (profit pool risk). Profit risk is higher if planned increases in profit come from competitors, and lower if it comes from growth in the total profit pool. Other profit risks include: unusually aggressive competitor reaction; volatile internal costs; or failure to control adequately marketing expenditure.

A more detailed look at the composition of risk in each of these areas is provided in Table 59.1.

TABLE 59.1   Factors contributing to risk

Overall risk associated with the business plan		
Market risk	**Share risk**	**Profit risk**
Product category risk, which is lower if the product category is well established and higher for a new product category.	Target market risk, which is lower if the target market is defined in terms of homogenous segments and higher if it is not.	Profit pool risk, which is lower if the targeted profit pool is high and growing and higher if it is static or shrinking.
Segment existence risk, which is lower if the target segment is well established and higher if it is a new segment	Proposition risk, which is lower if the proposition delivered to each segment is segment specific and higher if all segments are offered the same thing.	Competitor impact risk, which is lower if the profit impact on competitors is small and distributed and higher if it threatens a competitor's survival.
Sales volumes risk, which is lower if the sales volumes are well supported by evidence and higher if they are guessed.	SWOT risk, which is lower if the strengths and weaknesses of the organization are correctly assessed and leveraged by the strategy and higher if the strategy ignores the firm's strengths and weaknesses.	Internal gross margin risk, which is lower if the internal gross margin assumptions are conservative relative to current products and higher if they are optimistic.
Forecast risk, which is lower if the forecast growth is in line with historical trends and higher if it exceeds them significantly.	Uniqueness risk, which is lower if the target segments and propositions are different from that of the major competitors and higher if the strategy goes 'head on'.	Profit sources risk, which is lower if the source profit is growth in the existing profit pool and higher if the profit is planned to come from the market leader.
Pricing risk, which is lower if the pricing assumptions are conservative relative to current pricing levels and higher if they are optimistic.	Future risk, which is lower if the strategy allows for any trends in the market and higher if it fails to address them.	Other costs risk, which is lower if assumptions regarding other costs, including marketing support, are higher than existing costs and higher if they are lower than current costs.

The process of conducting marketing due diligence assessments starts with identification of the critical market segments for which marketing plans have been prepared. Projections of the future net free cash in-flows from these segments over a period of between three and five years should then be made. These calculations will consist of cost and revenue forecasts for each year, plus net free cash flow for each segment. Key factors that will increase or decrease future cash flows then need to be assessed for risk under the headings: market risk; share risk; and profit risk. The resultant probability factors should then be applied to the forecast revenues, costs and net free cash flows. Having ascertained the organization's cost of capital, the proportional cost of capital from the free cash flow for each segment for each year is deducted. An aggregate positive net present value indicates that the business is creating shareholder value – ie achieving overall returns greater than the weighted average cost of capital, having taken into account the risk associated with future cash flow. An overview of the process is provided in Figure 59.1

FIGURE 59.1 Marketing due diligence process

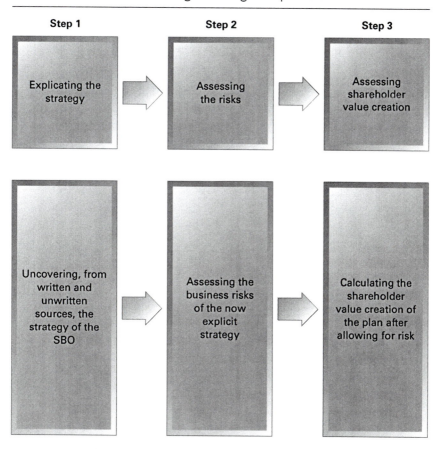

Marketing metrics

Greater accountability for marketing expenditure is one of the biggest issues facing the marketing community today, particularly as CEOs and CFOs are continually asking for costs to be cut, either because of economic circumstances or simply as a matter of good practice. The solution to avoiding *ad hoc* cost cutting is in establishing acceptable performance metrics for marketing activities. If those running organizations cannot judge the effectiveness of marketing expenditure, they will be more likely to make cuts in these areas and marketing managers will have a harder time resisting pressure to make cuts. As reflected in a Deloitte Report from 2007, which polled the opinions of CEOs and CFOs, those leading businesses have long had concerns about marketing expenditures. Comments included:

> Marketing has a tendency to be activity based – focusing on the number of campaigns it runs or how many people it needs to employ, rather than justifying the impact of marketing on the bottom-line and cash flow.

> There is still no consistent view on how to measure and report marketing success.

> Marketing have constantly hidden behind a fog of measures that are based purely on tactical marketing activity, rather than solid financial metrics that are relevant to the City.

The problem with establishing metrics that will measure the effectiveness of marketing is to find ones that reflect the broad range of marketing activity rather than simply the effectiveness of sales channels and promotional expenditure. These are tactical in nature and more akin to management than financial accounts. For financial impact, metrics have to reflect the pervasive nature of marketing's contributions:

- defining and understanding target markets;
- identifying viable and coherent segments within target markets;
- developing value propositions to meet the researched needs of the customers in target segments;
- communicating the value proposition to those responsible for overseeing the delivery of its component parts and gaining their commitment;

- playing a part in delivering the appropriate value;
- monitoring whether the promised value is being delivered.

These form the domain of marketing and can be represented as a series of interconnected activities moderated by the organization's assets that will act as the foundation for its competitive strategy, as illustrated in Figure 60.1.

FIGURE 60.1   Map of the marketing domain

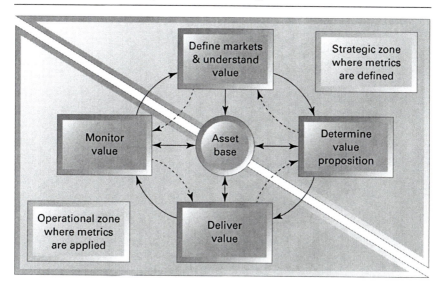

Level one metrics

The significance of activities in the 'strategic zone' in this representation is that the choice of target customers and the associated value propositions will underpin the longer-term objectives of the organization (usually incorporated into a three to five years strategic plan). These are high-level objectives and require metrics that can be used to communicate with a range of external stakeholders such as investors, market analysts, journalists and potential joint-venture partners. Their purpose is to persuade stakeholders of the true long-term value of the business. As such, the figures should have been subject to a due diligence process because their achievement or otherwise will either destroy or create shareholder value. In the same way that a takeover target would be subject to a due diligence process to assess the true value of the target, so marketing objectives should be assessed in terms the number of uncontrollable risks that could impact their achievement.

The process of marketing due diligence is addressed in more detail in Topic 59.

Level two metrics

At a second level, the output from activities in the 'strategic zone' will also determine the competitive advantage delivered by the organization. Competitive advantage requires that the organization provide value that is important to customers above and beyond those of its competitors. In a high growth market where there is excess demand, this may simply be activity that will provide future advantage, such as getting large amounts of product made and delivered quickly to establish market share. In more difficult markets, competitive advantage will derive from key aspects of the marketing mix.

The significant metrics here will therefore be whether the planned programmes and investments will deliver the competitive advantage claimed in the segments targeted by the strategy. These will be important for an organization's senior management team or board of directors, who will need to be convinced that the proposed courses of action have the potential to yield a return. A useful focus here is the critical success factors (CSFs) existing in each of the product/market segments being addressed by the organization. These lie at the heart of the marketing process as illustrated in Figure 60.2.

FIGURE 60.2 CSFs in the marketing process

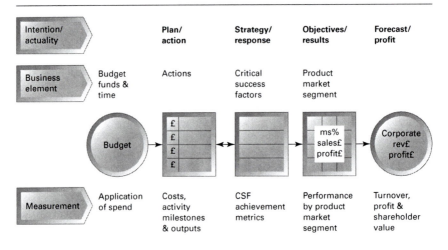

The evaluation required is the organization's position compared with competitors in customers' eyes. If the weighted scores for the CSFs indicate superior performance, senior management should have confidence that competitive advantage will be achieved. If the evaluation indicates inferior performance, then the analysis provides a focus for improvement and a need to advance the output from the relevant expenditure programmes in the 'operational zone'. All evaluations should be based on rigorous market research and objective assessments of performance rather than opinions and assertions. Too often there is a lack of relevant research and the opinions of senior managers overrule competent but data-light marketing executives. A template for CSF evaluation is illustrated in Figure 60.3.

FIGURE 60.3 Critical success factor analysis template

Critical Success Factors	Weighting factor	Your organization	Competitor A	Competitor B	Competitor C
CSF 1					
CSF 2					
CSF 3					
CSF 4					
Total weighted score (score x weight)	100				

* Strategies to improve competitive position/achieve objectives over time (4Ps)
* Metrics (each CSF) to measure performance over time in achieving goals

Such metrics move marketing away from the over-simplistic view of measures of marketing effectiveness based on the accounting notions of return on investment. These imply that taking profit and dividing it by investment as a simple input/output relationship can adequately assess marketing performance. As captured in an important *Harvard Business Review* article:

Measuring marketing performance isn't like measuring factory output – a fact that many non-marketing executives don't grasp. In the controlled environment of a manufacturing plant, it's simple to account for what goes in one end and what comes out the other and then determine productivity. The output of marketing can be measured only long after it has left the plant.

McGovern G, Court D, Quelch A, Crawford B, *Harvard Business Review*, November 2004

Clearly, there are many factors that impact on profit and which are beyond the control of marketing and a concentration on CSFs helps focus on issues that can be usefully controlled.

Level three metrics

The other side of Figure 60.1 is referred to as the 'operational zone'. This is where the money is actually spent on the activities that will determine the performance of the various CSFs. Many of these will be outside the direct control of a marketing department. For example, issues like product efficacy, after sales service, channel management and sometimes even price and the sales force are often controlled by other functions. The precise location of responsibility will vary from organization to organization. It is most likely, however, that marketing will be responsible for most promotional and market research expenditure as shown in Table 60.1.

TABLE 60.1 Typical responsibilities of a marketing department

- Generating market intelligence:
  - Mapping and reading markets/demand forecasting
  - Segmenting markets
  - Understanding customers
  - Defining new product opportunities
  - Positioning competitors
  - Monitoring performance

- Market communications:
  - Advertising, public relations, lead generation
  - Corporate communications
  - Managing social media communities
  - Promotions (merchandising, packaging, special offers etc)
  - Product launches, test marketing
  - Branding and impression management

Over the years, a number of metrics have been developed that will assess performance in many of these areas including:

- brand awareness;
- channel efficiency;
- cost per lead;
- customer satisfaction;
- growth and size of customer base;
- lead conversion rate;

- number, total and average order value;
- repurchase rate;
- share of customer spend;
- marketing cost per order.

Metrics for other marketing-based operational activities are beginning to emerge although there is still work to be done to provide more sophisticated measures of performance.

Overall, the issue of metrics for marketing performance becomes less of a problem if managers can focus on those areas that will be most helpful to the long-term survival and success of the organization. The three levels referred to above provide a way of thinking about metrics in terms of the organization's key stakeholders: external interests; internal senior management; and operational managers. By incorporating issues of due diligence, focusing on CSFs and monitoring operational performance, it becomes clear exactly what must be measured and why. It also obviates the assumption that a particular marketing action can be linked directly to profitability.

INDEX

NB: page numbers in *italic* indicate figures or tables

3M   10
7UP   181

A Classification Of Residential
      Neighbourhoods (ACORN)
      126
advertising   213–17
   advertising plan   216, *216–17*
   informative advertising   214–15
   legal issues   303
   market research   216
   media   213–14
   message   214–15
   persuasive advertising   215
   reminder advertising   215
Advertising Standards Authority   301
'AIDA' framework   88
Amazon   10, 67, 173, 263
   'channel captain'   255
   individualization   89
   micromarketing   296
   personalized portfolios   47
   single channel strategy   271
American Marketing Association   25
Ansoff Matrix   171–76, *172*
   existing products for existing markets
      172–73
   new markets for existing products
      173–74
   new products for existing markets
      174
   new products for new markets   174
Ansoff, Igor   171
Apple   182
   iPhone   26
   patent lawsuits   301
Arsenal FC   222
Avon Cosmetics   17

Badoit   180
BIC   174
Bing   90
Biro   180
Bluetooth   99
BMW   179, 214
   'Mini'   47

Booz Hamilton   87
Boston Matrix   *160*, 160–63
   Cash Cows   162
   cash flow implications   162, *163*
   Dogs   162
   drawbacks to   163
   experience curve   179, *179*
   Question Marks   162
   Stars   162
Brand Republic   301
branding   179–82
   brand personality   181–82
   brand positioning   180–81, *181*
   successful brand building   180
   vs commodity   179–80
British Airways   304
British Copyright Council   301
British Telecom (BT)   222
budgeting   297–300
   controllable and uncontrollable costs
      299
   costing marketing activities   299–300
   life cycle budgeting   298
   operating and opportunity budgeting
      298
   variable cost budgeting   298
   zero-based budgeting   297

Calvin Klein   83
capital goods   62–65
   customization   62, 73
   decision-making units   64
   innovation   62–63
   lead times   63
   order numbers   62
   pricing   63–64
   repeat business   63
Carrefour   66, 69
category management   70–73, 296
   customer information   73
   distribution systems   73
   evolution of   72, *73*
   limitations of   72
   mass customization   72
   vs brand management   71–72
Caterpillar   49, 179

channels
  channel management 252–56
    channel conflict 254–56
    intermediaries, motivating 252–53
    partnerships 253–54
  channel strategy 248–51
    forms of intermediaries 249–51, *250*
    intermediaries, advantages and disadvantages of 248–49
  marketing communication channels 266, *266–69*
  multi-channel integration 261–65
    channel-chain analysis 263–65, *264*
    channel segmentation strategy 262
    customer value curve 262–63, *263*
    customer value strategy 262
    discrete multi-channel strategy 262
    integrated multi-channel strategy 262
    migration strategy 261
    single channel strategy 261
Chivas Regal 131
Coca-Cola 71, 181, 184
  bottle shape trademark 303
  Dasani 221, 306
  global appeal of 131
  micromarketing 46
  product adaptation 288
  social media 95
  sponsorship 226
Committee of Advertising Practice (CAP) 301, 303
competitor analysis 155–59
  analysis framework 157, *158*
  bargaining power of buyers 156
  bargaining power of suppliers 156
individual competitor analysis 159, *159*
market competition 156–57
  market competitive position classifications *157*
  substitute products or services 156
  threat of new entrants 155
consumer buying behaviour 113–17
  buying decision, the 113–15, *114*
    'black box' 114
    buyer's response 114–15
    external factors 113
  decision-making process 116–17
    evaluation 116
    information search 116
    post-purchase perceptions 117
    purchase intention 116–17
  involvement 115–16

consumer products 43–47
  brands 45–46
  consumer durables 43–44
  direct mail 45
  'fast moving consumer goods' (FMCGs) 43
  markets 43–44
  mass customization 47
  micro marketing 46–47
  personal selling 44
  personalized portfolios 47
  retail outlets 45
  value chain management 46
Cranfield School of Management 33, 261
critical success factors (CSFs) 151–52, *152*, 312, *312–13*, *313*
customer retention 18–23
  benefits of 18–19
  customer defection, causes of 21
  customer values 23
  Net Promoter Score 20, *20*
  'promiscuous customers' 19–20
  'reasonable customers' 20
  strategies
    enhancing value 22
    interdependency 22
    validating choice 21–22
customer service 257–60
  creating a strategy 258–59, *259*
  electronic data interchange (EDI) 260
  elements of 257–58

Dannon 25
'Dark Patterns' 26
Data Protection Act 1998 304
databases 104–10
  components of *110*
  cross-functional co-operation 109
  customer relationship management (CRM) systems 104
  information flows 108, *108*
  legal issues 304
  myths and realities 105, *105*
  reconciling internal and external data 105, *106*
  segmentation methods *108*
Dell 46
  social media 95–96
Deloitte 310
Delphi forecast, the 275
Dexion 159
DHL 179
  Global Account policy 245
diffusion of innovation 189–92
  adoption process 189–90

categories of adopters
    early adopters   191
    'early majority'   191
    innovators   190–91
    laggards   191
    'late majority'   191
    rate of diffusion   191–92
Diffusion of Innovations   189
Direct Line   261
Directional Policy Matrix (DPM)   *164,*
        164–70
    business strengths   166–67, *167*
    market attractiveness   165–66, *166*
    steps in producing   *170*
    strategic business units (SBUs)   165
    strategic categories   *168*
Directive on Comparative Advertising   304
Disney   83
Drucker, Peter   6
DuPont   30

easyJet   181, 261
eBay   255, 261
Efficient Customer Response (ECR)   70
Emirates   222
Enron   24
Equality and Human Rights Commission
        302
Essential Law for Marketers   302
ethics   24–28
    American Marketing Association
        guidelines   25
    consumerism   27–28, *28*
    criticisms of marketing   25–26, *27*
Ethics Resource Centre   302
European Commission   301
Evian   180

Facebook   94, 101, 296
    B to C marketing   95
    Coca-Cola   95
    global appeal of   131
Federal Trade Commission   302, 303
Federer, Roger   222
FIFA   226
Financial Times   72
Fisher-Price   28
Five Forces Analysis   149
Flora   179
Ford   46, 181
four Ps *see* marketing mix
Fuji   221

General Electric   165, 263
General Motors   35

GKN   83
global marketing *see* international
        marketing
Google   10, 179
    data integration   89
    Google+   94
    search engine optimization   90
GSK   71

Hallmark   100
Harvard Business Review   123, 171, 313
Heinz   67
    category management   71
    customer database   73
Hewlett Packard (HP)   89, 267
high-pressure sales   25
high-tech products   57–61
    credibility   59
    defining 'high-tech'   57–58
    infrastructure   60–61
    life cycles   59–60, *60*
    positioning   60
    standards   59
    technology seduction   58–59
Hitachi   184
Honda   83
Hoover   180
HSBC
    First Direct   17, 44, 154, 261, 262
    money laundering   25
Hurricane Katrina   298

IBM   35, 184
IKEA   54
industrial products   48–51
    continuum of   48–49, *49*
    customer numbers   50
    derived demand   50
    key account management   51
    product evaluations   49–50
    product variability   50
    volumes   50
Information Commissioner's Office (ICO)
        302
Intel   35, 49
    'Intel Inside'   69
international marketing   79–84
    complexity   80–81, *81*
    control   82–83
    environment   79–80, *80*
    key questions   *84*
international product planning   287–90
    financial risks   290
    product characteristics   289
    product line choice   287–88

services 289
standards 288–89
internet marketing 87–93
  communities 92
  definition of 87
  engagement 92
  evidence of trustworthiness 91
  free information 88
  integration of data 89
  interactivity 90
  location and reach 90
  mass customization 89
  personal contact 92
  price 91
  referrals 91
  reputation management 91–92
  reviews 91
  search engine optimization 90
  security 92
  spam 88

John Lewis 14
Johnson & Johnson 47
Johnston Controls 49
Jordan, Michael 226

key account management (KAM)
    238–47
  Basic KAM 240–41, *241*
  Co-operative KAM 240, *241*
  Exploratory KAM 239
  future of 243
  implementing 244–47
    benefits of 245–46
    organizational positioning 247
    skills needed 246
  Integrated KAM 242, *242*
  Interdependent KAM *241*, 241–42
Kolah, Ardi 223, 302

Lehmann Brothers 24
Lentz, Jim 221
Levi's 248, 251
Levitt, Theodore 30
LinkedIn 94, 98
London 2012 Olympic Games 223
Lush 248

Mailing Preference Service 302
market segmentation 123–33
  analysis of benefits sought 126
  analysis of customer attributes 126
  analysis of customer behaviour 124
  clustering of groups 127
  consumer market *127*

industrial market 128, *128*
internationally 130–33
  e-commerce 133
  global products 131
  hybrid products 131–32
  implementation 132–33
  market variables 132
  national products 131
objectives of 129
marketing
  as a business process 6–7, *7*
  concept of 30
  definitions of 3–4
  due diligence 305–09
    market risk 307, *308*
    process *309*
    profit risk 307, *308*
    share risk 307, *308*
  environment, factors of 5–6
  legal issues 301–04
    advertising 303
    barriers to market entry 303
    databases 304
    direct marketing 303
    e-mail and mobile marketing 304
    law as a weapon 304
    sales promotions 303
    sources of information 301–02
  marketing management 8–9
  marketing orientation 8–10
  marketing tasks 8
  metrics 310–15
    level 1 311
    level 2 312–13
    level 3 314–15
    and the marketing domain 310–11,
      311
  as an organizational function 30–31
  philosophical, strategic and tactical
      levels of 6
  as a process 31, *32*
  world-class marketing, guidelines for
      33–40
    competitive advantage 34, *34*
    competitor surveillance 35, *36*
    environmental monitoring 35,
      35
    market dynamics 37, *38*
    market orientation 33–34, *34*
    market segmentation 36, *36*
    portfolio management 38, *38*
    professionalism 39–40, *40*
    strategic priorities 39, *39*
    strengths and weaknesses analysis
      37, *37*

marketing audits 146–49
  Five Forces Analysis 149
  outside consultants, using 149
  purpose of 146
  variables 147, *148*
marketing mix 4–5, 11–17
  place 5, 16–17
    see also channels
  price 4, 13–14
    variables *13*
  product 4, 11–12
    variables *12*
  promotion 5, 14–15
    impersonal promotion 15
    personal promotion 14
    sales promotions 15
  and relationship marketing 74–76, *76*
    customer service 75
    people 75–76
    processes 76
  and service products 56
marketing planning 277–86
  barriers to 282–86
    delegation 286
    detail level 284–85
    implementation plan 283
    integration of marketing into
      corporate planning 284–85
    line management support 284
    numbers 284
    planning as a ritual 285
    planning terminology 284
    short-term vs long-term planning
      285
    top management support 283
  and business plans 281
  as a managerial process 277–78
  planning timetable 279–81, *280*, *281*
  strategic marketing plans 278–79
  tactical marketing plans 278, *279*
marketing research 137–45
  desk vs field 140
  internal vs external 140
  main areas of *138*
  marketing information systems
    140–42
  passive research 139
  preparing a brief for 143–45
    accepting the proposal 145
    contents 143–44
    invitation to tender 144
    research proposal 145
  primary vs secondary 139
  reactive research 139
  topics *138*

Marketing Today 302
Marks & Spencer 80, 181
Marlboro 131
Maytag 159
Mazda 254
McDonald's 184
  global appeal of 131
  healthy eating 28, 154
  micromarketing 46
  product adaptation 288
McKinsey 87, 165
Mercedes-Benz 181–82, 184
Microsoft 97, 179
  Windows 193
Ministry of Justice 302
mobile marketing 99–103
  apps 100
  augmented reality 100
  legal issues 304
  marketing advantages of 101–02
  privacy 102–03
  security 103
  SMS marketing 99
  and social networking 100–01
  technology limitations 103
MySpace 94

Nescafé 179
Nestlé 24
Net Promoter Score 20, *20*
neuro-linguistic programming (NLP) 236
new product development 193–97
  new product classification 193–94,
    194
  risk 196, 197, *197*
  sources of ideas 194–96
  stages of development 196–97
Nielsen 73
Nike 214, 226
Nissan 83, 254

Office of Communications 302
Office of Fair Trading 302
Orange 44
organizational buying behaviour 118–22
  buying stages 118–19
  decision-making unit 121–22
    deciders 121
    gatekeepers 121
    initiators 121
    other influencers 121
    policy-makers 121
    users 121
  model *119*
  modified re-buys 120

new buy   119–20
   straight re-buys   120
organizational structure   291–96
   decentralization   293
   evolution of marketing function
      292
   marketing department structures
      293–95, *294*
   process focus   295
Orient Express   179

P&G   29, 71
   Charmin toilet paper   286
   Tide   298
Pareto analysis   140
Payment Protection Insurance (PPI)   25
PayPal   92
Pepsi   71, 181
   PepsiCo   194, 223
Perrier Water   179–80
Persil   179, 184
personal selling   228–31
   'ABC' sequence   229
   advantages of   230–31, *231*
   appointments   229
   objections   230
   SPIN approach   229
   trial closes   230
PEST (Political, Economic, Sociological
     and Technical) analysis   149
Phillips-Van Heusen   83
Pilkington Glass   83
Pinsent Masons   302
Porter, Michael   149, 155
   see also Five Forces Analysis
Poundland   200
pricing
   and capital goods   63–64
   price setting   204–07
      competitor changes   205
      customer discounts   205–06
      income 'leakage'   206–07
      new products   204–05
      price presentation   206
      rising costs   205
   strategies   198–203
      competitor pricing   201
      cost-based   201–02
      floor pricing   200
      market penetration   200
      market skimming   198–99
      micro-transaction pricing   203
      sliding   199
      value based pricing (VBP)   202–03
Primark   200

product life cycle   183–88
   alternative product life cycles   186, *186*
   impact on marketing strategy   187, *188*
   product categories and classes   183–84
   product life cycle curve   183, *183*
   stages in   *184–86*, 185
   vs market life cycle   183
public relations   218–21
   events   219
   expert opinion   220
   good causes   219
   news generation   218–19
   publications   219
   scope of   220–21
   visual identity   220

Quelch, John A   84

RBS   24
Reddit   94–95
relationship marketing   74–78
   and the marketing mix   74–76, 76
      customer service   75
      people   75–76
      processes   76
   six markets model   77, *77*–78
      customer markets   77
      influencer markets   77, 78
      internal markets   77, 78
      recruitment markets   77, 78
      referral markets   77, 78
      supplier markets   77, 78
Renault   181
Rentokil Initial   193
'reverse engineering'   195
Rogers, Everett   189
Rolex   184
Rolls-Royce   131
Ryanair   304

Sage Pay   92
Sainsbury's   80
   Active Kids schools vouchers   227
sales forecasting   273–76
   and uncertainties   276
   macro forecasting   274
   micro forecasting   274
   techniques   274–76
sales promotion   208–12
   definition of   208
   legal issues   303
   objectives of   208–09
   points schemes   209–10
   strategy and tactics   211–12
   types of   209, *210*

sales team, managing the   232–37
    motivation   235–37
    objectives   232–34, 234–35
Samsung   301
San Pellegrino   180
Schweppes   180–81
service products   52–56
    customer management   56
    examples of   52
    'fail points'   55
    and the marketing mix   56
    perishability   56
    quality   55
    relationship, importance of the   54
    tangibility   53, 53–54, 54
Shaw, Robert   110
Shell   165
Singer   180
Skype   87
social media marketing   94–98
    B to B marketing   96–97
    B to C marketing   95–96
    blogs   98
    community   98
    consistency of message   97
    expertise   98
    frequency   97
    interaction   98
    and mobile marketing   100–01
    most popular sites   94
    sales   98
    spread   98
    staff training   97
    transparency   97
Southwest Airlines   261
sponsorship   222–27
    growth of   223
    management cycle   224, 224–27
    objectives   224
    types of   222–23, 223
St Gobain   83
Standard Industrial Classification (SIC)
        126
Starbucks   100
State Farm Insurance   261
SWOT analysis   149, 150–54, 279
    opportunities and threats   153, 153–54
        market changes   154
        other suppliers   154
    strengths and weaknesses   151–52, 152
        critical success factors (CSFs)
            151–52, 152
        winning vs qualifying criteria   151

TalkTalk   222
Tate Modern   222
Taylor Nelson Sofres (TNS)   73
Tesco   47, 66
    Computers for Schools vouchers
        227
    Fresh and Easy   80–81, 84
    Home Plus   45
    private label products   72
    Race for Life   222
Thomas Cook   262
Tide   181, 184, 298
Timberland   219
T in the Park   222
Toyota   82, 83, 195
    'sticky accelerator' recall   221
Toys-R-Us   69
TPN Register   263
trade marketing   66–69
    future of   69
    intermediaries   66–67
        brand differentiation   67
        brand management   67
        e-commerce   67
        market fragmentation   67
        retail power   66–67
    strategies   68–69
    tactics   68
Twitter   94, 96, 98, 101, 102, 296

Unilever   222
United Technologies Corp   49
US Patent and Trademark Office   302

Vodafone   225
Volkswagen   181, 248
    Beetle   195

Walkers Crisps   194–95
Wal-Mart   66, 69
    'Sam's Choice' label   72
Warner Brothers   83
Wedgwood, Josiah   3
Weight Watchers   101
Westinghouse   83
Which?   78
Woods, Tiger   227
WorldPay   92

X Factor   222

Yahoo!   90
YouTube   101, 221, 296